PIANO REPERTOIRE
A Guide to Interpretation and Performance

BÉLA SIKI

SCHIRMER BOOKS
A Division of Macmillan Publishing Co., Inc.

NEW YORK

Collier Macmillan Publishers

LONDON

Copyright © 1981 by
SCHIRMER BOOKS
A Division of Macmillan Publishing Co., Inc.

SCHIRMER BOOKS
A Division of Macmillan Publishing Co., Inc.
866 Third Avenue, New York, N.Y. 10022

Collier Macmillan Canada, Ltd.

Library of Congress Catalog Card No.: 81-50526

printed in the United States of America

printing number
1   2   3   4   5   6   7   8   9   10

Library of Congress Cataloging in Publication Data

Siki, Béla.
  Piano repertoire.

  Bibliography: p.
  1. Piano music—Interpretation (Phrasing,
dynamics, etc.)   2. Piano—Performance.   I. Title.
MT235.S54   786.3   81-50526
ISBN 0-02-872390-2   AACR2

Contents

Preface ix

Johann Sebastian Bach 1

 Prelude and Fugue in C Minor, *Well-Tempered*
  Clavier, Book 1, No. 2 3
 Prelude and Fugue in D Major, *Well-Tempered*
  Clavier, Book 1, No. 5 8
 Prelude and Fugue in D Minor, *Well-Tempered*
  Clavier, Book 1, No. 6 14
 Prelude and Fugue in E Minor, *Well-Tempered*
  Clavier, Book 1, No. 10 20
 Prelude and Fugue in G Minor, *Well-Tempered*
  Clavier, Book 1, No. 16 27
 Prelude and Fugue in B Flat Major, *Well-Tempered*
  Clavier, Book 1, No. 21 32

Franz Joseph Haydn 37

 Sonata in C Minor, No. 20 38
 Variations in F Minor 49

Wolfgang Amadeus Mozart 59

 Sonata in A Minor, K. 310 61
 Sonata in B Flat Major, K. 333 75

Ludwig van Beethoven 89

 Sonata, Op. 10, No. 2 91
 Sonata in C Minor, Op. 13 100
 Sonata, Op. 27, No. 2 113
 Sonata, Op. 28 122

Franz Peter Schubert   133

Sonata in A Major, Op. 120 (D. V. 664)   134
Sonata in A Minor, Op. 164 (D. V. 537)   144

Robert Schumann   157

Papillons, Op. 2   159
Phantasiestücke, Op. 12   168

Frédéric Chopin   179

Etude in F Minor, Op. 25, No. 2   181
Etude in F Minor, Op. 10, No. 9   185
Etude, Op. 10, No. 12   189
Impromptu No. 1 in A Flat, Op. 29   194
Nocturne in F Sharp Major, Op. 15, No. 2   199
Waltz in A Flat Major, Op. 34, No. 1   203
Mazurka in A Minor, Op. 17, No. 4   209
Polonaise in C Sharp Minor, Op. 26, No. 1   213
Scherzo No. 2, Op. 31   217
Ballade No. 3, Op. 47   229
Berceuse, Op. 57   238

Franz Liszt   243

Sonetto 123 del Petrarca   245
Waldesrauschen   252
Paganini Etude No. 5 (*La Chasse*)   257

Johannes Brahms   263

Capriccio in F Sharp Minor, Op. 76, No. 1   265
Rhapsody in B Minor, Op. 79, No. 1   270
Capriccio in G Minor, Op. 116, No. 3   276
Intermezzo in B Flat Minor, Op. 117, No. 2   279
Intermezzo in A Major, Op. 118, No. 2   283
Ballade in G Minor, Op. 118, No. 3   286

Claude Debussy   289

Prélude (*Pour le piano*)   291
Jardins sous la pluie   295
Le Cathédrale engloutie   299
Minstrels   302
Bruyères   304
Ondine   306

Sergei Prokofiev   309

   Tales of an Old Grandmother, Op. 31   310

Béla Bartók   315

   Suite, Op. 14   317

Bibliography   329

Acknowledgments   331

Preface

This book offers guidance to the pianist in search of his own improvement, by proposing solutions to the various problems—technical or interpretative—that the pianist encounters while learning or performing. It discusses about fifty standard pieces from the pianist's repertoire, all of which are on a similar level of difficulty. This is, to say the least, an ambitious venture. To correct faults, give detailed technical advice, describe a specific sonority, portray details of interpretation—all this without hearing the reader's actual performance—may well seem incongruous. This book could be taken for a pianistic cookbook in which the concoction and taste of each dish are described, with particulars.

Assuredly, a musical performance must not be the result of a recipe; instead it should be carefully pondered, and much individual effort should be given to it. Then it should be performed under competent surveillance. Moreover words in print are hopelessly inadequate to relate the complex beauty of music in time.

Nevertheless this book may be of some assistance to many pianists. It is built upon years of teaching experience. It is conceivable that its usefulness will be felt, not only by those who learn, but also by those who teach.

Many of the comments in this book try to point out often-heard mistakes. If only a few mistakes that were unnoticed before can be corrected, the book has not been written in vain. A fingering, a redistribution of the text between the hands, or some small trick pointed out here and there may help those who want to play better. These finesses have been tested by many years of concert experience; usually they amaze pianists I have suggested them to by the mere fact that they serve their purpose.

The repertoire has been selected from the basic piano literature on the medium to advanced level of difficulty with the intention of helping as many pianists as possible. The selection was based on individual judgment and justified by the popularity of the pieces. As far as the post-Debussy period is concerned, the book offers only a limited choice from the huge output of piano music in the past thirty years. A selection from this output will depend on the personal taste of the performer, his affinities with the style of one composer or another, and on the accessibility of the music itself. Only large cities afford an almost unlimited availability of sheet music; anywhere else the choice is limited. Under the circumstances, the usefulness of a specific selection may be uncertain. Nevertheless the repertoire proposed is drawn from the two hundred most significant years of the keyboard literature, a period encompassing the widest variety of styles.

The formulation of pieces of technical advice may surprise some readers. There is repeated insistence on ''a free wrist'' and on the avoidance of ''excessive finger articulation.'' The meanings of these words may vary widely for the supporters of one technical method or another. Comments of this kind are not directed, however, toward conversion from one school to another; in broad outlines, if they are considered in their true essence rather than in a mere literal sense, they do not contradict any belief.

Bits of advice on fingering and pedaling are limited to the strictest minimum. The selection of a fingering for a tricky passage is a highly personal matter in which the conformation of the hand and the ability and proficiency of the performer are determining factors. Pedaling is an even more sensitive matter; the question of using the pedal in the works of Bach, Haydn, Mozart, or the young Beethoven has been debated many times. To offer a resolution of this historic dispute would be—to say the least—presumptuous. Furthermore even the most judicious pedaling needs to be adapted to specific situations: the possibilities of the instrument and the acoustics of the hall are two of the variables to take into consideration. The important point about the pedal is that errors lie at both extremes of the spectrum: too little pedal is just as damaging as too much. Unfortunately the reader cannot be initiated into some infallible system of pedaling that can be described in simple terms.

Not much is said in this book about practice habits, but it would be wrong to conclude that long practice hours can be done away with by the few tricks this book offers. In fact, regrettable as it seems, nothing can be proposed in lieu of practicing. However pianists have for too long and without much questioning accepted long, exhausting practice hours as an inherent, almost natural, burden of their art—as something fixed and wholly out of their power to modify or shorten.

A detailed study of practicing or practice habits—subjects examined in depth in many excellent books—goes far beyond the scope of this introduction. However it may be useful to bring up a few important points.

Practicing means to the pianist more or less what *rehearsal* means to the orchestra. It is the work necessary to produce the most perfect, inspired performance of a specific piece. The orchestra, however, is capable of giving a close-to-perfect performance of an entire program after three or four rehearsals, or roughly about twelve hours of actual practicing—a ridiculously short time for a pianist to prepare a recital. Most of the time, of course, the symphonic program includes standard pieces the orchestra has already performed on many occasions. Yet the orchestra may be able to put together, in the same amount of time, a whole program of contemporary music that it has never previously played. Although orchestra players deal individually with relatively minor technical difficulties, do not need to have a conception of the piece as a whole, and do not need to play from memory, the discrepancy in the hours needed is still flagrant and mostly unaccounted for.

The logical conclusion (secretly acknowledged but openly denied by many pianists) leads to the admission that pianists are either ill prepared technically to deal with the sovereign difficulties of the instrument or that they are wasting their time when practicing.

Many first-rate exercise books offer efficient remedies for surmounting technical shortcomings. There are études or exercises that single out specific technical problems, such as velocity of the fingers, flexibility of the wrist, and preparation for double notes, octaves, chords, and so on. The relentless playing of scales and arpeggios must be unreservedly recommended at this point.

Still, technical shortcomings alone cannot be held responsible for the waste of practice time. One of the principal causes of dispersion of effort in the course of practicing is that the pianist most often does not know what he is practicing *for*. Unlike the pianist, the orchestral conductor has constructed a distinct inner image of the work; at rehearsals his instructions to the individual players will mold the sound of the orchestra in accordance with this inner image. Unfortunately many pianists begin to practice before creating such an inner image. Hence, instead of imparting reality to the highest order of artistic imagination, their practicing degenerates into mere gymnastics through the senseless repetition of a phrase or passage. Practicing can be useful only if it helps to bring the actual performance—phrase after phrase—closer to the ideal mental image.

Time is often wasted when the pianist attempts to deal with too many difficulties at one time or when the section of the work he is trying to learn is too long. Human minds can grasp only a limited amount of data in a given time. Therefore technical difficulties have to be thoughtfully isolated, and sections have to be broken up into lengths that are simple for the eyes and mind to take in. Unwavering concentration also helps to eliminate the waste of practice time—a concentration that detects both technical and musical mistakes by constantly comparing the actual performance with the imagined musical structure.

Time can be wasted by unwisely breaking down the learning procedure into its components—seeking fluency first and "memorization" subsequently—when both elements might be gained at the same time without added effort if the sections practiced are short enough to be embraced by the mind at a glance. The sections can then be put together one after another, and the performance, inspired and fresh, emerges modeled after the inner image. Practicing in this manner makes it possible to improve (instead of worsening) details, both technically and interpretatively, at any phase of the work; it may also reduce practice time—which is still incommensurately longer than orchestra rehearsal hours—while improving practice quality.

Pianists throughout the world and at every imaginable level hope and relentlessly strive for improvement in their performances. The ambitious goal of this book is to encourage their steps along that rough path.

PIANO REPERTOIRE

Johann Sebastian Bach

Born 1685, Eisenach; died 1750, Leipzig

From the *Notenbüchlein für Anna Magdalena Bach* to the *Goldberg Variations*—from the first lessons to the pinnacle of virtuosity—Bach provides masterpieces in abundance for every stage in the development of the keyboard student; unceasing study of Bach has been proven beyond doubt to have the highest pedagogical value for all keyboard players.

A large part of Bach's work for keyboard instruments (unlike that of many other composers) is aligned in a hierarchical order of difficulty: one book prepares the student for success in mastering the next, which in turn prepares him for the one after it. The Notenbüchlein, the little preludes, the two-part inventions, the sinfonias (or three-part inventions), the French suites, and the *Well-Tempered Clavier* are listed here in ascending order of difficulty; each book builds on its predecessor. None of these works may be jumped over without endangering success in handling the next task. This is particularly true in the case (unfortunately much too frequent) of students who, having mastered the two-part inventions, pass over the sinfonias and immediately try the preludes and fugues of the *Well-Tempered Clavier*. Because of their lack of preparation, many young pianists never attain the ease that is necessary for part playing.

After a dozen or more preludes and fugues have been learned, the rest of the keyboard works (six partitas, six English suites, seven toccatas, the *Italian Concerto*, the *French Overture*—to mention only the most essential ones) may be approached without regard to any particular order. As for the *Goldberg Variations*, this work should be held in the highest esteem and touched only by an accomplished musician or virtuoso.

The *Well-Tempered Clavier*, Book 1, to which this book intends to introduce the student, not only exhibits the advantages of equally tempered tuning but also serves a distinct pedagogical purpose: the development of technique by using one specific kind of difficulty in each of the preludes and by calling for faultless rendering of a contrapuntal texture in each fugue. Besides manual dexterity in playing simultaneous voices that sometimes have different articulation or dynamics in the same hand, the skillful performance of counterpoint demands the intellectual capacity to understand and unravel complex musical constructions.

In common with other Baroque composers, Bach seldom specified tempo, articulation, or dynamics. In the entire *Well-Tempered Clavier*, Book 1, only a handful of markings of this sort are accounted original: Presto, Adagio, and Allegro toward the end of Prelude 2; the staccato mark in measure 2 of Fugue 6; and the articulation of the subject in Fugue 24. It is evident, however, that the absence of markings does not mean that these preludes and fugues may be played in any tempo, without regard to articulation or without dynamic changes. Performance in the Baroque period was in the hands of the composer himself or those of well-trained professionals; neither needed any more indications than the bare notes. But unfortunately the performance traditions of the Baroque era are lost for our day. A partial reconstruction of them is possible only through extensive reading of eighteenth-century writings (C.P.E. Bach, Quantz, Couperin, and Türk) as well as books by more recent authorities on Baroque music (Dannreuther, Dolmetsch, Bodky, Dart, Donington, and others). In addition, an extensive study of Bach's other music, instrumental and vocal, is strongly recommended. Comprehension of a musical style is based on knowledge of the musical literature.

Without pretending to supplant the intensive reading just recommended, this book presents suggestions pertaining to articulation, tempo, and dynamics solely to provide some guidance to those who may need it. The increases and decreases in dynamics proposed at specific points may seem controversial to the purist who cannot conceive of Bach on any instrument but the harpsichord (whose inability to render subtle changes of dynamics was recognized as a major weakness by most of its contemporaries). Dynamic shadings are inherent in our modern piano; they are necessary to mold a phrase. Without them piano playing is reduced to mere typewriting. Over and above dynamic nuances, a danger lies in unconsidered or wrongly applied "agogics" (i.e., prolonging slightly one beat of the measure and slightly shortening the other beats in order that the total length of the measure remains unchanged). Although Bach composed fantasias in a free style almost comparable to the Romantics', generally his works do not call for sizable agogic expression. Fugues especially require even tempos except for the few retardations, small in extent, needed only to mark the conclusions of the various sections.

Another controversial subject is the use of the damper pedal for playing Bach on the modern piano. The harpsichord had no such coloring device. Still, to avoid using the pedal altogether in Bach is senseless. Many preludes and fugues, particularly the slower ones, sound dry and inexpressive if they are played entirely without pedal. Pedal indications for the Bach works discussed in this book are omitted because even the most appropriate pedal indications, fastidiously marked, may be inadequate. The notated pedaling can be either too heavy or too light; it all depends on the condition of the instrument and the acoustics of the room. The final judgment on this point must be left ultimately to the ear, the musical taste, and the awareness of the performer.

BACH
Prelude and Fugue in C Minor

Well-Tempered Clavier, Book 1, No. 2

~~~~~~

The bold, toccata-like prelude shows persistent sixteenth figuration almost throughout the piece. The fugue is somewhat more pensive in mood, with an elaborate countersubject to the fairly simple theme. While the requirement for the Prelude is virtuosic finger technique, the fugue demands much finesse in phrasing and articulation.

Prelude

Form: Three sections

	MEASURES
Section 1	1 – 14
Section 2	15 – 28
Section 3	28 – 38

The strongly driving character of the prelude is supported by a persistent sixteenth-note figure that is difficult to render evenly while maintaining a well-balanced tone and perfect simultaneity of the hands. Metrical evenness depends largely upon the solutions brought to the problems of fingering. The simplest and most natural fingering for the right hand—consisting of 5-3-2-3 1-3-2-3—has to be discarded in measures where the ordinary span between the fifth and third fingers is unable to insure evenness in dealing with the extensions involved, as in measures 1, 6, and 8, where the fingering 5-2-1-2 1-2-1-2 is recommended.

Evenness of tone is just as important as metrical evenness in performance, but it is often disturbed by a heavy thumb or by excessive emphasis on the notes entrusted to the fifth finger, such that they display a moderate stress. Moreover the performer should constantly be aware of the goal of perfect simultaneity of the hands, which can be realized by establishing links between the fingers of the two hands for an impeccable simultaneous attack on the paired notes. Slow practice and steadfast listening help at this point.

It should be mentioned that use of the fourth finger of the left hand (instead of the fifth) is easier throughout measures 13–16. In measures 25–28 the pattern changes to a single-voice texture divided between the hands that presents problems of good connection, both in tone and in metrical evenness. Irresistibly virtuosic, these three measures of embellished arpeggios bursting upward from the lower register raise the tension of the work. Broadening the last arpeggio at measure 27 is a good way to prepare for the important downbeat of measure 28, which may be extended by a short fermata on the initial sixteenth rest of the right hand.

Then the Presto begins like an exuberant cadenza. The tempo change should be minimal—the Presto being only a shade faster than the preceding allegro. Exaggerated speed cannot do justice to the subtle details of the two imitative voices; moreover, it may turn the quick leaps of the left and right hands (measures 30 and 31) into disasters. The fingering problems in the Presto section are largely related to avoiding uncomfortable uses of the thumb on black keys. The suggested fingering is:

measures 28-33

Once again, the need for perfect simultaneity of the hands has to be pointed out; this goal is even more difficult to reach here than in the preceding measures because the broad leaps at measures 30 and 31 may get one hand behind the other. Linking the fingers of both hands in slow practice is an absolute necessity. Especially difficult is measure 32, where without warning the hands suddenly switch from parallel to contrary motion. This instantaneous change has to be mentally anticipated; disaster is almost certain if the performer is taken by surprise at this point.

The tempo slows down in measure 33 to introduce the declamatory Adagio at measure 34. The relation of the Presto to the Adagio is ♩ = ♪ (the quarter note of the Presto becomes a sixteenth note in the Adagio). Perfect continuity is thereby insured, for the sixteenth notes of the Allegro at measure 35 will proceed at the same speed as the immediately preceding sixty-fourths of the Adagio.

The closing Allegro section implies harmonies over a tonic pedal point. The last measure should include a sizable ritardando.

The energetic character of the prelude precludes an exceedingly fast tempo. The right choice seems to be around ♩ = 100–108. Keeping immutably to the adopted tempo (except for the suggested broadenings) will assure the grandeur of the interpretation. The Presto section is only slightly faster: say, ♩ = 120.

Dynamically, forte prevails throughout, with slight variations. The suggested dynamic scheme is:

MEASURES	
1 – 5	*f*
5 – 14	Gradual slight weakening of the sound
15 – 18	Lowest point, dynamically, but still close to *f*
18 – 27	Gradual increase of the sound to reach the initial *f*
28 – 33	Brilliant *f*
34	Declamatory character added
35 – 38	Measures remain strong (a final decrescendo would not do justice to the bold line of the arpeggios)

Fugue

Form: Three parts

	MEASURES
Exposition	1 – 9
Development	9 – 26
Recapitulation and coda	26 – 31

Differences between editions in their suggested articulation of the subject range from all staccato to all legato. Probably the most widely accepted articulation is the following:

measures 1-2

Allegretto

This articulation logically allows the eighth notes of the countersubject to be detached (nonlegato), while the legato suggested for the sixteenth notes binds all later sixteenth-note scales to be legato. Furthermore the legato suggested for the last fragment of the subject (second half of measure 2) turns its only quarter note into the most important note of the subject by bringing out its implied syncopation. A slight emphasis on the quarter note is a salient feature of the subject at every recurrence. Whatever articulation the performer may adopt has to be carried out consistently; this is the only real difficulty of the exposition.

At the opening of the development section, a problem of producing the right balance between the voices awaits solution. The sequential imitation between the two upper voices, built on the first limb of the subject and played in the right hand, needs precise articulation and a fine distinction in tone that is best described as the subtle difference in tone between first and second violins. Phrases of the sixteenth-note scales in the left hand are defined by the leaps, just as they are in measures 13–14 and in measures 23–25.

The interpretation of the entering subject in the treble at measure 11 has to take into account the masterly surprise prepared by Bach at this point: the entering subject can be regarded at first as the continuation of the sequential imitation established from measure 9 on. Beware of short staccatos in the voices of the left hand at measures 13 and 14: the eighth notes should be only slightly detached, matching the eighth notes of the subject.

The rendering of the subject entering in the alto at measure 15 requires good connection between the hands and an avoidance of excessive insistence. Measures 17 and 18 need good control of both tone and articulation. The left hand follows the articulation adopted for the first limb of the subject, while the right hand plays the ascending scales legato; these contrasting articulations impart more color to the short interjections in the soprano and thus underline the boldness of the harmonic progression.

The appearance of the subject in the soprano at measure 20 leads to difficulties of distinct articulations in the same hand in the second half of measure 21: the alto is to be played detached, while the last limb of the subject, in the soprano, must be strictly legato. A cloudless rendering of the sequence at measures 22–23 poses problems analogous to those of measures 9–10.

The recapitulatory entrance of the subject in the bass in the second half of measure 26 should be interpreted with great strength, and the adoption of a slightly slower tempo is conceivable at this point. (Pianists should resist the temptation to play this entrance in octaves, as suggested in several editions; the result can in no way match the use of the sixteen-foot stop on the harpsichord here.) The tempo should be further broadened at the approach to the eighth rest in measure 28, which is to be rendered as a well-defined, real silence in every part. The ensuing cadence, which it is possible to broaden still further, leads to the majestic coda, where the subject in the soprano is accompanied, over a tonic pedal point, by independent inner parts.

The spirited character of the fugue may lead to the adoption of an immoderate speed that fails to do justice to the refinement of harmony and articulation. A tempo of ♩ = 80 (with broadening for the coda) seems to accommodate both needs.

The following scheme is suggested for dynamics:

MEASURES

1 – 4	Subject, poco *f* (with countersubject meno *f*)
5 – 6	Interlude, meno *f* (the same as the countersubject)
7 – 8	Subject, poco *f* (with countersubjects poco *f*)
9 – 10	First episode, meno *f*
11 – 12	Subject, poco *f*
13 – 14	Second episode, meno *f*
15 – 16	Subject, poco *f* (with thoughtful balance)
17 – 19	Third episode, meno *f* (with crescendo)
20 – 21	Subject, *f*
22 – 25	Fourth episode, poco *f* (with crescendo)
26 – 28	Subject, brilliant *f*
28 – 31	Close and coda, più *f*

BACH
Prelude and Fugue in D Major

Well-Tempered Clavier, Book 1, No. 5

~~~~~~

Light and even finger technique and especially a flexible wrist are the requirements for the performance of this prelude. The fugue is energetic, almost pompous, without much difficulty in part playing.

Prelude

Form: Three sections

	MEASURES
Section 1	1 – 19
Section 2	20 – 26
Coda	27 – 35

Even at a first superficial glance, the main requirement for a good performance of this prelude strikes the eye immediately—smooth and even finger technique. However, finger articulation should not be confounded with finger gymnastics. Raising the fingers as high as possible before striking the keys will hinder the performer from reaching the supreme goal, tonal and metrical evenness, for raising the fingers exaggeratedly only accentuates their uneven strength. Here effortless finger articulation together with a laterally flexible wrist are the essential tools of the performer.

While the right hand maintains a light legato touch throughout the prelude, the left-hand notes are to be played as short staccatos; their flawless regularity will assist in preserving the tempo rigorously. The right hand's evenness may be impaired by clumsy articulation of the "weak" fingers or the thumb: it is unacceptable to bail out those fingers by a motion of the hand. Furthermore there is the danger that keeping the thumb over the key where it has been used, waiting for its next use in a "ready" position, will cause unwelcome stiffness in the hand. A number of difficulties can be eliminated in the course of the prelude if the thumb is kept relaxed in a natural position.

In measures 3 through 8, great flexibility of the hand is needed in dealing with the close position on the second and third beats of each measure, which is suddenly followed on each fourth beat by a large leap between the first and fifth fingers. The smoothness of execution also depends on the fingering used. The following is recommended:

measures 3-9

In measure 3, the first finger has to be prepared in advance for use on the third beat by pulling it under the hand while the other fingers execute the figure of the second beat. In the rest of this passage, turning the hand slightly outward (to the right) gives the fingers a greater advantage in negotiating some awkward figures. This hand position also grants a smoother use of the thumb on black keys, thus minimizing the harmful in-and-out motion of the hand on the keyboard.

An unskillful thumb, helped by a downward motion of the hand, is a particular danger in measure 9 because it impedes fluency and yields undue accents. The sudden reappearance of the closed position, which has not been encountered since measure 3, often ruins the execution of measure 14. The difficulty has to be foreseen and met with a flexible hand. Measure 17 again tests the flexibility and extendability of the thumb.

Measures 20–24 transpose into a new key the difficulties already met in the first measures. The recommended fingering for measures 25–26 is:

measures 25-26

In measure 27, the dominant pedal point appears; it is to be held without interruption or repetition until the beginning of the second beat in measure 30. Measures 29 and 30 are particularly difficult. The left hand has no opportunity for warming up; yet it has to match the speed of the right hand instantaneously. Measure 32 has part-playing problems in the right hand; meanwhile the left hand should play the tenor part without obtrusiveness. This measure should also include a distinct broadening of the tempo, allowing the rolled chord on the following downbeat to be handled in the grand manner.

The ensuing coda may be played in a slower tempo. The recommended execution of measure 33 is:

measure 33

Both diminished-seventh chords in measure 34 have to be rolled; the closing chords may have a full, organlike tone.

A lively allegro ($\downarrow$ = 120–126) seems appropriate to bring out the virtuosic brilliance of the prelude.

Dynamically, there is no opportunity for strong contrasts. A light, brilliant forte, with inflections to shape the outline of the figures, is recommended. At measure 20 a slightly softer tone may be adopted, favoring a build-up toward the cadenzalike coda and closing chords.

Fugue

Form: Four parts

	MEASURES
Exposition	1 – 8
Development	8 – 23
Coda	23 – 27

There is widespread controversy about the execution of the dotted rhythm in the subject. One of the rules pertaining to Baroque performance practices recommends double dotting (i.e., performing a double dotted eighth note followed by a thirty-second in this particular case) to avoid a spiritless, dull execution. Applying double dotting to this fugue is recommended by more than one respected authority; unquestionably it would invigorate the subject. But it would also deprive the episodes (measures 9–10, 17–18, and 21) of their inherent expressivity. To satisfy both needs, the performer has the choice—regardless of inconsistency—of adopting double dotting for the subjects and playing the episodes as written. A still better solution seems to be to play the fugue as notated, including the often-debated measure 22, in which the sixteenth note chord of the right hand at the end of the third beat has full harmonic significance only if it is considered together with the last thirty-second note of the third beat of the left hand.

A legato-marcato touch will bring out the unmistakable, straightforward character of the subject. The sixteenth notes of the dotted rhythm stand out from the line only too prominently if an undue emphasis is applied to them. In measure 3, the correct metrical execution of the first beat is as follows:

measure 3

The same solution applies to all further occurrences of this figure. The entrances of the alto in measure 4 and the soprano in measure 5 have to be played with a clearly distinct tone, with the right thumb holding on to the first note of the subject. In measures 9–10, the right-hand sixteenth-note groups have to be connected by the fingering and distribution of notes between the hands and be as legato as possible:

measures 9-10

(*cont.*)

measures 9-10 (*cont.*)

In measure 12, the left hand plays the first thirty-second note of the alto entrance with the thumb but should not hold on to it. With the increase of the volume to full orchestral sound in measures 14–16, the danger of a stiff wrist and arm increases as well and may produce an unacceptably harsh sound. The chords of measures 15 and 16 should receive melodic legato treatment through the use of a full, round tone. Meanwhile the part-playing problems should not escape the attention of the performer.

The episode in measures 17–18 has the same problems of legato playing that were discussed in measures 9–10. The recommended fingering and distribution are:

measures 17-18

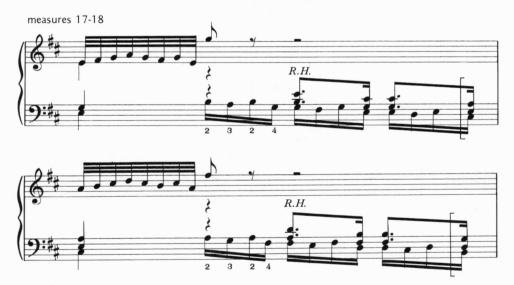

The ornament in measure 20 may be a short or long trill; for the one in measure 22, the following execution is suggested:

measure 22

The fingering for measures 24 and 25 is:

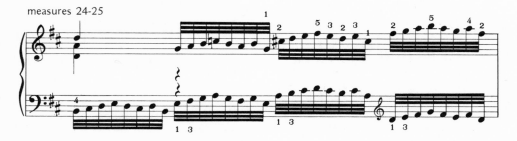

measures 24-25

The rhythmic precision of measures 25 and 26 is of the greatest importance: instead of careless speeding, the performer should broaden the tempo to emphasize the majestic ending.

There are not many of the usual contrapuntal difficulties or much intricate part playing in this fugue. The simple counterpoint results mainly in chords. The sparkling character and overwhelming rhythmic drive of this fugue cannot be mistaken. The recommended tempo is about ♩ = 60, or a little slower.

Two levels of dynamics are adequate, with both of them situated in the forte range: a healthy, strong forte for the subjects and cadences and an expressive, somewhat less brilliant sound for the episodes, with inflections to show the shape of the line and to emphasize a sensitive modulation, such as the appearance of the minor key in measure 9.

The suggested dynamic scheme is:

MEASURES

1 – 2	Brilliant *f*
3	Somewhat less (codetta)
4 – 5	Brilliant *f* with distinctive coloring of the entering voices
6	On second beat, sudden meno *f*
7	On second beat, brilliant *f* without heaviness of left hand
8	On second beat, lyrical *f* for the entering minor key
9 – 10	On first beats, *f*; the rest expressive meno *f*
11 – 16	Careful increase of volume to reach full sound at the close in E minor (on the first beat of measure 17)
17 – 19	See measures 9–10
20 – 23	*f*, increasing to the close in D major
23 – 27	Begin brilliant *f* and increase gradually; reach full sound for measures 25–27

BACH

Prelude and Fugue in D Minor

Well-Tempered Clavier, Book 1, No. 6

~~~~~~

An expressive, improvisatory prelude, built essentially on arpeggio figurations, prepares for a contemplative and elaborate fugue, which contains inversions of the subject and the answer.

Prelude

Form: Three sections

	MEASURES
Section 1	1 – 6
Section 2	6 – 14
Section 3	15 – 26

The difficulty of this prelude lies in the even, singing legato required for the sinuous line of the right hand, which is punctuated by smooth phrasings at points where the line shows a large leap. The first note of the right hand is to be played as a triplet, not as the sixteenth note notated. The legato necessitates well-chosen and solidly learned fingerings and a loose wrist and forearm, as well as minimal finger articulation, in order to produce a sound that melts the single notes into an expressive line. The articulation recommended for the first section of the left hand is *détaché* (separate long notes—the type of articulation that is achieved when one tries to play the repeated notes of measure 1 without the pedal).

In the second section, an expressive legato is recommended for the left hand, while in the right hand, the last note of each triplet group shares the melodic interest with the left hand. The sequential construction of this section has to be well brought out in performance: the phrase in measures 6–8 is followed in sequence by measures 8–10. In measures 10–12 the sequences are only a half measure long. Finally the previous long sequence reappears in measures 12–13. The left hand has the responsibility of defining the limits of the sequences by careful phrasings.

Over a tonic pedal point, the right-hand line recaptures full interest and begins a strong, intense drive to reach bold passion in turbulent arpeggios at measure 15; good coordination between the hands is needed to produce even triplets in the left hand at points where the right hand halts for one eighth note. The left hand returns to the earlier détaché articulation from measure 16 to measure 20, where the voice splits in two; the harmonic importance of the moving tenor will be emphasized if the left hand is played legato.

The right-hand arpeggios whirl more and more furiously in measures 21 and 22, accumulating diminished-seventh chords until the dominant pedal point is found in measure 23. From this point on, the right hand begins a new, decided climb to reach a rhetorical sequence of chromatically descending diminished sevenths where the tempo broadens considerably. The concluding chords are to be played in the grand manner of the full organ.

The main technical requirement of this otherwise simple prelude is a smooth, singing legato. As has already been suggested, the best result is obtained by producing series of notes shaped into long lines, rather than single notes played with excessive finger articulation. To this end, a loose and flexible wrist is the best ally throughout.

Whatever basic dynamic level is applied, it has to have dynamic inflections to do justice to the many expressive turns of the swirling line of the right hand. In comparison with the first section, the second may be interpreted in a more intense tone as a result of the left hand's joining the right in an expressive legato. Measures 10 and 11 include the opportunity for an echo dynamic, either between half-measure portions or between full-measure portions. Measure 14 gradually becomes weaker in order to reach the lowest point dynamically on the downbeat of measure 15, a decisive but still gradual increase of the volume beginning on the downbeat seems to be a natural way to underline the intensification of passion in the section. In closing chords, as has already been pointed out, the performer should seek the full sound of organ chords.

A sensitive rendering of the expressive turns and of the many harmonic refinements will be ruined by too fast a tempo. The recommended speed is situated in the neighborhood of ♩ = 60.

Fugue

Form: Three parts

	MEASURES
Exposition	1 – 8
Development	8 – 39
Racapitulation and coda	39 – 44

The slur over the sixteenth notes and the wedge over the first quarter note of the subject are among the few original articulation marks in the *Well-Tempered Clavier*. The staccato wedge is to be interpreted as an ordinary staccato: instead of indicating extreme shortness, the wedge takes away only half of the notated value. In this particular case, the wedge requires a portamento touch with a slight interruption of the sound before proceeding to the ensuing trill. The widely accepted interpretation at this point consists of a measured trill in thirty-second motion. The trill should begin on the main note rather than the upper auxiliary note; this solution is recommended for two reasons: (1) it does not obscure the deliberate skip of a falling third in the subject, and (2) it avoids the parallel fifth between the alto and bass that would result from beginning the trill with the upper auxiliary note in measure 12. Furthermore the expressive character of the trill requires closing notes in spite of the fact that they are not notated. The proposed execution of the trill is:

measure 2

For the articulation of the subject, an uninterrupted, singing legato is suggested up to the wedge on the B flat. In the countersubject the sixteenth notes should be played legato, while a ''breath'' should separate the two eighth notes in measure 4 to bring out their syncopated character. The strict legato required for the countersubject imposes a need for carefully considered fingerings that permit the best possible legato when the same key is played twice. The suggested fingering is:

measures 4-5

Measure 4 contains the first occurrence of the difficulty of playing the measured trill simultaneously with the moving sixteenths of the countersubject. The performance is often marred at this point by accents desperately employed with a view to keeping the hands together but impinging both on the expressivity of the trill and on the natural flow of the sixteenth notes. Though rhythmically unsophisticated, the trill needs to be rendered with independence in tone and expression.

In measure 6, the downbeat quarter note in the alto is best played with the thumb of the left hand, thus enabling the separation in the phrasing of the soprano between the eighth notes to be made more easily. Good voice leading is the main preoccupation of the right hand in measure 7. In measure 8, a break in the phrasing between the first and second eighth notes in the treble is essential to show that the entrance of the subject is in an irregular position (i.e., the subject has major or minor second steps on different points from those in its original version); the left hand ''breathes'' between the eighth notes of measure 9. From this point on, the left hand encounters problems similar to those met by the right hand in measures 5 and 6. The suggested fingerings are:

measures 9-12

measures 9-12 (*cont.*)

The thumb has to play as lightly as the other fingers in order to avoid undesirable accents.

In the soprano, several editions replace the turn over the last quarter note of each measure (measures 9-11) by a trill or a wedge. A wedge was placed by Bach over similar quarter notes in the inversion of this episode—the left hand in measures 30-32. A suggested execution of the turn is:

measure 9

From measure 12 through measure 14 there is a subject or its first limb in direct form or in inversion in every measure (measure 12, first limb in inversion in alto; measure 13, subject in soprano; measure 14, subject in inversion in alto and first limb in direct form in bass, both in irregular position). Each entrance has to be clearly rendered, with appropriate coloring.

At measures 15–16, the sequential progression leads to a momentous entrance in the bass at measure 17, where the tempo may be slightly stretched to gain the utmost clarity. At this point the right hand has problems in playing legato: a fingering analogous to that adopted for measures 4–5 is recommended. The entrance in the alto at measure 18 is awkward and should be played without undue insistence. The recommended solution for the long trill in the left hand at measure 20 is:

measure 20

The simultaneous use of the first and fifth fingers will contribute to the rhythmic stability of the trill, though a broadening of the general tempo in the measure is necessary.

The following stretto passage (measures 21–26) is difficult to execute with clarity if the performer seeks to bring out the overlapping subjects and inversions in their full length. But it is sufficient to bring out clearly the first limbs of subjects and inversions by careful separations between the first and second eighth notes of the measure in the appropriate voices (measure 21, bass; measure 22, soprano; measure 23, bass; measure 25, alto [preceded by an eighth-note rest]; and so on). Various editions add an unnecessary trill on the last quarter note of the treble in measure 23. The recommended fingering for measures 25–26 is:

measures 25-26

The execution of the trill in the alto at measure 29 is awkward. The recommended fingering is:

measure 29

An F sharp is possible in the conclusion because F would clash badly with the F sharp of the left hand on the downbeat of the following measure. The sequential episode at measures 30–32 does not require a turn in the left hand on the last quarter note of each measure, as some editions indicate. Careful separation of phrasing is essential between the first and second eighth notes (measure 34, alto and bass; measure 35, treble; measure 36–38, alto and bass). The sequential episode of measures 36–38 makes use of the three notes rising expressively on the first beat of each measure in the soprano, which the interpretation has to bring out in a sensitive way, with a slight insistence on the motive.

The entrance of the subject in the bass at measure 39 has to be carefully separated from the first eighth note of the measure; it may be played with a slight broadening of the tempo, while the entrance of the subject in the alto at measure 40 should not be too heavy. In the same measure, it is better to play the trill in the bass with an F natural, rather than an F sharp, in the closing notes. The execution of the long trill in measure 42 is similar to that of the one in measure 20. In the concluding measures, additional parts display two direct and two inverted motives from the first limb in contrary motion. The majesty of this conclusion should be well brought out by a considerable ritardando and full tone.

Only a moderate tempo can reveal the expressive character of the almost uninterrupted sixteenth-note motion. The suggested speed is: ♩ = 50–60.

The dynamic range of the fugue is rather narrow: the complex texture and the continuous presence of all three parts (except in measures 21–24) give almost no suggestion for dynamic change. In broad outline, however, it is most probably proper to make two continuing increases in volume—one from the opening to the close in A minor on the first eighth note of measure 21, and the other from the second eighth note of this measure, played suddenly less loud, to the majestic ending.

Here is the suggested dynamic scheme in more detail:

MEASURES	
1 – 4	*f* with appropriate shadings in the individual parts
5 – 11	Lighter *f*, including slight diminuendo
12 – 21	Continuous increase to the strong cadence
21 – 24	Lighter *f* from the second eighth note of the measure
25 – 29	Increase of the volume
30 – 32	Slight diminuendo
33 – 34	Continuous growth to the majestic conclusion

Because of the numerous full-subject entrances and limbs in both direct and inverted form, the texture of the fugue is fairly intricate. One is tempted to bring out subject after subject at the expense of the flowing line, thus losing the sense of unbroken continuity. Underlining each entrance only until it gives way to another entrance in another part will insure greater clarity in performance than rough insistence upon the full-length exposition of the subject each time.

BACH

Prelude and Fugue in E Minor

Well-Tempered Clavier, Book 1, No. 10

‿‿‿

The first half of the prelude has a broadly singing melody line, accompanied by a persistent figure, while the second half is a virtuosic toccata built on the persistent accompaniment figure of the first half. The fugue is the only two-part fugue in the collection and is closer to a two-part invention than to a fugue.

Prelude

Form: Two sections, with transition

		MEASURES
Section 1		1 – 21
First period		1 – 4
Second period		4 – 9
Third period		9 – 21
Transition		21 – 22
Section 2		23 – 41

The first part of the prelude resembles chamber music in that it is like a melody played on a stringed or wind instrument accompanied by a persistent figure in the bass and by chords in the middle parts. Each of the three layers needs appropriate treatment—a singing legato for the melodic line in the foreground; expressive shaping of the moving bass line in the second plane; and, finally, a light touch, precise in duration, for the middle voices on the softest level. In playing both the loudest and the softest parts, the right hand not only uses two distinct touches at the same time but also has to sustain long melodic notes for a full measure or longer.

Beyond the appropriate dynamic levels, the shaping of the phrases includes difficulties that involve the bass line. In fact, the notes of the bass line on the downbeat and the third beat of the measure carry harmonic significance that is completed by the middle voices. Each single harmony (especially the changing harmonies) needs a small, almost imperceptible stretching applied within the strict limitations of style and good taste: an actual rubato would overromanticize the noble melody beyond the line of acceptability.

A further problem is inherent in the realization of the ornaments. Obviously a long trill flowing directly into the written-out closing notes is needed every time, regardless of whether the ornament is notated *tr* or ∿ . A measured trill in thirty-second notes sensitively incorporated into the line and executed in the same singing legato, is recommended. The natural fluency of the left hand should be maintained during the trills in the melody to avoid accents that result from the effort of keeping the hands together.

In the performance of this prelude, much depends on the very first chord. If the desired tonal balance is well established and the bass line is sensitively shaped, the performance will most probably sail happily on undisturbed waters. Therefore the player's acute concentration before beginning the prelude will be even more important here than anywhere else.

In measure 3, the minute slurs need dynamic inflection more than real separation. On the last beat of the same measure, a smooth approach to the authentic cadence of measure 4, rather than sharp rhythm, should be the main preoccupation of the performer. Measures 4 to 9 (beginning on the third beat of measure 4) contain a harmonic sequence in which the changing points in the harmony need sensitive treatment. The recommended realization of the appoggiatura in measure 9 is:

measure 9

or

From this point on, the expression becomes more concentrated, as more unexpected modulations occur. The interruption of the trill by a sixteenth rest before the closing notes in measures 10 and 12 is a sign of deep emotion; at this point, a sensitive performance may convey the impression of a sudden lack of the physical forces needed to complete the trill. The expression deepens further from measure 15 on and reaches the emotional and dynamic climax at measures 19–20. Harmonic changes in this section should be well emphasized, along with the sinuosity of the melodic line. A broadening of the tempo at measure 20 will emphasize the conclusion of the first part.

A crescendo and an accelerando in the transition measures will lead spontaneously to the Presto, the toccata-like second part of the prelude built on the motive of the previous accompaniment figure. Achieving evenness and a perfect coupling of the hands are among the main difficulties. Although the harmony is still carried by the bass notes on the downbeat and third beat of the measure (in many instances separated by a considerable gap from the rest of the figure), a metric stress or even a slight delay would have a disastrous effect on the performance. The following suggestions for fingering ensure evenness:

measures 28-29

measures 32-33

measures 35-36

The choice of tempos should not only satisfy the separate needs of the contrasting sections, but it should also be appropriate for their relation to each other. In this particular case, it seems that the relationship is one of single to double: the recommended speed is ♩ = 60 for the first part and ♩ = 120 for the Presto, with measures 21–22 serving as a transition with an accelerando. The tempo of the first part bends slightly, in accordance with the sensitive curves of the melody, while the Presto is in strict tempo and only the last two measures have a conclusive ritardando. Furthermore, the contrast in tempo should be combined with a contrast in touch—a singing legato for the first part and brilliant finger articulation for the second part.

Contrasting dynamics applied to the contrasting sections are recommended—a singing legato with sensitive dynamic shadings for the first half and a brilliant forte for the second half. The suggested dynamic scheme is:

MEASURES

1 – 4	Cantabile (*mp* to *mf*) in the treble, *p* in the accompanying voices
4 – 9	Cantabile with broader dynamic inflections to mark the sinuosity of the melody

9 – 19	Continuous increase of the volume to the full, singing *f* at measure 19; accompaniment constantly less loud
20 – 21	Decrease of the volume with the ritardando to mark the end of the section
21 – 22	Increase of the volume with the accelerando
23 – 41	Brilliant, virtuosic *f* with some addition to the volume at measure 34 to underline the splitting of the treble voice; forceful conclusion.

Fugue

Form: Two parts

	MEASURES
Exposition	1 – 4
Development	5 – 38
Recapitulation	39 – 42

The lively subject seems very simple, at first glance; however further examination reveals that its last two beats (the second and third beats of measure 2) show more concentration of expression than the preceding segment. This difference may be skillfully exploited in the interpretation by applying a more legato and expressive touch to the tail of the subject. While the technical problems of playing the theme are fairly simple for the right hand, they are complicated and difficult for the left hand and need careful fingering. The complication becomes apparent as early in the work as measure 4, where a satisfactory solution for the fingering problem can be found only through taking into account the personal skill and manual abilities of the individual performer. The suggested fingerings are:

measure 4

Every recurrence of this problem is further complicated by the difficulty of synchronizing the hands in a perfectly even sixteenth-note motion. Sometimes the differing nature of the concurrent figures adds more complications, as it does in measures 5 and 7 where the open position of the arpeggiolike right-hand figure contrasts with the narrow position of the diatonically moving left hand. The recommended fingering is:

measures 5-8

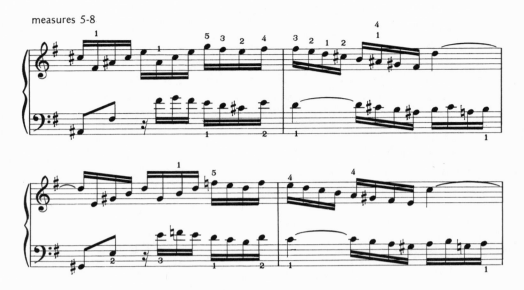

The large leaps in the left hand between measures 6 and 7 and between measures 8 and 9 may be played with elegant ease if the arm and shoulder are relaxed.

Measures 9–10 look simple; yet keeping the hands together here is not without problems. The faultless execution of these measures will to a large extent be the result of well-established and solidly learned fingerings. The recommended fingerings for measures 12 and measure 14 are:

measure 12

measure 14

The episode beginning at measure 15 fits the right hand better than the left. The recommended fingerings for the left hand are:

measure 16

measure 18

measures 20-21

The problems involved in measures 24–29 are similar to those of measures 5–10; here there is the complication that the usually less skillful left hand has to handle the arpeggio figure, and yet the synchronization of the hands should remain faultless. The recommended fingerings for measure 31 are:

measure 31

The frequency of black keys results in difficult fingerings for the left hand in measures 34 and 38:

measure 34

measure 38

At the last occurrence of the subject (measure 39 on), the imitation at measure 40 in the left hand has to be well emphasized. Most modern editions notate the closing (preferably major) chord in a rolled form.

The lively, spirited character of the fugue requires an energetic tempo; ♩ = 100 seems appropriate. To avoid an abrupt ending, a ritardando is needed from measure 41 to the end.

This simple, straightforward fugue does not call for sophisticated dynamic contrasts. In addition to shaping tonal inflections, the performer may wish to adopt the following dynamic scheme:

MEASURES	
1 – 4	Easy *f*, the left hand leading in measures 3–4
5 – 8	Slightly lighter; small, shaping crescendo-decrescendo embracing two measures may be adopted
9 – 10	Increasing the volume
11 – 14	Easy *f*
15 – 18	Slightly lighter, with emphasis on the sixteenth-note motive in either hand
19	*f*, to underline the unison
20 – 23	Easy *f*
24 – 27	Slightly lighter; shaping crescendo-decrescendo
28 – 29	Increasing the volume
30 – 33	Easy *f*
34 – 37	Similar to measures 15–18
38 – 42	*f*, gradually increasing toward the conclusion

BACH

Prelude and Fugue in G Minor

Well-Tempered Clavier, Book 1, No. 16

Sensitive musicianship is needed for the performance of this contemplative prelude. The fugue is in the same mood and requires much refinement in part playing and tonal shading.

Prelude

Form: Three sections and coda

	MEASURES
Section 1	1 – 7
Section 2	7 – 11
Section 3	11 – 18
Coda	18 – 19

An expressive, singing legato and flexible tone are required for the performance of this sorrowful prelude.

The opening trill is best executed at a free speed, with a slight prolongation of the principal note (with which it should begin). The trill should stop, without accent, when the left hand plays its last sixteenth note. The finished execution should be modeled after an expressive vocal trill; underneath, the left hand should outline the harmony softly. A perfect rendering of the singing line in measure 2 depends to a large extent on the evenness of tone quality between sixteenth and thirty-second notes, which is attained by avoiding inadvertent accents on the first thirty-second note. Such accents may, moreover, transform the calm pulsation of the 4/4 measure into a more agitated 8/8.

The execution of the trill in measure 3 is identical to the execution of the one in the first measure; the left hand, meanwhile, has to deal with part-playing problems: the dissonances between the overhanging tenor and the bass should be clearly audible in performance. Similar part-playing problems await the player in measures 4 and 5. In measure 7, the left-hand trill should be executed in the same way as the previous right-hand trills. Despite the fact that the pianist's left hand is usually not as well trained for the task as the right, the execution of this trill should sound light and easy, and its speed should match the speed of the previous trills in the right hand.

Among the variant textual readings of the last beat of measure 8 in the right hand, the one that suggests four even sixteenth notes seems preferable. Besides part playing, measures 9 and 10 include a refined difference between soprano and alto, somewhat like the subtle difference in tone between first and second violins of an orchestra. After another trill, the passion of the music intensifies in measures 12–13, where the motives are spread between bass and treble.

From measure 14 on, where the dominant pedal point is established, the soprano melody moving in quarter notes should dominate the persistent motive of the alto. The harmonic importance of the third beat in measure 15 requires a slight stretching; the small emphasis also points to the sudden warmth that invades the melodic line on the last beat of the measure. This is the emotional climax of the prelude, which is further emphasized by the left hand's suddenly moving in sixteenth notes for the first half of measure 16.

In measure 17 more stretching is required to bring out the accumulated harmonic tension on the subdominant. Good part playing is needed in the coda, where the motives seem to unwind after the previous tension. The ornament on the last beat of the concluding measure is best played in the following way:

measure 19

It is difficult to find a suitable tempo for this expressive prelude, especially because the first measure does not have the characteristic sixteenth-and-thirty-second-note motive; therefore the performer can easily be induced to take a too-slow tempo that may jeopardize the fluency of the performance. The right tempo, which must be flexible in many instances (such as at phrase ends or emotional climaxes), is situated in the neighborhood of ♩ = 60 and has a clear 4/4 pulsation.

A singing legato touch is required throughout, with a careful avoidance of nervous jerking of the thirty-second notes, both in tempo and tone.

Dynamics may vary between intense piano and solemn forte, with sensitive shaping applied to the figures to show their outline. The suggested dynamic scheme is:

MEASURES

1 – 4	Cantabile (between *mp* and *mf*, the left hand softer)
4 – 6	From third beat in measure 4, gradual increase of volume with careful shading of the melodic line
7 – 8	*f*
8 – 10	From fourth beat in measure 8, gradual decrease of volume to
11	Cantabile
12	Increase-decrease
13	Increase only

14 – 15   Decrease to third beat of measure 15
15 – 18   From third beat of measure 15, increase throughout to downbeat of measure 18
18 – 19   Gradual decrease to a concluding piano, with sensitive shading

Fugue

Form: Four parts

	MEASURES
Exposition	1 – 8
Development	8 – 28
Recapitulation	28 – 34

Most editions agree in suggesting legato for the second half of the subject, though they vary widely in recommending articulation for the first half. It is interesting to note that most editions recommend legato-staccato (portamento) for the countersubject, which is the inverted derivative of the subject. Therefore it seems logical to adopt the same articulation for the subject itself:

measures 1-3

The true portamento touch consists of long notes with almost no interruption between them; it is highly different from staccato, whose use here would contradict the majestic character of the fugue.

At the codetta of measure 4, where the eighth-and-sixteenth-note motive establishes its dominance over the rhythm for the rest of the fugue, both voices should be played legato in order to enhance the dramatic contrast with the entrance of the bass, playing detached and without heaviness or pounding in measure 5. By this point, the performer should have succeeded in imprinting the legato and portamento articulations conclusively upon the different motives.

The first episode (measures 8–12) contains the danger of a possible nervous jerking of the sixteenth notes, and it also hides a few surprises in the distribution of the motives between the hands. This latter problem should be solved smoothly, in a way that is unnoticed by the listener. Particularly tricky is measure 10, where the following solution is recommended:

measure 10

The following section (measures 12–18) contains many entrances and involves the temptation to pound out each and every one of them. The player has to show determined restraint by bringing out only the first half of the subject and playing the second half lightly. Furthermore the dynamic build-up of this section is crucial (see the suggested dynamic scheme on p. 31). An additional difficulty is hidden in measure 17, where a stretto between the bass and alto may endanger the clarity of the execution if both voices are played uniformly loud and with monochromatic touch. The short episode built on the eighth-and-sixteenth-note motive (measures 17–18) again involves the danger of nervous jerking.

The soprano enters at measure 21, with a slightly altered countersubject in the next measure that should be clearly shown in the performance; similar interpretation is to be given to the countersubject in measures 23–24. The following lyrical episode in measures 24–27 contains many problems of legato playing and consequently of fingering. It is absolutely necessary that the tied quarter notes in the soprano and alto be held for their full duration, including the first sixteenth note of the following beat to which they are tied—a requirement that complicates the fingering greatly. The suggested solution is:

measures 24-27

This fingering, though complicated, takes into account the various positions on the keyboard. As for the left hand, phrasings are needed, as the above example shows.

Measures 28–29 contain a difficult stretto involving all four voices that is further complicated by a crossing of the soprano and alto. An intelligent interpretation will only bring out the first half of the subject slightly and will not assign the same intensity to the second half. At measure 30, faultless voice leading should be coupled with a delicate distinction between the sounds of the alto and soprano. The entrance of the alto in measure 31 usually gets fair treatment, but the tenor entrance in measure 33 is often overlooked or drowned in the heavy texture of chords resulting from the splitting of voices. Only the following fingering is possible in the closing measure:

measure 34

The slight non legato touch (coupled with a ritardando) that is used here for the motive (previously played legato) makes the ending sound more majestic.

Based on the eighth-and-sixteenth-note motive, the tempo appears to be around ♩ = 80, but it is slightly broadened for more clarity when intricate strettos appear.

The majesty of this fugue is best served by using only two dynamic levels—a determined forte for the subjects and a lighter but still sonorous tone for the episodes. The forte adopted for the subject should be flexible and capable of underlining the inherent duality of the subject; the notes that are played portamento-tenuto should be forte, and those that are legato should be played poco meno forte.

The suggested dynamic scheme is:

MEASURES

1 – 3	*f* with the inherent differences just described
4	Sonorous *mf* for the codetta
5 – 7	*f*
8 – 12	Sonorous *mf*, increasing to *f* at the cadence
12 – 18	*f*, using various colors for the entrances, meno *f* for the second halves of the subject and for the other voices
18 – 19	Sonorous *mf*
20 – 24	*f* with various colors for the entrances, to the third beat of measure 24
24 – 28	From the third beat of measure 24, *mf*, the softest sound used in the fugue, with a clear difference between soprano and alto; measure 27 may increase to *f*
28 – 29	*f* for the first halves of the subjects, to the third beat of measure 29
29 – 30	On the third beat of measure 29, begin sonorous *mf*; increase constantly
31 – 32	*f*
33 – 34	The most majestic *f*

BACH

Prelude and Fugue in B Flat Major

Well-Tempered Clavier, Book 1, No. 21

~~~~~~

This toccata-like prelude requires fluent and easy finger technique and good coordination between the hands. The difficulty of the fugue lays in part-playing problems, involving a fairly fast speed.

Prelude

Form: Two sections

	MEASURES
Section 1	1 – 11
Section 2	11 – 20

The basic figure of the first section is one typically used for stringed instruments. Faultless execution of this figure on the keyboard is difficult. The necessary metrical evenness depends on maintaining good coordination between the hands, as well as on evenly executing the notes entrusted to the right hand. Jamming the right-hand notes together transforms the figure into inarticulate jerks, thus precluding any possibility of a decent performance. It is suggested that the fingers of the right hand be kept close to the keys so that they can play the figure in a relaxed manner, without excessive finger articulation or excessive forearm rotation. In fact, both these motions mentioned take part in the execution: it is only their employment to an immoderate extent that may be harmful to an even execution.

The eighth notes of the left hand are to be played in a light, *détaché* fashion. At measure 3, a more expressive legato-scale figure appears; it should be divided between the hands as marked in the music to avoid passages of the thumb. Good coordination between the hands will be assured here by preparing the hands over the keys ahead of time, before they take over their assigned portions of the scales; bumps and accents are thereby avoided. Together with a legato touch, the scales should have a sense of direction that is well underlined with appropriate dynamic shading, especially in measures 8 and 10. Measure 10 is further complicated by suddenly appearing arpeggio figures that only make metrical evenness more difficult to maintain. A sizable ritardando at the end of the measure will serve as preparation for the second section.

At this point, several editions indicate "Adagio" for the chords and "Presto" for the ensuing thirty-second-note figure at measures 11 and 13. Actually a change of tempo is less needed here than a great contrast in character. In addition to a healthy forte sound, the strong, dramatic nature of the chords should be emphasized by a dotting that is somewhat quicker than an ordinary ♩♪ rhythm but is not nearly as fast as double dotting. The tone should be full and brilliant, and it should remain free of harshness. The ensuing scale passage is to be interpreted with bold virtuosity. The figure in measures 11 and 12 is best played entirely with the right hand; only the downbeat of measure 13 will be entrusted to the left hand.

The rising figure of measures 13 and 14 should be started in the left hand and passed to the right on the third beat of measure 14. In measures 15–19, both the chords and the ensuing figures become declamatory, especially in measure 17 where a slight easing of the tempo is recommended. The chords of the same measure should be rapidly arpeggiated, bringing out the motion in eighth notes in the alto and tenor. The ornament on the downbeat of measure 19 is a mordent, which is to be played on the beat. The figure following it should be played with the utmost clarity and calm. Some editions without good authority add a twenty-first measure to the prelude consisting of a B flat bass note.

The tempo for this toccata-like prelude seems to be situated around ♩ = 80, with possible variations in the second section if the performer decides to obey the Adagio and Presto markings.

The dynamics should make a contrast between the first and second sections of the piece; particular care should also be given to the shading of the scale figures. The suggested dynamic scheme is:

MEASURES

1 – 2	Poco *f;* elegant sound
3 – 4	Expressive shading of the legato scale figures
5	On first and second beats, somewhat decreasing
5 – 6	From third beat of measures 5 to third beat of measure 6, a softer sound still in the range of an elegant, light *mf*
6 – 8	From third beat of measure 6, gradual increase to the poco *f*
8 – 10	Poco *f*, with expressive shading of scales and with special regard for conclusion of measure 10
11 – 20	*f*, with sonorous chords; scales constantly shaped by expressive dynamics
20	A slight decrease of sound in the rising arpeggio figure

Fugue

Form: Three parts

	MEASURES
Exposition	1 – 17
Development	17 – 41
Recapitulation and coda	41 – 48

The articulation of the first half of the fugue subject offers various possibilities. The following two examples show the opposite poles of these possibilities:

measures 1-3

measures 1-3

However different these phrasings seem at first glance, they both agree that the step of a sixth on the last beat of measure 1 and 2 should be disconnected and that the articulation of the subject necessarily decides the articulation of the first countersubject. Here is the suggested articulation for the subject and countersubject, with fingerings for the second half of the subject:

measures 1-9

(cont.)

measures 1–9 (*cont.*)

The phrasings involved should be smooth and tasteful; picking up the hand sharply at the end of a slur and falling heavily on the next key should be carefully avoided. In measures 7 and 8 the two voices have to be kept rigorously together, in both eighth-note and sixteenth-note motion.

The entrance of the bass at measure 9 brings in the second countersubject, with its lightly interjected sixteenth notes, at the ends of measures 9 and 10. This second countersubject brings some technical complications into measures 11 and 12. The disconnected repeated notes in the alto part of the right hand should be played with a light thumb, helped by only a minimal downward motion of the hand. The difficulty is more critical for the left hand in measures 15–16. The hands should be free of tenseness and stiffness at this point; extensive practicing of the passage in a slow and relaxed way is strongly recommended. The task is somewhat easier in measures 17 and 18.

The episode, measures 19–21, uses the first fragment of the subject in inverted form in the left hand; hence its articulation should match that adopted for the subject. The entrance in measure 22 is easy to overplay because it is divided between the hands. The tonal balance at the entrance of the bass in measure 26 is less of a problem. The same principle applies to the episode in measures 30–35 as to the first episode in measures 19–21. The only difficulty is that of good part playing in the left hand in measures 33 and 34. The entrance of the tenor at measure 35 is only a false entrance and should sound like one in the performance; it should give way to the complete entrance in the soprano at measure 37. The increased gap between the hands in measures 39 and 40 calls for good tonal balance.

At the recapitulatory entrance in measure 41, the tempo may slow down slightly, thus bringing a touch of solemnity to the last appearance of the subject. The recommended fingering for measures 43–44 is:

measures 43-44

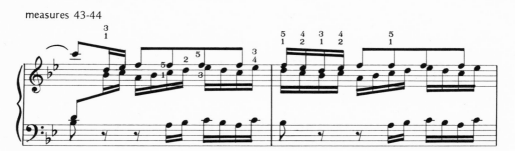

Measures 45 and 46 contain a problem of dividing the text between the hands in the most comfortable way. The recommended solution is:

measures 45-46

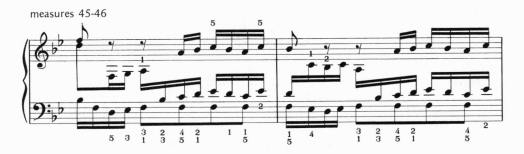

The touch of solemnity disappears in the concluding two measures, and the fugue ends on the jovial, cheerful tone used throughout.

This is a simple, unsophisticated piece that generates genuine good humor. A lively tempo, ♩ = 120, will serve this purpose.

There is no room for dramatic changes in dynamics in this straightforward fugue. The liveliness and wit are best rendered by appropriate articulation changes, rather than by dynamic contrasts. The suggested dynamic scheme is:

MEASURES	
1 – 4	Poco *f*
4 – 8	Poco *f* for the subject; the countersubject somewhat less but still crisp
9 – 12	Same as preceding
13 – 16	Same as preceding, with special care to preserve a light left hand
17 – 18	Good, singing *f* legato for the right hand, contrasting with the usual treatment of the second half of the subject
19 – 21	Slightly softer because one voice is missing
22 – 25	The softest poco *f*, with absolute clarity in voice leading
26 – 29	Poco *f*
30 – 32	Softer, since one voice is missing almost all the time
33 – 34	The same as previously; shaping of the right hand, clarity in the left
35 – 36	Softest poco *f* for false entrance
37 – 40	Poco *f* to mark real entrance
41 – 44	The loudest poco *f*, with a touch of solemnity, but still with elegant control
45 – 48	Poco *f*, keeping elegant control

Franz Joseph Haydn

Born 1732, Rohrau; died 1809, Vienna

A mistaken, though broadly shared, view of this great composer is the popular image of "Papa" Haydn, whose art, lacking in complexity, is even tempered, good humored, and therefore easily accessible, especially to children. Even in our day this view still prevails. The same half-dozen or so Haydn sonatas are diligently learned by young pianists, while the main core of Haydn's keyboard works is still ignored and almost completely excluded from the concert hall.

The number of Haydn piano sonatas varies from edition to edition. The Hoboken catalogue lists fifty-two, while the authoritative Vienna Urtext Edition has sixty-two of them. (The numbering in this book follows Hoboken's.) Even superficial sight reading reveals precious pearls among the sonatas that are worthy of rescue from oblivion, such as the *Sonata in A Major*, No. 12, with its syncopated Trio in the Menuetto movement; or the *Sonata in D Major*, No. 19, with its beautiful cellolike melody in the slow movement; or the magnificent *Sonata in A Flat Major*, No. 46.

Haydn's keyboard writing has its roots in the style of C. P. E. Bach and George Christoph Wagenseil (1715–1777), whose influence is distinctly visible in Haydn's early sonatas. Haydn was above all a violinist; his treatment of the fiddle is always original and virtuosic. As a keyboard performer he could not measure up to his virtuoso contemporaries Clementi and Mozart. But his treatment of the keyboard, which is less demanding in the early works, shows prolific fantasy and freedom of form. The late sonatas, inspired by and composed for such accomplished virtuosos as the Auenbrugger sisters (Franziska and Marianne), Marianne von Genzinger and Therese Jansen, display his best musical inspiration and attain perfection both in form and in instrumental writing. They call for strong technique as well as for the utmost sensitivity in performance—for power and poetry.

The study of Haydn's piano works is highly rewarding and should be strongly encouraged.

HAYDN

Sonata in C Minor, No. 20

~~~~~~

Dating from 1771, this sonata was composed in Haydn's *Sturm und Drang* ("storm and stress") period. Personal expression overshadows every other consideration in all three movements. A serious tone, heightened at times to tragic intensity, prevails throughout even the last movement, which has no affinity with the lighthearted finales usual with Haydn.

Moderato [Allegro moderato]

M.M. ♩ = 80–88

Form: Sonata

	MEASURES
Exposition	1 – 37
First subject	1 – 9
Transition	10 – 26
Second subject	26 – 31
Closing subject	32 – 37
Development	38 – 68
Recapitulation	69 – 100

Like sad sighs, the expressive slurs in both hands set the tragic-elegiac tone immediately, at the beginning of the movement. The serious, intense mood should prevent the performer from playing the slur endings or staccatos too short by picking up the hand sharply. Phrasings throughout the movement should be executed smoothly, with calm hands. In the second measure, successive intervals of the sixth have to be very carefully fingered to insure a smooth execution of the turn inserted before the third beat. It is most important to play the E flat (the low note of the fourth sixth) with the first finger, thus bringing the hand into the best position for the turn.

measure 2

In measure 3, the turns are preceded by upbeat eighth notes that should not be played with excessive shortness, even though they have to be slightly separated from the turns so as to give a pleading character to the suspensions on the first and third beats. If a polished execution of the inverted mordent in measure 4 is difficult to achieve, it can be replaced by a short grace note in the following way:

measure 4

The wedges appearing in this measure should not be played too short.

The second half of the main subject takes a new turn in measure 6 with a dotted-rhythm figure. From this point on, the melodic line gets longer; accordingly, the tone should also become more intense. In measure 7, the execution of the difficult inverted mordent should not alter the dotted rhythm, nor should it disrupt the melodic line. The left hand should play its part short and light, without interfering with the tone of the right-hand part. An emphatic, strong cadence will close the main subject in a decisive manner.

Measure 9 strikes up a resolute new motive. The answer is given to it by an expressive solo of the right hand, which is not in any way ready to give up the serious mood. The following example gives the approximate execution of the ornaments:

measure 9

The forte and piano alternating on the eighth notes in measures 11 and 14 do not imply dynamic extremes. The fortes should be interpreted more as meaningful sforzandos, with a slight prolongation of the note. The expressive mood continues undisturbed from measure 15 on. A good singing legato is needed here for the thirds in the right hand, while the left hand is only accompaniment (the piano is in the original). The forte that appears on the last beat of measure 18 is best introduced by a crescendo from the beginning of the measure.

The following sinuous single line seems to be unsuited to the pianoforte. In fact, it results from concentrating the expression in the melodic line. The performer needs all his interpretative power to render this single melodic line meaningfully, in a sensitive manner. The tempo may ease a little, but there should be no grouping accents to break up the flowing line. The repetition of the motive (it is repeated three times in the second half of measure 20 and in measure 21) poses a special challenge to the imaginative handling of this identical material, which is to be played with a different meaning each time.

The expressivity of the music is further enhanced from measure 22 on by the passionate triplets of the right hand and the harmonic ambiguity between major and minor mode. Measure 24 should gradually ease the tempo. The melody languishes as it becomes a recitativo at the Adagio, where the difference of duration between sixteenth notes and eighth notes should be clearly rendered. In measure 25, further rallentando is needed at the approach of the fermata (*smorzando* means slowing the tempo while making a diminuendo).

The Tempo primo explodes in a forte. In spite of the decided rhythm, the character of the music remains serious, even solemn. The wedges should be interpreted here as short staccatos; the dots following the sixteenth notes will become rests. The thirty-second notes should be played strongly, on the beat. In measure 28, the first E flat of the right hand should be executed as a thirty-second note, thus matching the rhythm of the similar motive in the same measure. The approximate execution of the ornament is:

The determined expression changes at measure 29 and gives way to some more feverish questioning. The phrase is left open in a dramatic manner on a dominant chord, which is followed by a no-less dramatic rest that should be held for its full length. The following closing section includes some technical difficulties, such as maintaining evenness in the left hand's triplet figure and independence and clarity in the right hand's five-note figure. Both tasks are easier with the fingers kept close to the keys. Further, the five-finger motive in the right hand may too readily be turned into inarticulate jerking if the hand is used in the manner of a wheel, without an independent but small articulation of each finger.

At measure 35 the expressive concentration on the melody is further intensified by chromaticism. The dominant-tonic cadence (measures 36–37) closes the exposition;

thus it has to be played very meaningfully. The following dotted motive should be played very softly, in a reflective mood—like a sad sigh.

The development begins with the main subject, and the sigh motives rise stepwise to an expressive suspension on the first beat of measure 39, which may have a slight prolongation. The passing of the motive to the left hand at measure 40 reminds one of Beethoven's compositional techniques. The sigh motives again rise stepwise from measure 43 on and climb even farther than before, arriving at another sorrowful suspension and the key of B flat minor at measure 45. The descending intervals should be played with a rallentando at the approach of the fermata, in complete resignation.

From this point on, the development is built on the closing subject. Evenness of the left hand is even more difficult to ensure here than in the earlier triplet figure because the passage is much longer and the figures involved are larger. The dynamics can be dictated by the imagination of the performer. (The only original dynamic markings for this section are: measure 55, *f* (*sf*) on the last beat; measure 61, crescendo; measure 62, *ff*; measure 65, *p*.) The D flat major scales of measure 51 are to be treated as bright melody, not as mere scales. The trill in measure 52 presupposes a suffix at the end. The following example gives the execution for the turns in measures 56, 57, and 58:

measure 56

The inverted mordents on the last beats of the same measures should be played lightly, respecting the slur ending. (The inverted mordent includes three notes: . In measure 58 there is a trill without suffix instead of an inverted mordent.)

The ornaments of measures 59 and 60 are best interpreted as turns, in the following way:

measure 59

Whatever dynamics the performer has adopted for the section, it is recommended that it be played piano from measure 59 on and kept at piano up to the crescendo in measure 61.

From this point on, tonal balance should be the performer's main preoccupation; the left hand should be kept softer than the right throughout the unison passage. The cadence in G minor (measures 64–65) should be rendered with clarity in spite of the missing tonic chord in the right hand. At this point the thoughtful solo motive returns in piano, and it is interrupted by the determined motive played forte. Here is the execution of the ornaments:

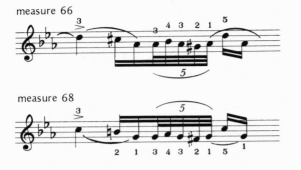

Measure 68 should broaden the tempo to prepare for the recapitulation.

After only four measures, the main motive passes to the left hand; it rises stepwise to reach a climax at the suspension on the first beat of measure 75, where it disintegrates (after the climax, a diminuendo and slight rallentando are recommended). The half-measure rest at measure 76 has to be of generous length. The pianissimo following is Haydn's own indication.

From this point on, the recapitulation does not exhibit any difference from the exposition until the coda enters on the third beat of measure 98. Containing short panting motives, the coda sounds exhausted from the heavy strain of past emotions. The dotted legato motive is like a sigh; the staccato eighth notes (beware of excessive shortness) express passive compliance.

There are many difficult details in this movement: the left hand's triplet sixteenth-note figures are not easy to play evenly, and the ornaments of the determined motive are only rarely executed with brio and ease. But as in many other works, in this one technique is less important than spirit. The consistently serious or tragic mood is difficult for the inexperienced pianist to render. The music, which is made up of many two-note slurs and short motives, too easily evokes a cute, joking expression. A good example of this pitfall is the closing subject with its five-note figures and simple tonic-dominant harmony; this music depicts terrifying obsession and should not sound like mere repetitions of a commonplace.

Andante con moto

M.M. ♩ = 50

Form: Sonata

		MEASURES
Exposition		1 – 25
	First subject	1 – 13
	Second subject	14 – 19
	Closing subject	19 – 25
Development		26 – 50
Recapitulation		51 – 67

A meditative mood prevails for the first subject, and this mood is further enhanced by the dignified, even motion of the bass line, which is similar to the bass part of a Baroque dance movement. This line has to be played with the expressivity of a cello, making the listener wonder (at least during the opening measure) which hand will carry the melody. The right-hand trill in measure 2 begins with the lower auxiliary note:

measure 2

A slight stress on the D natural underlines its dissonance with the bass.

From this measure on, the right hand has to capture the undivided attention of the listener: warm, singing tone for the melody is obviously indispensable. The original text for the last beat of measure 7 shows:

measure 7

The recommended execution is:

The inverted mordent of measure 8 coincides with a phrase ending; hence a light execution is necessary. The grace notes of measure 9 are short and slightly ahead of the beat. For the trills in measures 10 and 11, the performer may adopt from among many valid executions the following suggestion:

measure 10

In measure 12 the sixteenth notes on the last two beats are slurred by twos: the fingering should be 3–2 throughout. A smooth rendering of the phrase ending in measure 13 that closes the entire first subject is not easy. The combination of a noisy inverted mordent in the right hand together with the left hand obviously beginning a new phrase with the interval of a third on the second beat can have a disastrous effect at this point. The recommended fingering for the left hand in measure 13 is:

measure 13

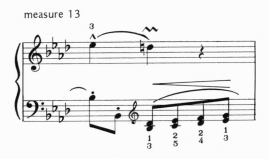

The second subject shows more personal involvement. The panting character of the almost constant syncopations effaces the original pensive dignity of the movement. Measures 14 and 15 may be played with an echo effect. The following four measures modulate through sorrowful minor keys. The suggested phrasing is:

measures 15-17

The second subject runs out of strength in measure 19.

The closing subject enters with the last two sixteenth notes of measure 19 and regains some of the solemn character of the opening subject. In measures 21 and 24, the bass line is strictly legato; the right-hand notes are separated by rests. The second version of the closing subject generates more intensity and climbs into higher regions, while the tempo broadens slightly.

The development opens in the pensive mood of the first subject, but it quickly runs out of force, and from measure 31 on, the panting syncopation takes over. Restless modulations lead through sorrowful minor keys, and the tonality of D flat major emerges from them in measure 36. In spite of the major key, the expressive sixteenth-note motive of the right hand adds supplication to the distress. The part playing of the left hand should be faultless in this section (measures 36–38), while the right hand has to show the two interruptions of the melodic line by sixteenth rests.

At measure 40, the second subject makes an appearance in the appeasing, stable atmosphere of D flat major, which settles in for the rest of the development. Measures 43–44 and 45–46 further confirm the tonality before the four-measure transition (measures 47–50) gets under way. The melody of this transitional section contains sensitive octave steps at the beginning of each measure (beware of picking the hand up sharply and marring the phrasing), while the bass rises in stepwise motion. Measure 50 should have a broadening of the tempo as it leads toward the recapitulation. The rendition of the development section is among the most difficult tasks in performing this movement.

The lasting comfort of the D-flat section in the development allows the recapitulation to brave the syncopation that cannot overpower the solemn character any longer. The recapitulation of the principal theme omits the first eight measures of the subject and states only the portion contained in measures 9 to 13 of the original statement; the second and closing subjects are restated without change.

The performance difficulties lie in sensitively rendering the differences between the solemn and the tormented passages. This rendering should express a soul torn between calm and distress, though a consistent tempo and good taste should be maintained. In spite of the "con moto," in the expression marking at the beginning of the movement, the tempo should not be too fast.

Finale: Allegro

M.M. ♩ = 144–152

Form: Sonata

	MEASURES
Exposition	1 – 46
First subject	1 – 12
Transition	12 – 20
Second subject	21 – 41
Closing subject	41 – 46
Development	47 – 78
Recapitulation	78 – 151

After the solemn slow movement, the tragic mood pervades the Finale, foreshadowing the last movement of Mozart's *Sonata in C Minor,* K. 457. Haydn's choice of sonata form instead of rondo or minuet form (more usual for finales in sonatas of this period) further points to the important message it contains.

The first subject instantly sets the listener in the midst of turmoil. The disconnected quarter notes and the falling five-note figure imbue the theme with a restlessness from which not even the longer line of measure 3 can recover. The wedges on the quarter notes (and, in general, throughout the movement) should not be interpreted with exaggerated sharpness. The trill in measure 5 should begin on the upper auxiliary note. The manuscript contains this notation for the first two beats of the right hand:

measure 6

The approximate execution of measures 5 and 6 is:

measures 5-6

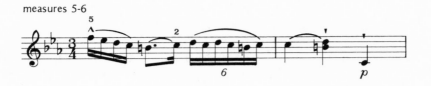

The performer should strictly obey the slurs and staccatos of measure 10 and should play the last two eighth notes of measure 11 long, with an almost tenuto touch. The transition, initiated by an impetuous sixteenth-note motive in the left hand, contrasts with the preceding main subject in its longer legato lines and in its use of imitation. The expression remains passionate, with the eighth notes preparing for the suspensions with small crescendos. In addition to elementary accuracy, the rendering should include the main ingredient of part playing—namely, the use of different colors for the upper and lower parts; here the part playing should be patterned after the sound of first and second violins.

The playfulness of the second subject is only apparent, for the seemingly innocent commonplaces soon turn to stormy figuration. From measure 27 onward, the last sixteenth note of each group obviously carries some melodic importance. In measure 29, when the left hand crosses over the right, one should refrain from picking up the hand sharply from the last quarter note of measure 28, so that an accent on it as well as a bump on the first quarter note of measure 29 can be avoided. Smooth, quick changes of position presuppose loose shoulders. The right-hand figure is uncomfortable and requires good finger technique.

At measure 31, the right hand regains full importance; measure 32 especially requires melodic treatment rather than empty scale work. Measures 33 and 34 should be played with conviction, and they should vigorously lead to the deceptive cadence on the first beat of measure 35, where the virtuosity explodes again.

The chromaticism of the melody appearing in measure 37 denotes strong emotion. The phrase ending on the first beat of measure 41 should be played conclusively, with some broadening of the tempo in measure 40. The inner motions of the closing subject imply the trepidation of a tormented soul. The development dies away with a sad sigh in the upper voices, calming down the tempo.

The development begins with the main subject in E flat major and stops with a dramatic question on the dominant; this passage is followed by an equally dramatic rest that should be given accurate, if not generous, length. At this point, the main subject reappears in F minor and leads to a contrapuntal section built on the staccato eighth-note motive that introduced the transition from the first to the second subject in the exposition. In spite of the staccatos, the mood remains gloomy and tormented by restless modulations. Beware of too-short staccatos and slur endings. The staccato quarter-note resolutions of the suspensions carry an expressive rather than a routine accent on the dominant harmonies (measures 57, 59, 61, and 63), and the subsequent measures with their tonic harmonies are lighter.

From measure 65 on, the apparently playful motive of the second subject shows growing anger that culminates in the cadence in G minor at measure 74. The fingering of this section needs to be solidly established and learned. The principle in fingering this broken-third passage is that the thumb is used on every lower white key, like this:

measure 65

Particularly good care has to be taken with the sudden change of span on the second beat of measure 68, where the usual distance of a third is suddenly broadened to that of a fourth. From this measure on, the last group of sixteenth notes in every measure carries an important melodic turn.

The transition to the recapitulation (measures 74–79) is like repentance after the angry outbreak of the preceding section. The thirds in the right hand are slurred without break; the wedge on the last third of the motive is to be interpreted without excessive shortness. During the rests separating the motives of the right hand, the left hand emits short sighs in its suspensions.

At the recapitulation (measure 79), the main subject has eighth notes throughout instead of the quarter notes of the exposition. Their chromaticism lends a subdued character to a theme that was strong and vigorous at its first appearance. The rhythm of the right hand at measure 81 is easily misread: the rhythm is that of even eighth notes slurred by twos, and every other note is shortened by a sixteenth rest.

The contrapuntal transition interrupts the main subject at measure 84 and leads to the recapitulation of the second subject at measure 90. There is no forewarning at this point that the subject will soon turn into an important fantasialike development. This section passes through different keys and finally reaches the dominant of C minor; it is followed by a meaningful rest with a fermata at measure 120. Perfect evenness of the continuous sixteenth notes is fairly difficult to obtain; a light thumb, moved without the help of the forearm, is the first condition for attaining this evenness. In measures 100 and 103, a new difficulty arises; the continuity of the sixteenths figure should not be broken by a bump at the point where the left hand takes over.

From measure 107 on, particular attention should be concentrated on the left hand's crossing over the right. If the octave is played excessively short, a crash on the top note is hardly avoidable.

The deviation from normal sonata form marked by this fantasia development of the second subject is important enough for Haydn to have felt that a new statement of the main subject following the fermata in measure 120 was necessary to bring order to the unfolding of the movement. At measure 128, the second half of the second subject (which was omitted up to this point) is recapitulated; everything seems to be following a normal path, when suddenly, at measure 138, the fantasia takes over a second time. The two-measure section of the exposition is extended here, and it covers a larger part of the keyboard. Thus the chord of the Neapolitan sixth is underlined much more strongly than it was in the exposition. The ensuing coda shows similar emotion to that of the exposition in its inner voices. The three closing measures try to be more affirmative, but they fail to be convincing.

There is no doubt that the Finale rivals the first movement in importance. In character, it is impassioned—even desperate. The intense emotion draws Haydn into altering his usual sonata form. Technically the difficulties lie in the passagework (which should be rendered with evenness) and in some demanding part playing. A renewed warning against interpreting the wedges with excessive shortness seems appropriate. The performance of the movement should give the impression of a soul driven by an unceasing storm.

HAYDN
Variations in F Minor

~~~~~~

Called by Haydn "un piccolo divertimento" and composed in 1793 for Barbara Ployer (for whom Mozart had written two piano concertos, K. 449 and K. 453), this set of variations shows Haydn at the height of his creative powers. The main theme is in F minor; it is followed by a second theme in the parallel major. Each theme has two variations. The work then concludes with an extensive coda—a sort of development built on the subject in minor.

Andante

M.M. ♪ = 96–100

Form: Variations

	MEASURES
Theme A	1 – 29
Theme B	30 – 49
First variation on theme A	50 – 78
First variation on theme B	79 – 98
Second variation on theme A	99 – 127
Second variation on theme B	128 – 145
Coda	146 – 228

The serene theme, which reflects a combination of elegant charm and submissive melancholy, is propelled by a characteristic dotted rhythm that should be perfectly precise in performance. Overdotting the rhythm is just as unacceptable as a too-soft rendition, which would deprive the theme of its right amount of nervous spark. The dotted sixteenth note, which is sometimes written out as an ordinary sixteenth followed by a thirty-second rest, is to be played consistently staccato; the suggested fingering for measures 1 and 2 serves this purpose:

measures 1-3

Any weight or accent should be avoided on the eighth-note F of the melody in the middle of measure 2, since it is the last note of the first motive. The second motive begins with the ensuing dotted rhythm.

    Measures 4 through 6 have to be as legato as possible, and they should contain an expressive crescendo-decrescendo. The turn in measure 5 begins with the note above:

measure 5

The sorrowful dissonance of the suspension at the beginning of measure 6 has to be brought out in a sensitive way, and the middle voice in the right hand should be played softly, without disturbing the suspension in the melody. The left hand in these first six measures has to deal with some part-playing problems: the quarter notes of the bass line are a guide to the pedaling. There should be two pedals per measure in the first three measures; then in measures 4 through 6 there should be a fresh pedal every time the left hand plays a note in either voice. Though the hands exchange roles at measure 7, beware of too loud a left hand. The part playing in the right hand should be strictly executed in these measures; the same holds true for the part playing in the left hand in measures 10–11. Beware of making a noticeable ritardando in measure 12, where the first half of Theme A ends; it would break the continuity.

    The second half of the theme shows a more elaborate melodic line that brings in new technical difficulties. Among them the four-note thirty-seconds figures (measures 14 and 15) need close attention. Carelessly tearing through these figures is intolerable because it turns these notes, which are an important part of the melody, into inarticulate jerks. The ornament in measure 17 is to be played on the beat; the middle voice needs the same care it received in measure 6. The legato thirds of the left hand should be separated from the resolution on the third beat of the measure by a break in the phrasing. They lead into the reappearance of the first motive, which is split at this point between low and high registers and carries expressions differentiated by the timbres themselves.

The music takes a more decisive path in measure 20 with a turn toward the subdominant harmony. Measure 22, in spite of its apparent emptiness (there are only two chords, which are separated by rests), has high intensity; the exact count should be observed rigorously. On its reappearance in measure 23, the main idea shows growing anger; the anger explodes in the syncopated Neapolitan sixth, which should be rolled, accented, and played with a tenuto touch. The ensuing dotted arpeggio takes the edge off the chord and brings the melancholy mood back.

The chords of the left hand in measures 27 and 28 should be of precise duration. The F minor subject concludes on a tone of resignation.

The second theme, which is in F major, has a smiling, expressive character. The rising chromaticism of measure 30 builds up tension that unwinds in the cascade of arpeggios in measure 31. The ensuing graceful turns add to the relaxed mood. The arpeggios are best played here with small and independent finger articulations that are helped by the lateral bending of the wrist. Notice that the left hand plays legato only in measures 30 and 34; all other eighth notes (with the exception of the last two in measure 36) should be played detached, but not staccato.

At the end of measure 36, a short breath pause, much in the manner of a comma in a sentence, is necessary. Measure 37 is to be played with the strictest legato in both hands. To bring out its expressive chromaticism, a crescendo may be included that leads to a brilliant forte in measure 38 (with sparkling articulation for the arpeggio); it is followed by a sudden piano that is to be taken seriously.

The second half of the theme has a difficult accompaniment (measure 40): the left hand has to produce graceful turns similar to those of the right hand in the following two measures. Measure 43 is reminiscent of measure 17 as far as the phrasing of the left hand is concerned. The performance of measures 44 and 45 should reveal the answering chromaticism between the rising left hand and the falling right. From measure 46 on, the elegant charm of the staccato eighth notes has to be brought to life. Particular care must be taken with the left-hand arpeggio in measure 48, which often receives clumsy treatment due to excessive armweight. The three notes of the left hand in measure 49 are to be played staccato and with the same elegance it received at the end of the first part of the second theme.

The alternation of the hands gives the first variation a restless, agitated character to which the almost-always-present chromaticism adds a dark, pessimistic color. Although they are separated by rests, the portamento notes of the right hand should form a long line. The deep and sorrowful sforzandos underline the dissonances in measure 52. In the following measure, the cascading chromatic scale is to be played without accents that break up the long line. In measures 54 and 55, the melodic line becomes intensely legato, and many grinding dissonances result from the overlapping voices. In measure 56, the hands exchange roles—the left hand plays the motive portamento and the right hand plays legato; the right hand has some part-playing problems here.

At measure 62, the line in the soprano becomes legato although the alternation of the hands keeps on. The phrasing of measures 62–64 is:

measures 62-64

The sorrowful harmony on the last eighth note of measure 65 needs sensitive rendering.

The returning first idea (measure 67) closely follows the changes in mood observed in the theme—the more decisive direction that appears in measure 69 (which should be coupled with a crescendo toward the downbeat of measure 71 and immediately followed by a piano) and the growing anger from measure 72 on. The Neapolitan chord in measure 75 is even more salient than it was in the theme, because at this point it is alternated between the hands. This arpeggio figure distributed between the hands may sound ragged if the left hand is sharply accented. The coordination between the hands should be well established, both tonally and rhythmically.

The subject in F major reappears and continues without change to measure 83, where a difficult chain of trills embellishes the melody. Naturally there should be no gap or slowing down in the constant, even speed of the trill while switching from one main note to another. The best solution lies in a free, unmeasured trill with as many shakes as possible. If the technical limitations of the performer make the adoption of this solution impossible, the recommended approximate execution is:

measures 83-84

(The chain of trills in example 57 has no tail or complement.)

measure 87

At measure 89 the left hand begins a trill that has to be executed without clumsiness at an even speed and in an accompanying tone while the right hand molds the melody independently. The left-hand trill should end on the downbeat of measure 92, and it should coincide with the first note of the trill in the right hand. The chain of trills written for the top part of the left hand in measure 93 has to be played with the right hand. Only the smallest gap is tolerable between measures 93 and 94 while the helping right hand flies at lightning speed into its new position to begin the trill in the soprano. The difficult trills in the left hand at measures 95 and 96 often disrupt the melodic line and overpower the trills of the right hand. A light, skillful left hand is a basic requirement for the successful execution of this variation.

The delicate lacework of the second variation calls for good scale and figure playing in both hands and for great sensitivity. The sinuosity of the swift line of thirty-seconds is to be executed expressively in a singing, legato tone. Measure 99 is difficult to finger:

measure 99

Excessive finger articulation counteracts the "molto legato" recommendation, especially in the large figures of measures 103 and 104.

From measure 105 on, the left hand has to deal with awkward turns; the awkwardness results from being obliged to use the "weak" fingers often. In the second half of the variation, there is an uncomfortable fingering for the right hand in measure 113. Only a relaxed thumb permits an easy rendering of this measure.

measure 113

Beware of tearing through the arpeggio divided between the hands in measure 115. Good coordination between the hands and appropriate finger articulation will insure evenness. Small hands may welcome the following suggestion for measure 118:

measure 118

Measures 125–127 need careful consideration by the interpreter. The number of notes in the arpeggio groups looks different only at a first superficial glance. Each group in measures 125 and 126 occupies the length of an eighth note, while the group in measure 127 extends the length of a full quarter note; for this reason there is practically no difference in their speed. The suggested grouping of the arpeggio in measure 127 is:

measure 127

Light finger articulation together with a flexible wrist will insure shape and clarity in the arpeggios.

The second variation of the F major subject has complicated rhythmic subdivisions that emphasize the fantasia character. The resulting technical difficulties are severe. The first of these subdivisions occurs in measure 129. Each group of triplet thirty-seconds lasts the length of one sixteenth note in this measure—these notes go at a very fast rate. The fingering for the measure has to be carefully established and adapted to the player's ability. Three possible fingerings are:

measure 129

The top fingering is recommended to the performer with a light, agile thumb; the third suggestion is only diffidently recommended because the use of two hands usually cannot be fast enough to cope with the required speed, and furthermore it may impair rhythmic and tonal evenness.

Measure 130 is often misunderstood and ill interpreted. The performer has to show that the left-hand entrance on the last sixteenth note of measure 129 is not a downbeat. The following articulation of the left hand in measures 129–130 may advantageously serve this purpose:

measures 129-130

It is taken from the articulation of measures 133–134. Owing to the fast speed and rhythmic complication of measures 129 and 130, many performers lose the tempo at this point; then they desperately try to reestablish it with unacceptable accents on the groups of thirty-second notes in measure 131.

Throughout the second half of the variation, the thirty-second figures reign undisturbed, making it easier for the performer to keep a steady tempo. The main difficulty in this section is keeping the thirty-seconds in left hand consistently light (as in measures 136 and 139). Particularly difficult is measure 143, where the left hand joins the right a tenth lower and accompanies it with delicate restraint. In measure 145, the chromatic figure of the left hand is to be played with tactful significance and a slight ritardando.

The coda is built entirely on the F minor subject; here its tragic, or dramatic, elements are emphasized. The coda starts off by quoting the first twenty-one measures of the theme, which are unchanged except that the repeat mark is eliminated. The significant measures where the music takes a decisive new path (measures 165–166) are followed by a meaningful rest instead of a resolution. The turn toward G flat major at measure 168 is a first timid try; it is also followed by a rest charged with electricity. Then the storm breaks out for good in the explosion of forte at measure 170. The feverish chromaticism and broken melodic line reflect fiery passion. The reappearance of the key of F minor in measure 180 brings the drama to its paroxysmal climax with an obsessive repetition of the dotted rhythm.

The main difficulty of the coda is reached in measures 186–189. Many otherwise acceptable performances collapse at this point because of the lack of rhythmic independence of the hands. Instead of trying to divide the scales of the right hand mathematically into four beats, the player should concentrate on the rhythm of the left hand, giving full length to the quarter-note octave and the ensuing eighth rest. The right-hand scale should be divided into two parts, with the highest note of each scale on the second beat in measures 186–188. In measure 189, the second beat will coincide with the high G in the following manner:

measure 189

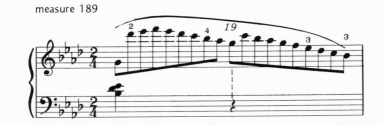

Here is a suggestion for preparatory practice of this passage:

measure 186

Measures 190–193 should be played in the strictest tempo. The passage, reminiscent of cadenza texture, contains still-fiery passion; it should be rendered with the utmost ardor and brilliance. The high intensity relaxes only in measure 193, where the safe haven of the dominant chord of F minor appears together with the familiar dotted rhythm. At this point it no longer contains the previous aggression and drama, and it seems to prepare for the resignation of measure 205. Measures 201–204 have to be molded into a long line by an expressive crescendo-decrescendo. Measure 204 should

ease the tempo. The last three chords of this measure are to be played legato, and they should lead expressively to the resolution in F minor. Sensitive performers will find the right significance for the even thirty-second figure that replaces the dotted rhythm in measure 206.

Still another revolt occurs with the syncopated chords, which are increasingly accented, of measures 212 and 213. The tempo should linger in measures 215–219 in preparation for the small-print free cadenza notes of measure 219, the last of which has a meditative fermata. The ensuing forte (measure 219) brings the dotted rhythm back in tempo primo. The closing phrase with its sombre diminished-seventh chords, sinks the piece into deep sorrow. Only a little consolation is drawn from the dotted motive that the right hand gives out coaxingly in the next-to-last measure.

This work equals the very best of Haydn's piano sonatas. The technical difficulties, which are mainly a question of the relaxed and graceful rendering of figures and trills in the left hand, seem modest in comparison with the difficulties of interpretation. Fluctuating among charm, melancholy, and dramatic revolt, the moods need a rendering that is full of character but avoids facile exaggeration. The tone quality should have no harshness in the dramatic passages, and it should be able to sing expressively in the figurations. All repeat marks should be obeyed in the finished performance.

Wolfgang Amadeus Mozart

Born 1756, Salzburg; died 1791, Vienna

The piano works of Mozart give many people the impression, at first, of ready formulas repetitiously applied, of conventional turns without real feeling or life, and even sometimes of banalities—the impression of superficiality that is characteristic of the so-called Rococo style. It is most unfortunate that many younger pianists never try to penetrate more deeply into the mind of this genius, who was one of the most remarkable musicians of all time. These pianists either consider Mozart's piano works too easy and uninteresting (because they do not pretend to achieve a musical revolution with stunning novelties), or, with a knowing air, declare them to be the most difficult of all music and strongly not recommended.

As is so often the case, the truth lies somewhere in the middle. It is a fact that Mozart's piano style is based on technical formulas, such as the Alberti-bass and broken-chord accompaniments that were established by his predecessors. To these formulas, however, Mozart added the contemporary Italian style of vocal writing, which is evident in his melodies as well as in his figures and fiorituras. Even a short study of his work (especially of his slow movements) permits us to realize the deep feeling that permeates it. Further study will reveal his extraordinarily rich and expressive harmonic language, his concise developments sections, and such novelties as vigorous themes that are full of character, audacious dissonances, and melodies transplanted to the bass. These are the areas where Mozart laid down some of the foundations of the modern piano style.

In his piano works (as in Beethoven's), the music shows constant hints of its possibilities for orchestration; the interpreter should exploit these possibilities as far as possible in the domain of dynamics and sonority. Therefore a study of Mozart's symphonic and operatic oeuvre is highly recommended to pianists.

Mozart was recognized as one of the greatest virtuoso pianists of his time: he played the harpsichord and the pianoforte with the ease of genius, as one speaks his mother tongue. He never tried or even thought of formulating a method of pianoforte playing. It was only later that Clementi opened the real era of the piano and established the principles of a systematic piano technique. Some of his principles have survived till our day, such as the ones that apply par excellence to the performance of Mozart—calm hands, even fingerwork, and only minimal use of the forearm.

Purists of our day often question the use of the modern grand piano, with its rich sound and its pedals, for the performance of Mozart. The dispute, though not so vehement as that concerning the instruments for which Bach wrote his keyboard music, is mostly in vain. Style concerns the way the instrument is used much more than it concerns the instrument itself, and on this point Clementi's principles probably constitute the most valuable advice that can be given the performer.

MOZART
Sonata in A Minor, K. 310

~~~~~~

Composed in Paris in 1778, this sonata has something exceptional about it, as have many other works by Mozart written in a minor key. It is a dark, tragic work with a decisive, main subject that is full of character in the first movement. The slow movement gives an impression of peace and resignation until a powerful outbreak of tragic sorrow occurs in its development. The presto, written in a form that is hard to identify, passes by at breathtaking speed. Throughout the sonata, Mozart treats the instrument in an unusually virtuosic way, involving great technical difficulties for the performer.

Allegro maestoso

M.M. ♩ = 104

Form: Sonata

	MEASURES
Exposition	1 – 49
First subject	1 – 15
Transition	16 – 22
Second subject	22 – 45
Closing subject	45 – 49
Development	50 – 79
Recapitulation	80 – 133

The mood of the entire movement is set by the strong, tragic main subject. The initial grace note is to be played short, ahead of the beat, and without attaching a specific value to its length. The grace notes of measures 2 and 4 are long: each is to be played as an eighth note. Because Mozart gives the subject an unusual chordal accompaniment—more in the manner of a string quartet than in any typical piano style—tonal balance has to be among the main preoccupations of the performer.

The second half of the subject, which begins at measure 5, is to be played piano. This section is difficult to play because of the imitation between the hands of the sigh-motive slurs: when the right hand is playing the second third of the slur light and short, the left hand is playing the first, heavy note with a sforzando. Usually this left-hand sforzando invades the right hand also, robbing the sigh motive of its typical dynamic relation.

measures 6-7

The dotted rhythm of measure 8 has to be precise throughout. A commonly observed mistake consists of playing the last sixteenth note of the measure too soon in order to make room for the grace note of measure 9.

The first repetition of the main subject has an even darker character: the slurs and staccatos, as they occur in measure 13, are expressing dramatic revolt rather than the teasing charm they manifest elsewhere. The "calando" indication in the following measure calls for a slight ritardando—a hesitation in the tempo like a manifestation of fright after expressing such anger in the preceding measure. The original tempo is resumed with the piano in measure 15.

The dynamic changes of the transition section offer also hints for color changes, similar to alternating tutti and solo woodwind passages of a symphony. The forte in measure 16 comes on the second beat, just as the piano does in measure 18, while the forte in measure 20 begins on the first beat. The last left-hand octave in measure 22 is not a real forte: it has the strength of a well-controlled accompaniment forte. It also has to be played longer than an ordinary staccato, in order for it to contrast more with the short staccatos of the second subject in the right hand.

Instead of the customary, more singing second subject, here we have to deal with an uninterrupted flow of sixteenth notes. Performing them presupposes a light, even finger technique. Instead of excessively articulating the single notes, the player should be able to connect them in a long line. Learning the correct fingering of the zigzagging diatonic passages is especially important here because the passage recurs in more complicated keys later on. The C major tonality involves only white keys and therefore allows the use of practically any fingering without inconvenience. The fingering should always be:

measure 23

Learning the correct fingering here has important consequences later on—in measure 37 for the right hand and in measures 42–43 for the left hand (the fingering for the left hand is: 4–1–3–2 4–1–3–2 and so on). The eighth notes in the accompanying intervals and chords of the left hand should be played staccato; the quarters have to be held for their real value.

Sensitive interpreters won't miss the more expressive character of the music from measure 26 on. The left hand adds to the expressiveness in measures 28–32; part playing in this passage should be faultless. Avoid accents on the beats in measure 32 (which would only slice the beautiful soaring line), and in the next measure, bring the left hand in discreetly, joining it to the right without a heavy entrance. The trill of measure 34 should begin on the note above; it has no resolution on the downbeat of measure 35!

The trill of measure 39 begins on the main note. Its resolution in measure 40 causes the problem of delicately repeating the same note in the space of two sixteenths while changing from the right hand to the left. Unskillfulness easily occasions a heavy bump on the C played with the left hand.

Measures 42 and 43 contain difficult trills and some part-playing problems. The trills begin with the note above. The part playing involves, not only the correct holding of the keys, but also a difference in sound between the upper and lower voices. In measure 43, the fingering of the trill is:

measure 43

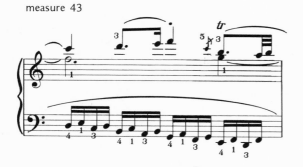

The forte indication in measure 44 (probably a later editor's dynamic rather than Mozart's) belongs to the whole line; a heavy left hand or right thumb should cause no accents on the beats. The closing subject has a long line in the left hand that is fairly difficult to finger. The recommended fingering is:

measure 45

The right hand has to be played with determination: a loose wrist will avoid harshness in the tone.

Although the development begins in major, the tragic mood attached to the subject prevails and is even more emphasized by the fortepianos (which are to be played as sforzandos) in measures 54 and 55. The subsequent two measures (56–57) contain a beautiful enharmonic modulation. Here the performer faces an impossible task—to make a difference, somehow, between the B flat of the first measure and the A sharp of the second. Besides this highly refined musical task, the performer has to deal effectively with difficult passagework. In the broken arpeggios of measure 56–57, the hand must be firmly set in the position of each successive inversion of the dominant seventh chord. This is necessary to deal successfully with the changing intervals between the fingers. The left hand has three beats of rests in measure 56 and a chord to be sustained for the whole length of measure 57.

These two measures lead to the most difficult part of the movement. The left-hand motive has to be kept at an even speed to give a solid background to the dotted rhythm of the right hand. The low notes are to be played with a quick opening of the hand into octave position at lightning speed. The rest of the time the left hand remains in closed position to deal with the trill-like figure. The right hand has even greater problems to solve. The dotted rhythm has to be firmly maintained throughout: even the slightest deviation can have disastrous consequences. It is extremely difficult to keep the rhythm unaltered here because the figure also contains serious problems in part playing. Throughout the passage, the player has to insure perfect synchronization of the hands.

The dynamic indications ff at measure 58, pp at measure 62, and ff again at measure 66 are vital for correct interpretation of this passage. Any departure from these dynamic extremes is unacceptable in that it takes away from the grandeur of this unique development. The excitement rises to a paroxysm of emotion in measure 70. The sixteenth note in the right hand should be rigorously together with the corresponding sixteenth of the left hand. The trills begin on the note above: the fingering 3–5 on them is a possibility. No accents should be given to the beats in measure 73; rather, the player should bring out the tormented harmony in the right hand. In measure 74, the left hand takes over the difficult motive played up to here by the right hand. A successful rendition presupposes the performer's ability to play a good, effortless trill in the left hand. Usually pianists have several good "trill fingers" in the right hand, but they are limited in the left hand to one possibility, normally either 1–2 or 2–3. The performer has to use his best (that is, his fastest) fingering here and play the trill as effortlessly as possible. There is a real danger that an unmeasured pulsation of the trill may affect the speed of the sixteenth notes in the right hand and transform the last group in the measure into an inarticulate broken chord. Both hands have to be listened to carefully in order to control the different speeds. Avoid accents on the beats at measure 78, and bring out the excited line of the right hand.

At the recapitulation, the first grace note of the subject is missing. The theme appears unchanged as far as measure 88, when suddenly a new, more orchestral version takes over with a tremolo (which should sound like the upper strings) in the right hand and the subject (which should sound like the cello) in the left hand. The pulsation of the tremolo has to be at the correct speed: it should be moving at the same rate as the sixteenth-note figures of the left hand. In measures 90 and 92 of the left hand, beware of playing the eighth notes preceding the sixteenths scales of the subject too long: this lengthening would impede synchronization of the hands just as badly as a too-fast tremolo would.

The "calando" is valid for measures 94 and 95; the tempo resumes with measure 96. The second subject, appearing this time in minor, has a number of melodic and harmonic alterations that often exploit sorrowful chromaticism. The accompanying left hand is legato in measures 104 through 108, adding to the more serious atmosphere. The part playing in the same hand should be faultless between measures 109 and 112. Meanwhile the right hand has some uncomfortable turns to deal with. The recommended fingering for measure 111 is:

measure 111

The suggestion of some editions to put the first finger on the G sharp is not to be followed.

Accuracy and ease are difficult to attain in measure 119. The fingering is:

measure 119

The most difficult passage in the movement occurs in measures 126–127. Not only is the downward zigzag arpeggio difficult to finger, but it is followed by a jump to a five-note chord in the right hand. The player may play the passage as notated by Mozart with the following fingering:

measures 126-127

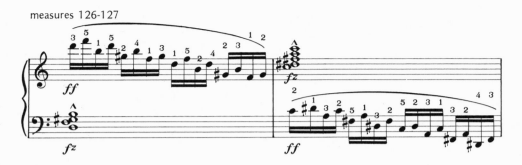

or he can slightly alter the distribution between hands; this solution makes the right-hand jump easier but the left hand somewhat more complicated.

measures 126-127

The only alteration of the closing subject is that the closing chords are not rolled. They have to have a rich, full sound without hardness.

The difficulties of this movement are manifold. It projects a rendering of passion and revolt, and at the same time, it demands the mastery of such wide-ranging technical difficulties as an even finger technique, tremolos, chords, and perfect synchronization of the hands. The difficulty of this coordination in the development section cannot be overemphasized. Also the wide dynamic contrasts indicated throughout the movement must be followed literally; their softening would only weaken the character of the subject involved. The "maestoso" in the indication at the beginning of the movement is to be taken most seriously in determining the tempo.

Andante cantabile con espressione

M.M. $\flat$ = 69–76

Form: Sonata

	MEASURES
Exposition	1 – 31
First subject	1 – 15
Second subject	15 – 29
Closing subject	29 – 31
Development	31 – 57
Recapitulation	57 – 86

The noble, singing line of the Andante begins in sharp contrast with the character of the preceding movement. One of the characteristic features of this movement is a certain soaring type of crescendo that appears immediately in the upbeat. The grace note before the fortepiano completes the harmony; it is to be played before the beat (otherwise it weakens the following dotted rhythm), but nonetheless in an expressive manner. The double thirds at the end of the first measure need a good legato. The second beat in the second measure has to be light in spite of the use of the thumb. The preceding thirty-seconds have to be played at the correct speed, neither too slow nor jerked.

The feeling of soaring toward the fortepiano is evident again in measure 2. It is somewhat more difficult to extricate the top line in measure 3 from the chordal accompaniment. The thirty-seconds of the measure are part of the melody; therefore they should not be played as a run. The left hand should join the right on the last thirty-second note without a bump. The trill that some editions indicate on the first beat of measure 4 can be omitted here as well as in the recapitulation. The half phrase ends softly on the second beat, and the thirty-second-note scale is the upbeat to the second half phrase. Some editions prolong the slur to the first note of the scale as a pleasing way to sustain the sound of the quarter-note E until the first note of the scale is sounded. The upbeat thirty-second-note scale again has a soaring crescendo to the fortepiano. A heavy thumb on the lower voice in the right hand can easily ruin the melodic line.

The trill in measure 6 begins with the main note; for its fingering, use 5–3. The second beat of measure 6 should be light; the forte that appears in the next measure mainly means that the passage should be played cantabile. The turn of measure 7 should be executed as follows:

measure 7

The trill begins with the grace note.

The second part of the main subject (which begins in measure 8) has an Alberti bass as its accompaniment that lends more motion to the music. The trill of measure 8 begins on the main note and contains only five notes (or one turn). The staccatos are also part of the singing line: beware of a dry, short sound. Sensitive players can detect the change of color between the upward and downward motive of the subject as they could if they were played by different instruments of the orchestra. The grace notes of measure 9 are to be played long, like this: ♪♪ . The fingering should be 3–2 throughout.

At measure 11 the fortepianos are played off the beat. They should not be violent: rather, they should be expressive and should include a slight prolongation. The trills of the next measure are to be executed as turns, like this:

measure 12

Measure 13 is to be executed as follows:

measure 13

The nervous speed of the sixty-fourths in measure 14 should be rigorously exact but still singing; the left hand then leads meaningfully to the next section.

The second subject does not have the usual singing character. The repeated sixteenth notes seem to have a calming effect on it. The difference between sixteenth-note and eighth-note staccatos has to be clearly exhibited, with the staccato sixteenths being shorter. The thirty-second-note figure is expressively legato, but it does not have crescendo swells. At the repeat in measure 17, one has to take good care to maintain constant speed in the trill, while the left hand deals with quite serious part-playing problems. It is especially difficult to avoid an accent in the thirty-seconds' line when one is playing the last staccato eighth note of the lower voice. One should be wary of a downward motion of the hand at this point. If these two measures (measures 17 and 18) are well executed, they can have the perfection of an outstanding chamber-orchestra performance.

In measure 19, the trill is once more reduced to a turn beginning on the main note. The fortepianos avoid heaviness on the thumb of the right hand or in the bass. The turn of measure 20 is played as follows:

measure 20

The staccatos should be singing, as they were previously.

In measure 21, the trill begins on the note above. The offbeat fortepiano can easily be overdone in measure 22, especially in the left hand. The chordal progression of measure 23 has to be played as legato as possible, with a soaring crescendo that leads to a triumphant ending in the following measure. In measure 25, the turns begin on the upper note, and therefore they contain only four notes. The hands have to be perfectly synchronized for the turns. The usual clumsiness of the left hand will be minimized by the use of the fingering 2–3–4–3 on the turn; it is recommended even to players with small hands.

In measure 26, no crescendo is applied to the rising scales. Editions differ on the articulation of the last eight thirty-second notes of the measure: some indicate legato, and some go on with the staccato. However they all agree that the forte of measure 27 is sudden. Here the chord of the right hand should sound as if it were played by the woodwinds, and it is to be held exactly as written: the two lower voices rest from the second beat on, while the top third is held over into the next measure. Below the chord, the three scales of the left hand can suggest the sound of three different groups of instruments.

The beginning of measure 28 can expand in time in order to give the impression that the top C can be reached only with difficulty. The trill begins on the note above and involves difficult part playing; avoid heaviness of the thumb. When the left hand joins the right, it should have the same speed in its trill; the grace note is played ahead of the beat. It is especially important that the tails of the double trill be well synchronized. The trill of the closing subject also has a tail. The ending chords bring the forte back; this dynamic should be executed with special care to avoid heaviness in the low register.

The development begins in bright C major, and it seems as if the serene mood will last for ever. In measure 35, the dynamic marking is unclear in many editions. The forte enters with the first G of the right hand. The turn on the first beat of the measure, preceding the forte, is to be played softly and in the manner of a Baroque ornament placed on the end of a phrase. The C-major cadence in measure 36 needs to be stretched slightly: it sounds like a farewell to the happy times.

In sharp contrast, C minor brings a blast of cold air to the music. The new dramatic mood should suddenly chill the listener, like a ghostly apparition. Over the excited triplets of the left hand, the phrase advances with a soaring crescendo to a forte, which is followed by a hesitant piano answer. The trills begin with the main note. The grace note in measure 39 is long: it should be executed in the same manner as the written-out version in measure 52.

From measure 41 on, the insistent questioning gets louder and louder as we reach the climactic section of the movement. The sound is that of the full orchestra. The right hand articulates the triplet sixteenths with exasperation: the first two of the group of six are slurred, and the others are not too short—(they are played in a sort of lazy staccato that does not require the finger change that many editions indicate). The interest is focused on the left hand; yet the relation between the hands is not that of melody and accompaniment. The main problems of the rendition are rhythmic stability and the execution of the trills in the left hand. Mozart clearly wants double dotting throughout; but instead of a double dot, he inserts a thirty-second rest, indicating clearly that he wants the thirty-second note of the left hand to be played after the last triplet chord of the right hand. An accurate rendering of the rhythm is further complicated by the fact that the subsequent trill (in measures 46 and 49) has to be started on the main note, as must the trills on the last beat of both measures. Thus the left hand is involved in the difficult problem of playing a precise rhythm on repeated notes. Here changing the fingers is indispensable. Furthermore the speed of the trill should not have any influence on the speed of the right hand. This section displays fierce passion and passes through audacious dissonances until the calando occurs in measure 50. Here the right hand gets full control of the melody, and by means of expressive slurs, it leads to the dominant of F major.

In measures 51 and 52, sensitive interpretation can make a beautiful effect of the diminished seventh (51) or augmented sixth (52) chord on the third beat. Notice the simple dotting of the rhythm, which thus loses all aggressiveness and pathos.

In the recapitulation, the first part of the main subject is unchanged; however the second part (beginning with measure 61) modulates frequently, giving the section an agitated character. Changes of dynamics are also frequent: the fortes and pianos alternate regularly. There is an interesting dynamic change in measure 66: the scale moving upward is forte, as if it were being played by the full orchestra. Then, suddenly, on the second sixteenth note of the second beat, a solo instrument is left alone. The second subject group has an extension (measures 72–74) where orchestration changes are again obvious. Otherwise the recapitulation remains unchanged to the last measure. By the way, this measure is often misread and played at double speed.

The tempo and character indication at the beginning of the movement—*Andante cantabile con espressione*—is explicit for its interpretation. The main requirement for the performance is a good, singing legato coupled with a good sense for the rendering of the refined changes in orchestration. The development taxes the performer both musically and technically. Without a perfect mastery of all the difficulties in this section, the performance of the movement must remain unacceptable. The suggested tempo is fairly slow in order to permit the sixteenth and thirty-second notes to be played cantabile. The movement needs discreet pedaling to color the sound.

Presto

M.M. ♩ = 104–108, middle episode (C) ♩ = 96

Form: Rondo (free)

		MEASURES
A		1 – 20
B		20 – 106
	Transition	20 – 63
	B proper	64 – 86
	Transition	87 – 106
A		107 – 142
C		143 – 174
A		174 – 194
	B group	195 – 244
	Coda	245 – 252

The entire movement is built on one subject with a characteristic dotted-quarter-

and-an-eighth-note meter. The rendering of the slurs drawn between the dotted quarter and the eighth should be modeled after the bowing of a stringed instrument rather
than played in the pianistic tradition; the slurs here indicate changes in the direction of
the bow, with only a minimal interruption of the sound at the bar line. This interpretation will lend fluency, smoothness, and line to the subject if the thumb of the
right hand is kept light. Off-beat entrances of the bass should be made without a bump
in every instance; to avoid this accent, the left hand should be close to the keys and
prepared to play. The grace notes have to be played long, with the exception of the one
in measure 25, which should be short.

The phrasing for measure 8 differs in the various editions; it is best to play four
legato eighth notes, as in measure 63. The last three eighth notes of measure 16 raise
the sound to forte, which prevails to the end of the first subject. (In some editions, instead of fortes there are fortepiano indications in measures 17 and 18.)

At measure 21, the melody shows a long, uninterrupted line for the first time.
There is a sort of supplication in these eight measures; the tone should be warmer and
the crescendo natural, without sounding strident. The inverted mordents in measure
27 are in fact triplets on the corresponding eighth notes, played like this:

measure 27

Suddenly a colder, more mysterious mood is felt at the appearance of C minor in
measure 29, even though the subject is the same as the one at the beginning of the
movement. The uneasy fealing does not last long. The explosive forte at measure 37 is
like a paroxysm of anxious agitation. This passage is difficult to finger in the left hand;
editions differ in their recommendations. The fingering the performer adopts here settles the fingering, not only for the corresponding passage of the recapitulation (which
begins at measures 210), but also for the passage at measure 127. Thus the decision is
far-reaching. Two possibilities are:

measure 37

The same fingerings are to be used at measure 210. Two possibilities are shown for
measure 127:

Often measures 43 and 44 sound heavy because the top voice of the chords is drowned by the too-loud lower voices. The two voices appearing in measure 52 and, later, in measures 56–59 in the right hand can cause some part-playing problems if they are not played on two different sound levels. This is the reason for taking the fortepiano indications in measures 56 and 58 seriously: the first note of the melody should be loud, and the lower voice should be piano.

From the forte at measure 60, a diminuendo prepares the sound for the B section (which uses the same theme as section A) emerging in the bass in octaves. Although the subject is the same, the mood seems different: it is more solemn now. It is interrupted by a forte explosion of agitation at measure 72. The right hand has no problem in fingering this passage: the fingering is 1–2–5–4 throughout. In the left hand, the fingering $3\overset{1\_2}{}4$ most closely imitates the bowing of stringed instruments.

The transition section beginning at measure 87 has serious part-playing problems. Its texture reminds one of string-trio writing. Two kinds of sound for the two voices in the right hand are vital, especially from measure 95 on. A careless performance can transform the beautiful imitation into a simple figure.

At first the recapitulation of the A subject unfolds without a change; then the sadness contained in the phrase overflows with the crescendo (measure 124) and reaches exasperation with the forte (measure 127). The fingering for the right hand is $2\overset{4\_3}{}1$ throughout (the fingering for the left hand has been discussed in the remarks for measure 37). The slurs and staccatos that appear in measures 132–133 and 140–141 express exhaustion rather than rococo charm.

The major mode brings only pale sunshine and little warmth to section C; the character of the music remains ghostly. Technically the right hand has a definite problem in fingering the thirds. It is possible to play them $2\overset{4\_3}{}1$ throughout, which would emphasize the slurring by pairs within the longer legato sign. This solution, however, presupposes an ability to use the thumb indiscriminately on white and black keys—a difficult task in such an intricate texture. There is another, more complicated fingering that takes into account the use of the black keys:

measures 143-150

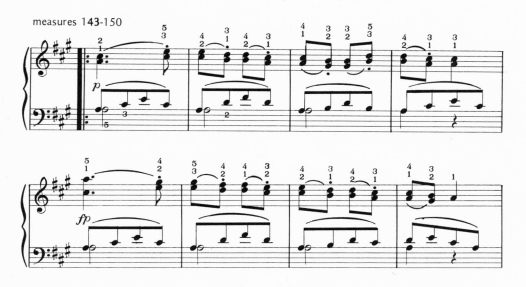

The slurs that connect the thirds in groups of two do not need to be heavily emphasized (some editions do not even indicate them). The fortepiano of measure 147 is like a sad sigh.

In measure 155, the grace note is to be played long, in the following way:

measure 155

The left hand should play the tenor (the low voice of the right hand) in measure 157; this distribution of notes will facilitate the execution of the trill.

The second part of the middle episode begins with a modest single line. The accompanying thirds should be performed as follows:

measures 161-162

The inverted mordent of measure 163 is a triplet that has the duration of the eighth note. Both repeat marks of the section are mandatory. At the second ending (measure 174b), the last three eighth notes of the measure are to be treated as upbeats to the recapitulation that appears in measure 175.

At measure 233, the appearance of the theme in a high register makes it seem that it is escaping from reality; the subsequent forte chords try to attract it back to earth. The trumpet call of measure 245 announces doomsday. A good performance will clearly show the imitation of the motive in the bass (at measure 247). Notice that Mozart's dynamic indication is only forte for this passage, and that he refrained from indicating fortissimo, even though he did use fortissimos in the first movement. The chords should be played without brutality: their top voice should clearly carry the melodic line. The last chord should have the length of a quarter note, and the movement should end with a quarter-note rest that is part of the performance.

The dismal mood of this evanescent, breathless movement is unmistakable; not even the major mode of the middle episode brings significant change to it. The fact that the main subject is used for episodes and transitions only complicates the task of the performer. He has to be able to play the same subject at different moments with different meaning or character, as if it were appearing in a different light. A smooth rendition of the slurs is the principal technical difficulty of the movement. A good understanding of part playing is also needed in some important passages. To a much greater extent than the preceding two movements, the Presto lacks the usual Rococo atmosphere of the other Mozart sonatas. To the highest degree this sonata is a unique personal expression.

MOZART

Sonata in B Flat Major, K. 333

This sonata is usually accepted as being one of the so-called Paris sonatas. However it shows some important differences in style from the other Paris sonatas: it is less decided in character, and its lines are long and singing. It also shows a great deal of chromaticism, harmonic boldness in the slow movement, and innovation of form in the Rondo, which was composed on the model of a concerto rondo and even includes a cadenza.

Allegro

M.M. ♩ = 116

Form: Sonata

	MEASURES
Exposition	1 – 63
First subject	1 – 10
Transition	10 – 22
Second subject	23 – 38
Transition	38 – 50
Closing subject	50 – 63
Development	63 – 93
Recapitulation	93 – 165

The main preoccupation of the performer for the opening ten measures should be the elegance of the sound and the balance between the hands, in particular. The usual mezzo forte for the opening reproduced in most editions is the result of a convention: where there is no dynamic indication in Mozart, play mezzo forte.

The grace note of the opening upbeat measure is to be played as a sixteenth note, like this ♩♬. Furthermore the interruptions of slurs in the first four measures do not mean an interruption of sound in the phrasing. On the contrary, the player has to hear the full length of the dotted quarter notes. The first real rest occurs in measure 4, but it should not be a pretext for raising the hand and then falling back heavily on the first sixteenth note of the next phrase. Too often in the performances of Mozart's works, the sixteenth notes are played too fast, no matter where they occur. Bear this in mind when playing measures 6 and 8. The danger of playing these measures too fast is even greater because there is no accompaniment to the bare sixteenths of the right hand.

Between the measures with singing sixteenths, syncopation (in measure 5) adds to the expressive quality; in measure 7, it turns into teasing slurs. The dynamic level finally rises to forte in measure 9, and the subject ends in an affirmative tone.

The transition, in piano, has a darker character; it begins like the main subject, but it is played one octave lower. A modulation takes place almost immediately. Measures 13 and 14 are often rushed—especially if the performer forgets about the singing quality of the sixteenths. The right-hand fingering is also delicate in those two measures. The recommended fingering is:

measures 12-13

The break in phrasing between the first and second sixteenth notes on the third beat of measures 15 and 16 can be ugly if it is overdone. The first sixteenth note in each case has a staccato dot in addition to a slur ending. Played as a short staccato, this note can stand out from the line like a sharp accent. The fingering itself can be responsible for this accent, if it calls for a quick lateral motion of the hand. The suggested fingering is:

measure 15

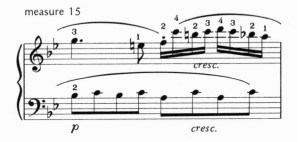

Some editions suggest an unnecessary crescendo from measure 15 on, to prepare for the forte in measure 18. Note that in spite of the forte, the tone remains happy and relaxed, especially through measures 19 and 21, where a heavy left hand can easily interfere with the elegant charm of the right hand's part. The turn in measure 21 begins on the upper note (some editions show a trill here, but a turn of four thirty-second notes is sufficient).

The second subject starts off with a sforzando chord. Take care to give it good tonal balance by bringing the soprano out! The two ensuing sixteenth notes can easily become an inarticulate jerk if they are not heard as part of the melodic line. The staccato eighth notes should sing; avoid playing them too short. The sforzando in measure

24 has a more expressive ring. A longer legato line follows, with luscious syncopations and a trill that can spoil everything if it is played too tensely or too loud. The grace notes of measures 27, 28, and 35 are to be played long, like this:

measure 27

The phrasing of these measures varies from edition to edition; the eighth notes appear as legato in some editions and staccato in others: ♪♪♩ or ♪♪♩ . Which articulation to adopt is up to each performer, as long as he puts the preceding sixteenth notes into the melodic line.

The sixteenth notes of measure 30 are also often troublesome. While the right hand usually carries out its task well, the clumsier left hand often stumbles or turns this uncomfortable figure into an inarticulate jerk.

At measure 35, the second exposition of the subject reaches another sudden forte. Just as before, the cantabile is to be maintained in spite of the forte. The left hand of measure 35 is provided with different articulation marks in the various editions:

The following transition begins with a charming slurred and staccato subject over a busy accompaniment figure. The fortepiano should not be overdone: the forte is closer to a moderate sforzando in piano. The dynamic changes, calling for piano in measure 43. The tempo should be carefully controlled in measures 43–44; it is very easy to play these measures too slowly; it is also easy to play measure 45 too fast, because of the sudden entrance of the forte. Measure 46 brings the piano back. In the following two measures (47 and 48), the performer should clearly show the relation between slurs and dynamics that exists between the left-hand chords like this:

measure 47

There is a textual discrepancy in the bass note of the second beat of measure 49 in the different editions; some have a B flat, and others have a B natural. The B natural is correct. The closing subject can easily be started at a too-fast tempo. Also the closeness of the hands can result in poor tonal balance. The right hand alone plays singing sixteenths in measures 52 and 56: beware of rushing. The broken-third figure in this subject can be troublesome. It is important to establish a fingering that can be used subsequently. Two possibilities are:

measures 50-51

Crescendos are indicated in most editions for measures 51 and 55, reminding one of the legendary crescendo of the Mannheim orchestra, which Mozart heard on his way to and from Paris. Both the speed and the sound of the Alberti bass of measures 57 and 58 should be kept well under control. The performer should beware of rushing the bass, especially during the cadential trill (which has to begin on the note above). The following codetta calls for sharp dynamics; here piano and there forte. The melodic line is interrupted several times by eighth rests that should be clearly audible in the performance. The turn in measure 62 begins on the upper note and should be incorporated into the melodic line.

The development begins with the main subject, which is unchanged except for the octave jump between the motives, giving the performer the opportunity to demonstrate his artistry by imposing different colors on them, as those produced by different instruments of the orchestra. This is emphasized even more by the expressive crescendo-decrescendo associated with each of the answers. The importance of the grace notes in measures 65, 67, 68, and 69 is mainly harmonic; they are to be played short and ahead of the beat, but expressively. These ornaments should be played in the manner of an instrument that is unable to play two simultaneous notes and instead uses the quick arpeggiation of an interval to suggest harmony.

The forte enters in measure 68 (some editions indicate it only at measure 70), and the happy mood of F major seems to last forever; suddenly, without warning, F minor appears at measure 71. Over a busy Alberti bass, the right hand enunciates a long phrase, full of sorrow and exasperation and complicated by the most expressive syncopation. Throughout the passage, the Alberti bass should be even but sensitive, in order to insure the harmonic foundation for the expressive, personal quality of the right-hand part. But above all, the left-hand figure should not be obtrusive. The despairing syncopation in measures 73 and 74 has to be played more closely to a portamento than to a simple finger legato.

In measure 76, the clouds are getting even darker; the trills make it appear as though the whole earth will tremble. The trills begin with the upper note, while the preceding sixteenth note must have its precise length. The staccatos of the next measure (measure 77) are heroic rather than gracious. The most expressive moment of the phrase is reached at this point; from here on, the clouds seem to break away, and some blue sky is already in sight. The ornament of measure 79 begins on the main note in spite of the fact that it repeats the preceding note. The syncopations are back in measure 80, but they express resignation instead of revolt. We reach the dominant of G minor, which will be confirmed for five measures (measures 81–86). The right-hand figure in measures 81 and 83 is especially difficult.

The music has not yet been able to recover from the previous outbreak, and it still shivers with emotion. A matter-of-fact treatment would reduce its refined melody to a senseless run. From the purely technical standpoint, the player has to have a light thumb that can work by itself, without the help of the forearm or hand. The left-hand accompanying intervals have the same slur and dynamic relationship as the figure in measure 47. In measure 85, the alternation of the hands shows that the heartbeat has not calmed down yet. The left-hand chords, which contain the harmony, should be a little longer than the right-hand single notes. The bridge to the recapitulation begins at measure 86 with a broadly singing phrase reminiscent of woodwinds. Wherever sixteenth-note pasages occur, the performer should be sure about their correct speed and their singing quality.

In measure 93, a little hesitation in the slightly detached eighth notes preceding the recapitulation is necessary to bring out all its charm. After the presentation of unaltered main subject, the transition (beginning at measure 103) turns harmonically in another direction and explodes in a forte at measure 106. This is followed by an unusual concentration of chromaticism—in the melody as well as in the harmony. Aside from this, the recapitulation brings only a few changes—the extension of the phrase (measures 142–152) by a diatonic sequence (measures 144–146) followed by chromaticism.

Measure 150 is quite a technical problem for heavy-handed players. The use of the arm has to be limited here to bringing the fingers into position ready to play; excessive arm weight would ruin this delicate passage. The turns (in some editions, trills) are to be started on the main note—a melodic necessity—and to contain five notes, like this:

measure 150

The correct reading of measure 159 is:

measure 159

The beauty of a singing legato is the most important requirement for the performance of this movement. Very special care has to be brought to the sixteenth-note passages, which should sing the same way the rest of the music does. In the midst of a happy, smiling mood, the dark passage of the development should stand out, fully doing justice to this most emotional outbreak. Throughout the hand should be light, allowing the fingers to cope better with some of the uncomfortable figurations. The singing quality of the movement leads to the use of a spacious tempo.

Andante cantabile

M.M. ♩ = 56–60

        Form: Sonata

	MEASURES
Exposition	1 – 31
First subject	1 – 13
First part	1 – 8
Second part	8 – 13
Second subject	14 – 21
Closing subject	21 – 31
Development	31 – 50
Recapitulation	51 – 82

The character indication "cantabile" added to the tempo indication is the most valuable direction for the performer. The first measure also has "dolce," which in some editions is completed with a "piano." Do not rush the quarter notes in the second measure, but do not make beats out of them in order to keep the tempo. Listen carefully that the sounds of these quarter notes are sustained for their full length, holding them will help achieve the perfect legato. The quarter notes point with a small crescendo toward the dissonance on the downbeat of measure 3, which is (within the required piano) the dynamic high point of the phrase. A little prolongation of that dissonance is in order, and the performer has to make up the time in the last four sixteenth notes of the measure. The interval of a sixth at the beginning of measure 4 is often played with a heavy fall that results from the quick move of the hand to find the new position. If this motion seems unavoidable, the player should consider the following distribution (the sixth on the downbeat is divided between the hands, while the sixth on the second beat is in the right hand):

measure 4

The phrasing here should be especially smooth, and the thirty-seconds leading back to the subject should be played with a light thumb and with imagination.

Measure 5 contains a fairly wide jump in the melody; avoid a heavy bump. If all else fails, one could consider the following distribution of notes here:

measure 5

The trill in the ensuing measure is to be incorporated into the melodic line: it should be singing and relaxed and followed by smooth phrasing. In measure 7, the grace notes have to be played long and on the beat, like this:

measure 7

The fingering is 3–2 throughout; avoid heaviness of the hand.

The phrase calms down here to show the end of the first part. In the second part, the accompaniment should be very soft and sensitive, slightly prolonging the notes where the sforzandos fall in measures 9 and 11. The right hand sings happily, and there is no heaviness in the slurred 16th notes, whose fingering is always 3–2. The upbeat eighth-note thirds are expressive portamentos. The ornament in measure 12 is executed as follows:

measure 12

At the end of this measure, the expressiveness of the contrary motion of the thirds should be brought out.

The second subject begins mezzo forte with a short, yet expressive grace note. The main characteristic of this subject is that its motives are interrupted every other measure (measures 15 and 17) to give way to three eighth notes that should sound as if they are played by a different group of instruments. The thirty-seconds in the soprano motive have the same singing tone as the rest of the phrase.

In measure 19, the expressive chromaticism in the tenor must not be overlooked. The triplets of the following measure have to have dignity and grace in order to prepare for a calm, round phrase ending. In the closing subject, the dynamic indications point once more to the orchestral treatment of the piano: the forte means tutti, and the piano means a group of solo instruments. The left-hand line begins as a simple accompaniment; it then turns out to be an expressive line, and it should not be treated with undue haste. The thirty-seconds in the right hand are to be incorporated into the line in the best vocal tradition. At the end of the repeat, in measure 28, the thirty-seconds' line has a longing crescendo. The last note of the measure, a thirty-second, should not be played too short, but rather with a teasing charm.

The development begins with a daring dissonance that is emphasized by a forte-piano that should be interpreted as a *sfp*. A good legato is very important for the thirds; the fingering is:

measure 32

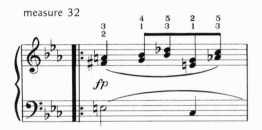

The phrase shows a jump upward in the following measure that indicates a change in color. The last three eighth notes of measure 35 have to be softer than piano, and they should be played without any delay despite the wide jump for the left hand. To avoid a bump here that would spoil the mysterious quality of the low Fs, the following solution can be considered:

measure 35

At this point, the minor mood, which has been well prepared for in the preceding measures, establishes domination and turns the beautiful dreaming into deep sorrow, as though it were passing through a zone of melancholy (measures 36–43). The melody has an outspoken, improvisatory character over the chromatically rising bass line. The sorrow is only emphasized by the constant crescendo that raises the sound from a mysterious piano to a sonorous forte in measure 41, where the tonality of A flat major is established. The piano reenters suddenly, on the first beat of measure 42.

The dreaming seems to begin again in measure 43, but strong emotions color the phrase darker and darker by means of expressive sforzandos. The distance between soprano and bass widens; the modulation passes through the sorrowful key of D flat minor to reach, finally, the dominant of E flat. In this measure as well as in those following (measures 48–49), the repeated eighth-note chords have a calming effect on the throbbing heart. In measure 50, a cadenzalike figure improvises its way back to the recapitulation. There are a few minor changes from the exposition here: these include an Alberti bass accompaniment in the left hand in measure 52 and embellishments that make the right-hand line more interesting in measures 53–55. Measure 56 has expressive syncopation, while the cadence measure (measure 57) shows more determination than its counterpart in the exposition. Measure 61 has an embellishment that can be uncomfortable for many players in its first form, where there is no way to avoid the use of the weak fingers.

In the second subject group, measure 68 also shows a different, more insistent melodic line, while the underlying harmony is also somewhat changed. In measure 70, the grace note is short but expressive, after the penetrating chromaticism of the triplets.

There is an octave jump in measure 75 of the closing subject, which points to further refinement in color. The charming change in the figuration in measure 77 is due to the limitation of the eighteenth-century keyboard and has to be accepted as it stands in Mozart's text. The second ending and concluding measure stand in place of a coda. These measures contain the only pianissimo in the movement. The slur and dynamic relation between the last two chords has to be well observed.

A singing legato and smooth phrasing are needed for the performance of this dreaming slow movement. The "dolce" indication of the first measure has to be understood as applying everywhere, even in forte passages. As in the preceding movement, the sorrowful mood of the development is in sharp contrast with the rest of the Andante. The tempo should not be too slow: Mozart prescribes "andante," not "adagio." The tactful use of the pedal will help to avoid dryness.

Allegretto grazioso

M.M. $\downarrow$ = 66–69

Form: Rondo	MEASURES
A	1 – 16
B	16 – 40
A	41 – 56
C	56 – 111
A	112 – 127
B	127 – 171
Cadenza	171 – 198
A and coda	199 – 224

Mozart uses a charming *Gassenhauer* (literally, "street song") as the main subject (A) of this rondo, which is in an irresistibly joyful mood. The entire rondo is composed on the model of a concerto movement, with solo and orchestral tutti contrasts. It is interesting to note the similarity of the harmoy, the appearance of the G as the last note of the left hand in the first measure of both the first and last movements. There is a danger of overdotting the dotted-quarter and eighth rhythm of the melody and thus robbing the phrase of its relaxed jauntiness. The precise rhythm of this phrase is very important at its every occurrence and should be a main concern of the performer.

According to some editions, the text of the second and tenth measures of the main subject shows an eighth-note upbeat to the following measure, thus adopting the text of the sixth and fourteenth measures, which have the upbeat eighth note in every edition.

The fingering for measures 3 and 11 is a series of 3–2s that emphasize the teasing slurs but avoids heaviness; the left hand here shows the harmonic skeleton. In measure 4, the two sixteenth notes are part of the melody and should not be turned into fast, inarticulate jerks; the same remark applies to the triplets in the following measure. A nice, smooth phrasing is needed after the first eighth note of measure 8, where the solo instrument finishes the phrase leading to the full orchestra's entrance with an exhilarating crescendo scale.

The repeat of the subject is for the orchestra in forte, with a noisier Alberti bass. The solo is back in measure 16 with the first episode. The observance of articulation—staccato eighths and legato quarters—is most important. The solo then raises its voice to forte in measure 20. In the following measure (measure 21), the triplet figure of the right hand is often begun together with the last eighth note of the left hand, thus turning the triplet eighths into sixteenth notes.

The performer has to observe the correct speed for the sixteenths entering in measure 23; they are usually played too fast. A new subject enters graciously in piano in measure 24. The happiness is at its pinnacle. The two sixteenths of the subject should be part of the line and not jerked, while the left hand should maintain a light piano accompaniment. The first finger, in particular, should be devoid of heaviness.

At measure 29, the forte is back. This passage corresponds to a bravura passage in a concerto; the left hand plays the orchestral accompaniment chords, with the chord on the last quarter of the measure slightly shorter than the one on the downbeat. The zigzag arpeggios of the right hand can cause problems to the performer with a heavy hand. The frequent use of the thumb makes these passages uncomfortable. The key to ease of execution is in the early preparation of the thumb: it should not remain too long on the key where it was first used but must move under the hand, ready for its next use.

The trill in measure 31 begins on the main note, while the turn before the trill in measure 35 has to be incorporated into the value of the main note: the first note of the turn is played on the beat together with the first note of the left hand. A light and spirited marchlike motive that will play an important role in the subsequent development of the movement and in the cadenza leads back to the recapitulation of the main subject. The performer has to render the soprano's eighth notes interrupted by eighth rests evenly: the notes and rests must all be their proper length and played at the cor-

rect speed. The left hand has a similar task, but it has quarter notes that are complicated by slurs and part-playing problems.

The "flute solo" of measures 39–40 is to be played with the fingerings 2–4 and
4–2 throughout; it can have a slight ritardando at the end of measure 40. The second
exposition of the main subject is unchanged: even the middle episode begins the same
way the first episode did. It takes a different direction only at measure 61, where an
expressive crescendo prepares the sforzando downbeat of measure 62 and introduces
an eighth-note motion with slurs in the alto and then in the tenor. The slurs (which
should be played without heaviness) invite the player to slow down the tempo of this
phrase, whose character is that of a sad question. The answer comes with the sorrowful
phrase beginning at measure 64 in forte. In spite of the dynamics, the Alberti bass has
to be light to allow the right hand to be more prominent. Even more than in the main
subject, the sixteenth triplets of the melody should be devoid of the undue haste that
could easily transform them into jerks.

The same warning applies to the thirty-second notes of measures 69 and 70. Also
the left-hand chords should not be obtrusive in these measures, while the right-hand
articulation of alternating slurs and staccatos should be rigorously carried out. The
passing of the clouds does not last long. It yields to a new, rather nonchalant subject in
E flat major at measure 76. This subject has a disjunct line and a dotted rhythm. The
B flats of the line should be soft enough not to disturb the longer notes carrying the
more interesting part. A more expressive phrase begins at the second half of measure
84 with slurred eighth notes that are reminiscent of string writing. The chords in the
left hand can be played like pizzicatos, but they must still be given harmonic importance. The forte of measure 87 is like an exclamation that is followed by a dramatic
pause. The answer in measure 88 and 90 is rather indifferent.

Suddenly and without warning, a sorrowful version of the first subject begins at
measure 91; here it appears in the minor mode. The change of mood is also reflected
in the change of orchestration: one can hear the penetrating sound of the woodwinds
in measures 91–92, the strings answering in measures 93–94, the woodwinds again in
measures 95–96, and then the strings in measures 97–98. The character of the music
becomes more and more disconcerted; the confusion increases in the modulatory
passage begining at measure 99, which gives the impression of great difficulty in finding the right key and the right mood in which to bring back the main subject. A
crescendo culminates in forte at measure 102, where the expressiveness also seems to
climax. The turn is to be played as follows:

measure 102

The marchlike motive brings the recapitulation of the main subject back in the
usual way. However there is a major change in the second episode, where pressing
questions emerge in the form of theatrical chords (measures 132 and 135). The answer

is a naive staccato line (measures 133 and 136). Some editions wrongly give B naturals in the tenor on the second and third beats of measure 132; these should be B flats. The tonal balance of the forte chords should be good, avoiding heaviness in the left hand and bringing the soprano out.

The subsequent passage in triplets has the same difficulty mentioned in measures 21 and 22. The sixteenth-note scales beginning at measure 144 have two witty staccato eighth notes at the end. Here there is also a definite danger of playing the sixteenths too fast. In measure 152, there is an uncomfortable leap to the higher octave. The left hand is often either late or too heavy on the second eighth note of the measure. The jump has to be foreseen and executed with ease. If the left hand cannot handle the leap successfully, the right hand can play the second eighth note of the left hand.

The bravura passage is extended here, and it reminds one even more strongly of the passage in a concerto before the closing trill. The difficulty of the zigzag arpeggios has already been mentioned; still, the figure of measures 160–161 needs special work in bringing the thumb into the next position after its first use. In spite of the trium- phant forte, the performer should not force the sound, since forcing can easily cause stiffness in the hand and fingers and thus ruin the passage. The close of the section (measures 162–163) expresses the greatest possible hilarity.

After the usual marchlike motive, a real orchestral tutti enters at measure 168. The left hand is important but not brutal; the Alberti-like figure of the right hand is the keyboard version of an upper-string tremolo. The fermata should be prepared by a ritardando in the manner of an orchestra before a cadenza. "Cadenza in tempo" means that the basic tempo is that of the entire movement. However it should be kept in mind that any cadenza presumes a certain amount of improvisatory freedom in the performance. There is room for flexibility as early as measure 175, where the sudden change to minor can be emphasized by a slower tempo and a sudden softening of the sound. Measures 177 and 178 have a definite improvisatory character and may be played with hesitation.

The tempo should be reinstated suddenly at measure 179, with the entrance of the march motive. A small amount of freedom (a slightly slower tempo) can be brought to measures 182–183; the tempo resumes at measure 184. Enthusiasm rises with the crescendo, and it climaxes in the forte at measure 189, where the necessity of keeping the harmony clear calls for a slightly slower tempo again. The forte should be main- tained throughout this chordal sequence, and then the dynamic level should suddenly be dropped to mezzo forte at the second half of measure 193 so that it can rise again to the forte at measure 197. This measure slows down considerably as we approach the fermata.

The subsequent part in small print is most improvisatory; it has to be played in the style of Mozart's concerto cadenzas. There are traditional figures here that occur in practically every one of his cadenzas. The three-octave B flat scale can be played with a crescendo or a decrescendo and, depending on the dynamics adopted, with an accelerando (exclamation) or a slight ritardando (question). The four-note sequences beginning with sixteenths that come after the second short B flat scale contain slurs and staccatos. When the figure switches to eighth and quarter notes, it should be understood as a continuous slowing down rather than as a sudden change in speed. The two fermata notes of the cadenza should be played with charm and innocence.

Solo and orchestra evenly share the recapitulation of the main subject. The entrance of the tutti at measure 203 should be unmistakable. The repeated notes of measures 206 and 207 should be played with finger changes:

measures 206-207

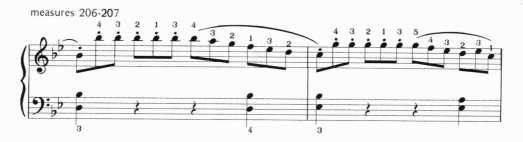

Beware of mistakenly playing the sixteenths in measure 209 too fast. In the last closing subject (measure 214), the staccatos should be played with a smiling charm. The sixteenths triplet of measure 218 should not be jerked, and the trill of measure 219 should be played with ease. Measures 221 and 222 may have a slight ritardando and calando; the closing orchestral chords are in the slower tempo.

This rondo is without doubt the most interesting movement of the sonata; it shows the inventive power and originality of Mozart at his best. Its performance calls for high spirits and wit; constant control of rhythm and tempo; brilliant, effortless finger virtuosity for the bravura passages; and imagination for the improvisatory parts. The tempo, which is not easy to feel, should be a relaxed alla breve. Thinking in terms of solo and tutti helps the interpretation; however, beware loud, heavy imitations of the orchestra and feeble, inarticulate solos without projection.

Ludwig van Beethoven

Born 1770, Bonn; died 1827, Vienna

Beethoven is one of the great geniuses of all time. His name and his masterpieces have become symbols for mankind, and his influence on the development of music—on composition, interpretation, and aesthetics alike—has been felt to the present day.

A celebrated pianist, Beethoven wrote for the pianoforte from his early youth into his late years. The thirty-two piano sonatas are certainly among the most important single contributions to the piano repertoire. His twenty-one sets of variations represent another important group. There are also the five piano concertos (eight, if the Triple Concerto for violin, cello, and piano; the transcription of the Violin Concerto; and the *Choral Fantasia* are counted), and a number of miscellaneous works including the bagatelles (Op. 33, 119, 126), three rondos (Op. 51, nos. 1 and 2, and Op. 129), the *Andante in F*, the Fantasy, Op. 77, the Polonaise, Op. 89, plus a large amount of chamber music with piano.

The structural innovations Beethoven brought to the various musical forms are too well known to require discussion here. The stunning development of his pianistic style cannot be separated from the development of the pianoforte itself during the first three decades of the nineteenth century. Whereas the virtuosity of Haydn and Mozart is more or less limited to scale and arpeggio figures, that of Beethoven includes double thirds, fourths, sixths, and octaves. Chords appear to be the most important single element in his piano writing: they can be either legato in choralelike melodies or furiously hammered out in passionate outbreaks. His Alberti basses take widely extended forms. Long trills (for which Beethoven shows a genuine predilection) are combined with melodies, sometimes in a way that involves the difficulty of playing the trill with the outer fingers while using the strong fingers for the melody.

The innermost essence of Beethoven's piano style, however, is its absence of virtuosity for its own sake. All the difficulties—which are often more taxing than those to be found in "virtuoso" works—are inherent in his musical style to the extent that technique and the musical message cannot be separated. For this reason, the performance of Beethoven's works is exceptionally difficult; it requires the seldom-achieved perfect balance between impeccable technique and musical understanding.

All in all, Beethoven's oeuvre remains unequaled.

BEETHOVEN

Sonata in F Major, Op. 10, No. 2

Composed and published in 1798, this charming work is often regarded as a rather unimportant product of Beethoven's creativity and used as a good "teaching" sonata. Indeed the image of the "dramatic Beethoven" does not fit this light, spontaneous work. But even considered only as a "teaching piece" it reveals a great many high-level difficulties requiring well-developed dexterity and fluency.

Allegro

M.M. ♩ = 104–112

Form: Sonata

	MEASURES
Exposition	1 – 66
First subject	1 – 37
Second subject	38 – 54
Closing subject	55 – 66
Development	67 – 116
Recapitulation	117 – 202

Preciseness of attack and rhythm and conciseness of sound are the main problems of the first subject. The chords have to be well balanced, with all the notes sounding, and yet they must be in piano. Also a distinct difference in duration has to be revealed between the staccato eighth and quarter notes. The triplet motive has to be perfectly timed and played with accurate speed; it should be devoid of nervous jerking. The legato required in both hands from measure 5 on is particularly difficult to achieve in the left hand. Finger substitutions offer only limited help: the legato will be achieved mainly by maintaining quietness in the left hand and arm.

The dotted rhythm is missing from measure 5 in some editions. Whereas the phrase in measures 5–8 develops expressive tension along with the crescendo-decrescendo, the phrase in measures 9–12 dissipates all seriousness with its dancing dotted rhythms. The trill in measure 9 begins on the main note; the ornament in measure 10 is played on the beat and incorporated into the melodic line. Throughout the phrase, the dotted rhythm should remain sharp and spicy.

Ill temper appears with the rinforzando of measure 13. In the almost exasperatedly repeated triplet motives in measures 16–18, the concluding right-hand octave of each slurred group should be played lightly and without undue abruptness.

A singing legato and good tonal balance are required for the ensuing more lyrical section (measures 18–30). Finger substitutions to insure legato in the right hand are less helpful than smoothness of the hand and arm motions. The climaxing sforzandos in measures 21 and 25 mark only the high points of the dynamic swells; they have to be devoid of roughness. Perfect evenness of the left-hand figure is difficult to attain, unless the thumb can match perfectly the sound produced by the other fingers. The fortissimo in measure 27 is an explosion of joy rather than high drama; it has to be achieved with a full, singing tone and proper tonal balance.

The accompaniment figure at measure 30 has discouraged many pianists from going deeper into this sonata. For its effortless execution, the fingers—especially those that do not take part in the action—need to be kept relaxed and close to the surface of the keys. High finger articulation will turn this discreet accompaniment into a loud noise. Furthermore the lightness of the hand has to be preserved by not putting any arm weight on the first notes of the groups (which are also stemmed as quarter notes). Special care is recommended for the rhythmic division of the figure. When practicing the left hand alone, it is easy to turn the 2×3 portioning into 3×2, which makes it impossible to put the figure together with the right-hand part. Of course, grouping accents should be avoided in performance. Playing the passage hands together is difficult because of the problem of playing four against six.

The cheerful staccato sforzandos of the right hand in measures 32–35 should be played in a witty rather than an aggressive manner. The right-hand sixteenth notes in measures 36–37 carry the melody; their line should be sensitively molded. Slurs and staccatos should be accurately rendered in measures 38–39, where the ornaments on the last eighth notes have to be played with melodic importance, beginning on the main note each time.

In measures 41–43, good coordination between the hands has to be established. The danger is that the thirty-second rest before each right-hand figure may be overextended so as to reduce the figure to a mere broken chord played much faster than necessary. The alternating intervals of measures 47–50 need perfect metrical evenness: both hands should play witty rather than hammered staccatos, and the interest should focus distinctly on the top line. Measures 51–54 should be played in a graceful forte, without roughness in the phrasing. In measure 53, the sixteenth notes should be kept to an accurate speed.

The difficulty of the closing subject lies in the accompaniment figure. Only a light finger articulation that avoids excessive motions can assure perfect tonal and metrical evenness. Some complications may arise at measures 58, 62, and 64, where the unrestricted speed of the trill often influences the left-hand figure to be faster. The octaves of the closing measure should show wit and elegance.

The closing octave motive remains the driving force throughout the development. The difficulty here lies in establishing a feeling of connection between this figure and the following triplet or sixteenths motive, where any extension of the initial rest will be detrimental to continuity and will turn these delicate shivers into inarticulate jerked figures. The accuracy of the sudden forte chord on the downbeat of measure 73 is often spoiled if a small caesura is not inserted on the preceding bar line or if the forte is exaggerated.

A longer melody hidden in the broken octaves appears at measure 77. Again the rests in the right hand should be accurate to insure perfect coordination between the hands. The bass notes on the downbeats are light, yet sonorous enough to carry the harmonic foundation. The fifth finger of the left hand should be reserved for these bass notes exclusively and never reused on the chords. Expressive crescendos point toward the fortepiano in measure 83 and the fortissimo in measure 89 marking the new key areas.

It is particularly difficult to keep good coordination between the hands the entire length of the crescendos. Though the chord in measure 99 is to be played piano, a small caesura will help here just as it did in measure 73. The dynamic shading of this section (measures 95–116) has to be strictly obeyed. The coordination between the hands is more and more difficult to maintain from measure 110 on because of the large gap between the hands. The decrescendo at measure 113 quickly dims the sound to piano and pianissimo, and there is also a considerable ritardando. The ensuing silence should be of great intensity. The tension—without foreshadowing earthquakes—is full of expectation.

The first subject returns in D major (measures 117–129); it has no crescendo-decrescendo indication here, and the omission is most probably intentional. The timing of the silence in measures 129–130 has to be precise, if not generous. Measure 135 may have a slight ritardando; the tempo resumes in measure 136. The dynamic swell is also missing from the phrase in measures 136–140. From this point on, the recapitulation shows only two differences from the exposition. The left hand plays the melody in measures 153–159. The quarter notes of the left hand form an expressive chord, while the ensuing eighth-note chords are light. The right hand takes over the leading role in measures 160–161. A slight prolongation of the sixteenth notes on the first and second beats of these measures underlines the modulation effectively. The other difference is in measures 187 and 188, where the following fingering is recommended for the left hand:

measures 187-188

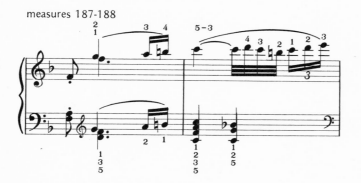

Elegant and effortless, this movement is reminiscent of Scarlatti in its conciseness. The performance requires effortlessness, not only in the busy, technically difficult figures but also in the accumulation of tensions and in the holding of fermatas. Along with the technical equipment, artistry is also under a severe test in the section comprising measures 117–136, a real touchstone of imaginative interpretation and projection in piano and pianissimo.

Allegretto

M.M. ♩. = 66

Form: Minuet, trio, minuet

	MEASURES
Minuet	1 – 38
Trio	39 – 124
Minuet	125 – 170

Tonal balance and part playing are the principal difficulties of the minuet. The unison theme in the lower register has to be led by the right hand, while the left hand remains subdued. At measure 5, the part-playing difficulties begin to emerge. If the grace note of measure 6 is interpreted "long," it fits better into the melodic line:

measure 6

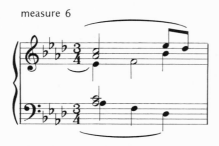

No crescendo is indicated for the first eight measures; yet the melody should pass from the scarcely audible, mysterious beginning to the radiant warmth of A flat major without a driving crescendo that would wipe out the idle quality of the first phrase.

In the second phrase (measures 9–16) (which should also be played without a prominent crescendo), the sorrowful sforzandos will reach a higher sphere at the point where the last sforzando overflows to the downbeat of measure 16; this last sforzando is topped by a fermata. The sforzandos on the third beats are marked staccato; however if they are played too short, they can easily transform sorrowful exclamations into ridiculous hiccups. The trill in measure 15 begins on the main note. Only a moderate duration should be assigned to the fermata in measure 16.

The piano for the ensuing right-hand solo and the pianissimo where the left hand joins the right should be rendered distinctly; the poignant rinforzandos and slurs in measures 23–24 should also be clear. Small hands encounter serious difficulties in playing the sixths of measures 25 and 29 in a smooth legato. If using the second finger in the low voice proves to be troublesome, part of the alto may be taken into the left-hand part. A full-scale crescendo is supposed to take place between the piano of measure 30 and the fortissimo of measure 33; it is helped by the extra voices entering along the way. At the trill in measure 34 (starting on the main note), a new, smaller crescendo begins, but it is stopped by the sudden piano on the graceful closing chords.

A warm, full tone and good tonal balance are the requirements for performance of the trio. The gently rocking rhythm is reminiscent of a popular Ländler. The first two phrases (measures 38–46) should be played with relaxed simplicity. The ornament in measure 42 is best started ahead of time in order to preserve the rhythm of the upbeat eighth notes.

measures 41–42

The next phrase (measures 46–54), which is twice as long as the two preceding phrases, shows a prominent crescendo toward the deep sforzando on the downbeat of measure 49. As an effect of the ensuing decrescendo, the G naturals in the middle voices of measure 50 have to be played very softly—just like harmonic corrections under the overhanging soprano. Furthermore, the sforzando chord and its resolution in measures 49–50 may have a slightly broader count, and the tempo should resume on the third beat of measure 50. The left-hand sforzandos that appear with the second statement of the subject should not be exaggerated.

In measures 57–58 and wherever else this figure appears, the slurs and staccatos have to be articulated precisely, yet without getting into the foreground. Meanwhile the right-hand chords at the phrase endings (measures 57–58, 61–62, and 65–66) have to be in the proper slur relationship dynamically (last chord softer than the preceding one)—a matter easily overlooked while the attention is drawn to the articulation of the left hand.

A light crescendo in the left-hand chords reminiscent of horns paves the way for the expressive sforzando of the right hand in the section comprising measures 71–78. The resolution of the left-hand chords on the downbeats of measures 74 and 78 requires great finesse in exactly matching the sound of the overhanging decayed harmonies. The crescendo at measure 83 should be made quite prominent, and the resolution of the right-hand sforzando chord on the downbeat of measure 86 requires the same finesse as measures 74 and 78 required of the left hand.

Although they are marked pianissimo, measures 87–93 must have distinct clarity and a well-focused melody. The rests of measures 93–94 (and of measures 117–118) should be generous rather than short. The restatement contains only two novelties: one is the addition of grace notes to the right-hand sforzandos (they are to be played expressively as part of the melody). The other is a chilling chromatic step in the soprano at measure 114. The passage leading back to the minuet is played in ponderous pianissimo; the last left-hand octave before the double bar may serve as an upbeat to the minuet.

The returning minuet contains some slight variations on the original statement, such as the use of alternate hands for the repeat of the first phrase (measures 132–140), which tests part-playing ability more severely than at the phrase's first appearance.

The busier eighth-note accompaniment of measures 141–148 should not cloud the imitative game of the right hand. The alternation persists to the end of the minuet, causing minor problems of tonal balance; in measures 155–156 and 159–160, for example, the alternating accompaniment should be kept well below the level of the soprano. The closing chords have to be played forte, but without excess.

Smooth phrasing without abruptness and part-playing problems are the principal difficulties of the Allegretto. It has to be played—in strong contrast to the virtuosic outer movements—with an intimate tenderness and fervor.

Presto

M.M. ♩ = 144–152

Form: Two themes alternated, with elements
of development and recapitulation

			MEASURES		
	A		1	–	22
	B		23	–	32
Development	{ A		33	–	68
	{ B		69	–	86
Recapitulation	{ A		87	–	124
	{ B		125	–	150

Firm rhythm and crisp staccato playing are the basic requirements of the entire movement. A proper speed for the sixteenth notes of the fugato subject, which are often inarticulately jammed together or rushed, is a problem throughout the Presto. The crispness of the staccato notes can be assured by a finger change on the repeated notes, like this:

measures 1- 8

In the absence of detailed dynamic markings, it is customary to begin the movement piano and raise the level slightly at each subsequent entrance. The sforzandos of
measures 15–16 and 19–20, while exhilarating, should still be far from the volume of
the forte at measure 21, which strikes in as a complete surprise. This forte is modeled
after the sudden entrance of an orchestral tutti. The left hand has the responsibility of
lucidly enunciating the harmony in measures 15–20; the eighth- and quarter-note
chords should be assigned their proper length. The recommended fingering for the
right hand is:

measure 21

The sudden piano in measure 23 is presumably meant to apply to the second
eighth note on, since the downbeat is the resolution of the preceding phrase and is
therefore played a light forte. The soprano has a leading role in measures 23–26; it is
often overpowered by the other voices and needs distinct focusing. The sixteenth notes
in measures 26 and 30 may turn into inarticulate figures. Preliminary practice in the
following way

measure 26

usually helps to keep the sixteenths in proper tempo.
    The sudden outbreak of loud forte together with the unison in measures 33–36
usually incites thoughtless brutality or full martellato treatment in the left hand. The
witty elegance of the subject has to be preserved at every dynamic level. In the section
comprising measures 37–40, it is difficult to keep the subject and the Alberti accompaniment perfectly synchronized; this is especially true at measure 40, where the sudden change in the position of the left hand often results in an unacceptable delay. The
fugal exposition in diminution at measure 41 has to be kept in an animated
pianissimo; keep the sudden forte of measure 45 for a surprise. Often this explosion is
spoiled by stumbling on the right-hand interval. The following fingering helps accuracy:

measures 44-45

From measure 51 on, the right hand needs (in addition to faultless part playing) two distinctly colored voices. The downbeat of measure 54 is also a frequent victim of inaccuracy. The recommended fingering for it is:

measures 53-54

The left-hand sforzandos pointing to the tonic, dominant, or subdominant of the different key areas have to have the depth of a string bass but none of the hardness so easily produced in this particular register of the piano. Still, the sixteenth notes of the right hand need the principal attention of the performer; it is too easy to transform them into inarticulate jammed figures and consequently to increase the general tempo to the extent that measures 63–66 (where new difficulties in synchronization of the hands appear) are reached in an unmanageable tempo. The section comprising measures 45–66 should be played in strict tempo, yet with the utmost temperament; it should have the virtuosity and clarity of the solo instruments of an orchestra. The motive ♪♪ ♬ turns into an obsession here.

Perfect simultaneity of the chords in piano from measure 69 on is a severe test of tonal control. A relaxed wrist and the avoidance of too much tension in the fingers will help. Piano should be maintained throughout measures 76–80, instead of anticipating the crescendo that eventually appears in measure 81. In spite of the crescendo, the left hand should remain light and unobtrusive to allow the playful imitation in the lower voice of the right hand to be clearly brought out at measure 84. Forte should be reached only in measure 85; it prepares for the whimsical main subject, which enters with a comical triplet upbeat in measure 86. Many otherwise acceptable performances are marred at this point by the absence of a firm tempo. Beginning with the comical triplet upbeat, the speed of both the main motive and the sixteenth-note scales has to be under rigorous control; if the upbeat is jammed together, suddenly and without warning the tempo can be pushed ahead. The pianist is surprised, and his right hand dashes ahead in pursuit; it not only follows but even overtakes the left hand, further ruining the tempo.

Even if none of this happens and the performance follows a well-established, happy course, traps like measures 94 and 102 still await the inexperienced performer. The unexpected shape of the right-hand figure strikes the player—or the tempo—like lightning. If entanglement of the fingers can be avoided, sudden panic may hasten the tempo to the extent that a sizable portion of the measure will be missing and the downbeat of the following measure will arrive too soon. The effect is like that of stumbling on an obstacle during an otherwise smooth sprint. Slow practice and intense concentration are strongly recommended. Dynamically this section may be given a stunning brightness by passing the fortissimo from one hand to the other at the entrances of the subjects.

At measure 107, still another new difficulty is to be found—broken octaves synchronized with a tremolo accompaniment figure. High finger articulation in the broken octaves may be a source of stiffness in the hand and forearm and, consequently, a source of fatigue when the passage is extended. Fatigue may also be due to the stiffness of the middle fingers, which, instead of being satisfied with their inactive role in broken-octave playing, curl up in a paroxysm of activity. In this particular sonata, not only the length of the passage but also the required increase of the volume to forte and fortissimo is taxing. In broken octaves, the fingers should strike the keys from a very small distance above them, while the wrist, slightly raised, transmits a slight rotation of the forearm to the fingers. The crescendo to forte and fortissimo will be produced by a slight increase of the rotation.

Still, synchronizing the broken octaves with the tremolo accompaniment of the left hand reveals itself to be very difficult. The position changes on the keyboard—from parallel to contrary motion—further complicate the execution. Measures 123–124 are particularly difficult: the right hand's scale, rushing on as usual at breakneck speed, does not give the left hand's broken octaves a chance to follow. Without doubt the section comprising measures 85–124 contains the most severe difficulties in the entire movement and should be the object of serious and intensive study.

The forte downbeat of measure 125 is followed by a piano on the second eighth note. The uncomfortable position change for the left hand at measure 133 may be helped by leaning the body slightly to the right during the preceding one or two measures, thus giving the left hand the room necessary for a smooth switch. The left-hand downbeat in measure 133 is played with the fifth finger, while the thumb crosses over the right hand. The separate stems for the first eighth note of the right hand on the downbeat of measures 141 and 143 are meant as phrasings. The crescendo and fortissimo of the concluding measures have to be kept elegant: a ritardando should be limited to a slight delay of the concluding octave, which should be played rigorously as a quarter note.

The elegance and exhilaration of the Presto depend on effortless sound, faultless rhythm, and firm tempo. The conciseness of the form and texture requires impeccable solutions for all the technical difficulties and wit and imagination for the interpretative problems.

BEETHOVEN
Sonata in C Minor, Op. 13

~~~~~~

Although the subtitle *Sonate pathétique* appears in the first published version of this work, this descriptive term was probably not Beethoven's. However the powerful concentration of tragic passion and pathos in the opening movement fully justifies it. The Rondo finale, in a somewhat less passionate vein, is preceded by a lyrical and nobly nostalgic slow movement. The work was composed and published in 1799.

Grave

M.M. ♪ = 66

Allegro di molto e con brio

M.M. ♩. = 144

Form: Sonata, with introduction

		MEASURES
Grave Introduction		1 – 10
Molto allegro Exposition		1 – 122
	First subject	1 – 24
	Transition	25 – 40
	Second subject	41 – 78
	Closing subject	79 – 122
	Development	123 – 184
	Recapitulation	185 – 284
	Coda	285 – 300

The Grave is referred to as an introduction only to simplify matters. The inclusion of this material in the development and coda proves that it is an integral part of the movement and implies improvisation every time it occurs. The three components of the main motive—the opening forte chord, the ensuing dotted rhythm, and the concluding sigh motive—are equally important and have to be faultlessly rendered for successful performance. The dotted chord has to be played with tragic depth, yet with well-balanced sound. To insist on impeccable precision in the dotted rhythm probably will not be superfluous. The identical treatment of similar motives is an absolute condition for a satisfactory performance of this movement; this condition can be fulfilled here only if the correct rhythm is solidly established and reproduced in the identical manner at its every occurrence. The difficulty usually arises in connection with keeping the thirty-second notes of the motive rightly proportioned: a too-long thirty-second note would deprive the rhythm of its solemn pathos, while a too-short one would not suit the singing quality of the melodic line. Finally the emotionally entreating slur at the end of the phrase that is like a sorrowful question has to be played thoroughly legato and with care for the dynamic relation between the slurred notes (i.e., last note softer than the preceding one).

In measures 3 and 4, the important difference between fortepiano and sforzando has to be well understood and interpreted: the sforzandos of measure 3 and the downbeat of measure 4 are meant to be in piano and therefore are less sonorous than the preceding fortepianos. Measure 4 has a crescendo; as a result, the last two sforzandos are almost fortes. The left hand's rest on the sixth eighth note of the measure must be obeyed by both the hand and the pedal, while the following left-hand sforzando octave should be moderate enough not to cover the overhanging A flat of the soprano. The shape and nobility of the succeeding scale are more important than metrical exactness: the concluding five notes, especially, should have the line of a vocalise.

From measure 5 on, the opposition of characters, which is further stressed by dynamic extremes, suggests a dialogue. The sorrowfully imploring motive is interrupted with fury by the fortissimo chords in the lower register. An imperceptibly slower tempo for these violent outbursts will draw more attention to the moving bass line. The downbeat octaves of the left hand, which are notated on separate stems in measures 5, 6, and 7, should be slightly prolonged. In measures 7 and 8, the uninterrupted chordal accompaniment should be kept dynamically well below the melody line, especially during the crescendo in measure 8.

The full duration of the rests at the end of measure 9 appears painfully long to inexperienced pianists; panic-stricken by the seemingly interminable silence, they cut short measure 9 and proceed far ahead of time to measure 10. Relying solely on counting at this point usually does not give a satisfactory result. The following suggestion may insure a proper duration for the silence (the notes in lighter print are to be heard by the inner ear):

measure 9

The portamento required in measures 9 and 10 for the repeated sixteenth notes is very close to a legato. The execution of the virtuoso chromatic scale in measure 10 is often marred by in-and-out motions of the hand when the fingers move between the white and black keys; curving the fingers helps to avoid this unnecessary motion. A sizable crescendo toward the sforzando fermata heightens the dramatic tension at the moment of passage from the Grave to the Allegro.

The first sixteen bars of the Allegro include the main technical difficulty of the movement—a metrically even octave tremolo in the left hand. Often performers are carried away by the impetuosity of the music and expect that without taking the time and pains to solve the basic technical problems, the left-hand part will miraculously fall into place just by being played over and over. The correct speed of the tremolo is best assured if the lower notes played by the fifth finger are heard as pulsating quarter notes in alla breve. Intervals and chords of the right hand consistently coincide with the left-hand fifth finger. It is advantageous to reduce finger articulation of the tremolo to a strict minimum. A slightly raised wrist and a small rotation of the forearm at the proper speed will prevent stiffness and tiring. The crescendo, coupled with the diatonic motion in measures 5–8, further complicates the task of the left hand: the piano at measure 9 should appear as a sudden drop back. The use of the fourth finger on the black keys is recommended when the tremolo moves in scale pattern.

As well as being perfectly fitted to the pulsation of the left hand, the right-hand intervals and chords should also have overwhelming drive. The difference in length between the staccato quarter and half notes of the right-hand line should be clearly rendered. The syncopations of measures 3 and 11 may be emphasized by accents, although sforzandos appear in these passages only in the recapitulation. The middle voice in measures 7 and 8, in contrary motion to the bass, raises the harmonic tension; it should not be overplayed, however. The accompaniment figure of measures 17 and 18 is often erroneously phrased, in the following way:

measures 17-18

Even if it is a trifle too soon, the accompaniment third on the downbeat of measure 19 precipitates the right-hand arpeggio, ruins the tempo for the ensuing measures, and makes it virtually impossible to coordinate the left hand with the right in the middle of measure 20. At measure 25, the driving motive and tremolo reappear; they are interrupted by sforzando chords whose duration should be rigorously correct while the left-hand pulsations are kept even. The impeccable rendering of the sigh motive, without the slightest heaviness on the resolutions, is most important in measures 35–38.

At measure 41, the left hand approaches the B flat with the fifth finger under the right hand, leaving the right hand in the *sopra* position to reach for the lower register, where the second subject begins. The main difficulty of the second subject lies precisely in the quick changes between low and high registers. To secure smoothness in these changes, the adoption of a particular physical position is recommended. It consists of leaning the torso as far to the left as is comfortably possible with the right foot still on the pedal. If this position is maintained until the last crossing is passed, it will greatly facilitate a smooth reaching for the motives in the lower register; yet it creates no disadvantage in performing the upper part of the subject. The imploring slurs, further enhanced by the sforzandos, contrast with the staccato quarter notes. The ornament is to be played as a triplet on the beat; the same fingering should always be used, even when this means using the thumb on a black key.

measure 47

The accompaniment in the left hand is to be kept soft throughout, while the bass line is to be clearly sensed in measures 65, 69, and in similar measures elsewhere. Small hands are undeniably handicapped in the figure from measure 79 on because the stretch between the fifth and second fingers of the right hand becomes quite taxing. Early releases of the fifth finger at these points are acceptable. The staccatos appearing from measure 83 on are to be interpreted as slight accents emphasizing the lines of the soprano and bass as well as the increasing gap between them. The driving crescendo included in the passage should not cause stiffness or impair the beauty of the tone. The recommended fingering for measures 103–107 is:

measures 103-107

Keeping the right arm and wrist relaxed in measures 115–120 will insure a full, rich sound without hardness.

The repeat has long been a subject of heated debate. In the absence of authentic evidence to the contrary, it seems logical to include the Grave if the repeat is taken. In this particular case, however, doing away with the repeat may be the best solution.

The Grave at the opening of the development should be interpreted identically in all ways to the one at the opening of the movement. The enharmonic modulation to E minor in measure 125, specifically marked piano, can have a magical effect in sensitive hands. The ensuing quarter-note chords are often mistakenly played too fast, thus not only ruining the tempo but also making the necessary ritardando (when approaching the fermata) impossible.

The Allegro combines the explosive main motive with the imploring motive of the Grave. The strict observance of the prescribed dynamics is of the utmost importance in this section (measures 127–138). At measure 139, the octave tremolo is entrusted to the right hand; it is more difficult here because of the offbeat slurring of the left hand. Reducing the tremolo to the pulsation of the thumb and putting this together with the correctly slurred left-hand part is a useful exercise to begin with. Accents on the main beats that conflict with the slurring of the left hand should be avoided. A further complication involving the tremolo appears from measure 150 on; the downward diatonic motion implies hidden slurs like these:

The dynamic in measure 153 is a subito piano. Measures 157–160 contain the troublesome task of keeping the right-hand figures strictly synchronized with the left-hand tremolo. Usually the tremolo (in fact, here it is really only a pedal point) has difficulty keeping up the required speed with the seemingly more active right hand. The alla breve grouping has to be rigorously preserved, even in the slowest practice tempo. The sudden change in speed and the part-playing difficulties in measures 163–164, often makes the left hand stumble. The strict enforcement of the tempo in these measures should prevent unrhythmic limping. The right-hand trill in measure 164 begins on the main note and is executed with the fingering 3–5; at most it contains seven notes, including the tail. Finally care should be taken to maintain a good tonal balance here by playing the left-hand part only moderately loud in order not to cover the right hand. The right-hand solo in measures 177–184 has to be played piano; however it should have the appropriate shading. This passage is more like a melody line than a virtuosic run.

In the recapitulation, the troublesome octave tremolo lasts eight measures longer than in the exposition, severely taxing the endurance of the performer. While the recapitulation of the second subject group brings no new difficulty, measures 245–246 (and similar passages elsewhere) contain a particularly uncomfortable stretching between the fifth and second fingers. The recommended fingering for measures 267–271 is:

measures 267-270

There is an important change in the outlook of the Grave motive introducing the coda: the heavy opening chords of the motive fail to appear. Laborious counting may be avoided if the weight of the rests replacing the chords is mentally felt; this is especially true on the downbeat of measure 285, where a sharp-edged termination of the preceding fortissimo chord will draw more attention to the importance of the silence. The crescendo in measure 287 leading to the sforzando should be prominent and followed by a well-gradated diminuendo. The tempo of the closing measures has to be the same as at every other occurrence, and no faster. In particular, the tempo of the closing chords has to be closely controlled.

One cannot insist enough on a perfect balance between musical expression and faultless technical rendering—a balance that is particularly difficult to achieve here where a strong and appealing dramatic content might make the performer unaware of technical shortcomings. Without the long and patient work that alone can bring solutions to the manifold technical problems, an acceptable performance cannot be expected.

Adagio cantabile

M.M. ♪ = about 54

Form: Rondo—A-B-A-C-A-Coda

	MEASURES
A	1 – 16
B	17 – 28
A	29 – 36
C	36 – 50
A	51 – 66
Coda	66 – 73

Tonal balance is the problem from the very outset of the piece: to the right hand is entrusted the melody (appearing in the middle register) and an accompaniment moving in sixteenth notes; the left hand has a single bass line for the first exposition of the theme. These three layers of sound have to be firmly established: the melody is in the foreground, the bass line is in the second plane, and the sixteenths motion is the softest. A truly sensitive performance of the theme would include a refined rubato in the execution of the sixteenth notes; if they were played with metrical evenness, they would encase the melody in a strait jacket. Very small, almost imperceptible prolongations on points where the harmony changes will make the structure clear and allow a natural breathing of the melody.

It is particularly difficult to maintain strict legato along with good tonal balance in measure 5, where thirty-second notes appear in the soprano. The following suggestion insures a smooth blending of the thirty-seconds into the melody line and at the same time avoids an unacceptable hesitation on the bar line, which is the result of the fingering that is normally used—crossing the fourth finger over the fifth.

measures 5-6

In measure 7, the portamento sixteenth notes should be almost legato. The conclusion of the phrase on the downbeat of measure 8 needs generous prolongation. The time lost can be made up in the other triplet sixteenths in such a manner that the total duration of the measure remains unchanged. The tone color also should change after the prolonged conclusion, in response to the intimation of a different orchestration that pervades the second exposition of the main theme with a richer texture; in it even the bass line has a quasi-soloistic comment in measures 12 and 13. There is no way in which the left hand can help out the right in measure 13 when the difficult thirty-second notes occur in the melody line. Only the above-mentioned finger crossing is possible. It can be avoided in measures 5 and 33, but it is unavoidable at measure 13. The conclusion of the theme at measure 16 should be played with a slight easing of the tempo.

The first episode (which is really more of an interlude) begins with a thirty-second-note upbeat that is often modified to a sixteenth. The right hand, freed from part-playing problems, can use a broadly singing tone for the melody over the accompaniment chords of the left hand. A suggested solution for the ornaments in measures 20 and 21 is:

measures 20-21

A little time taken before the downbeat of measure 22 will allow a smooth blending of the grace-note slide into the melody line. At measure 24, the melody lies in the expressive slurs of the sixteenths motion; there should be a small crescendo. In measures 27–28, the chromaticism underlined by slurs has to be sensitively rendered, while the tempo may be eased in measure 28 to prepare for the reentry of the main subject.

The middle episode, which is in the dark parallel minor and has an impetuous triplet motion, provides a strong contrast. Here also tonal balance should be among the main preoccupations of the performer. The particular difficulty lies in playing the melody and the repeated-chord accompaniment in the same hand with a well-balanced tone. Instead of using finger articulation exclusively, the player can best play the repeated chords by making a slight motion of the forearm while the fingers remain on the surface of the keys to insure a simultaneous attack on the notes. The soprano and bass are conversing in a dialogue. A small emphasis on the bass entrances will sustain the line of the ensuing triplets. These notes have to be correctly articulated: first legato, then portamento.

The crescendo in measure 41 leads with sudden dramatic intensity into three dynamically growing, wild sforzandos. A common mistake at this point is to play the right-hand triplets in measure 42 legato and to attach them to the following sforzandos. The pedal used on the sforzando octaves should be released at the beginnings of the second and fourth eighth notes of measure 42.

The cadence in E major in measure 43 may receive a fierce interpretation. Only the first chord on the downbeat of measure 44 is forte; its sound, however, has to be prolonged by the pedal for one eighth note. The right-hand part of measures 48–50 is difficult for small or weak hands since they have to be outstretched and used in an uncomfortable position. The dominant chord in measure 50 is especially awkward; using the thumb on the two lowest keys is recommended. In these measures, the left hand's comment is staccato for the first time. The authenticity of the rinforzandos appearing in some editions at measures 48–49 is doubtful. The genuine crescendo at measure 50, bringing along a slight easing of the tempo, drops back to piano suddenly on the downbeat of measure 51, where the tempo is resumed.

In spite of the triplet motion in the accompaniment, the last statement of the main subject should have the same serenity as its previous occurrences. The correct articulation of the accompaniment triplets is of the utmost importance: two triplet notes are slurred, and one is staccato. In particular, the last staccato note of each triplet group should be closely watched, inasmuch as it is easy to slur it to the following group. The slur endings and the following staccato notes should not be sharply detached or too short; their execution should be modeled on the way stringed instruments would handle the motive. The thirty-second notes of measure 63 will coincide with the last triplet note of the accompaniment figure.

The conclusion of the main subject at measure 65 has to be given a sizable ritardando: the downbeat of measure 66 needs an important prolongation to mark the passage to the coda. The dotted motive in measures 66–67 and 67–68 is often spoiled by an unacceptable hesitation on the bar line that is due to clumsy searching for the new left-hand position. This hesitation is easily avoided if the thumb is used on the last three E flats of measures 66 and 68. The suggested solution for the ornament in measure 68 is:

measure 68

The left-hand slurs and the rinforzandos pervade the interpretation of the closing triplet motive from measure 70 on; give special care to the lightness of the downbeat chords. In the last measure, the graceful effect of the motion of the middle voices coupled with a considerable ritardando should not be overlooked.

Except for the violent outburst of the middle episode, the whole movement unfolds in imposing calm. The three appearances of the main subject (always in an intensely singing legato) are tied together by similarity rather than difference in expression at each occurrence. The noble line of the melody requires an intense, full, but still mellow tone, while the other voices are kept well below the melody level.

Rondo: Allegro

M.M. ♩ = about 96

Form: Rondo

	MEASURES
A	1 – 17
B	18 – 61
A	61 – 78
C	78 – 120
A	120 – 134
B	134 – 170
A	170 – 182
Coda	182 – 210

The left-hand figure accompanying the elaborate melodic line is difficult to keep even if the wrist does not follow the activity of the fingers with a slight lateral motion. The use of the third and fourth fingers in the fingering of the arpeggios should be as classically prescribed. The right hand has the responsibility of molding the long, sinuous melody. The upbeat should not be played exaggeratedly staccato. The grace notes of measures 2 and 3 have to be executed short but without causing any accent on the ensuing main notes.

The main part of the subject is reached in measures 5–6 (and in measures 9–10), where the two-grace-note slides are to be played clearly ahead of the beat to avoid an octave parallel between soprano and bass. An almost imperceptible hesitation on the bar line in the left-hand part will give time enough to complete the grace-note slide, which should be played considerably softer than the heavy-printed note in order to incorporate it into the melody line. The difficult transition from measure 10 to measure 11 in the left hand often separates the leading upbeat motive of the right hand from the downbeat. The phrasing of the right hand following the downbeat of measure 12 should be smooth, and special care should be taken to avoid an accent on the downbeat, which—in spite of the staccato—should not be played too short.

Beethoven scored only a few dynamic markings in this movement, so the rest of them have to be supplied by the performer. The suggested dynamic scheme is:

MEASURES

1 – 4	*p*
5 – 6	*mp*
7 – 8	Diminuendo to *p*
8 – 10	*mf*
10 – 11	Diminuendo
12 – 17	Crescendo from *mp* to *f*

The powerful conclusion of the main subject leads directly to the fortepiano in measure 18. Zigzag arpeggios (measures 19 and 23) often occasion difficulties, especially if the thumb is used more often than is necessary. The fingering of these measures should adhere to the fingering of chords, with the thumb released immediately after each use and moved under the palm of the hand toward the key where it has to be used next.

Measures 19–20 and 23–24 need good-sized dynamic shaping swells. The singing legato of the right hand should be the prominent feature of the next section (measures 25–32) in spite of the very difficult part-playing problem of measures 29–30. Measure 29 should be played with the hand turned inward to allow the thumb to reach under the hand toward the C of the soprano (second eighth note in measure 30). At this point, pointing the elbow way out is commendable, for this action helps the thumb to reach farther. A crescendo in measures 31–32 followed by a sudden piano on the downbeat of measure 33 is recommended.

The virtuosic triplets appearing at this point are often played too fast, in total disregard for the general tempo. The passage should indeed sound virtuosic—but not hurried. The following phrasing, recommended by most of the editions, is almost impossible to realize at the required tempo; however its main implication—a light triplet note on the downbeats—should be well understood.

measure 37

The soaring line of measure 39, together with the bold arpeggio of measure 41, should have a shape far beyond the piano that is the only dynamic indication supplied by Beethoven, and the conclusion of the section at measures 42–43 should remain vigorous. A heavy left hand and clumsy slurs may make the staccato notes of the melody inaudibly weak; the melodic line, correctly articulated, should sing forth with clarity and vigor. The piano indicated again at measure 43 presumably means that measure 42 should be played considerably louder than piano. The expressive theme with the repeated chords (measures 43–51) should by played *legato possibile* with the fingers constantly kept as close as possible to the keys. The touch is a portamento that is greatly inspired by the portamento of stringed instruments. The crescendo in measure 49 may begin earlier, thus making the sforzando—which should be placed on the half-note D flat in the middle of the measure—sound more natural. The phrase ends in a conclusive forte.

The triplet motive reappearing in the left hand at measure 51 should have the same slight separation in the phrasing that it had in the right hand at measure 37. The sforzando of measures 54 and 55 should be enthusiastic but not overpowering. The recommended fingering for the right hand is:

measures 56-57

The dotted half note on the downbeat of measure 58 should have an accurate duration, and the ensuing scale passage should be played with the utmost passion. It climaxes in the sforzando on the downbeat of measure 60, and this chord has to be generously extended on the fermata of measure 61.

The theme of the strongly contrasting middle episode requires a relaxed, singing legato combined with smooth, refined phrasing. Special attention has to be given to the end of measure 94: the right hand concludes the phrase on the last quarter note while the left hand, having finished its phrase a quarter note earlier, begins a new phrase at the same point. Usually the left-hand phrasing draws the right hand along, thus causing the last sixth interval of the measure to be played too loud for a phrase ending.

The staccato scales from measure 98 on are, in general, played with too much tension because of the performer's desire to play the staccatos sharply—a feat that is scarcely manageable at the required speed. For these scales, finger articulation must be reduced to a minimum while the forearm performs a slight downward motion similar to that used in octave passages. The syncopated sforzando of measure 105 should not be played exaggeratedly loud or sharply separated from the preceding note.

In many performances, the passage beginning in measure 107 shows serious rhythmic inadequacies that turn the broken arpeggios of each hand into inarticulate, quick jerks—if the proper speed in alla breve can be kept up at all. Coordination between the hands has to be well established and maintained for the full passage. The coordination of the passage is made more complicated by the fact that the right-hand figure consists of three sixteenth notes preceded by a sixteenth rest while the left-hand figure has two sixteenth notes preceded by an eighth rest—a difference the performer has to be fully aware of. Practicing should begin in a slow but nonetheless alla breve tempo in which the metrical regularity of the sixteenth is constantly controlled; then it should be sped up gradually until the required tempo is reached. Equal attention has to be given to the accuracy of the speed of the suddenly appearing triplets in measure 113. The sforzandos from this point on should be emphasized by prominent dynamic swells.

The recapitulation of the main subject contains the beautiful variant of the left hand taking over the melody with the last two eighth notes of measure 128. The accompanying right-hand broken triads should be metrically precise and without accents when the hand flies from one position to another. The right hand resumes the melody with the rising arpeggio at measure 132; a slight crescendo toward the sforzando is recommended here. The downbeat of measure 133 may be slightly delayed in the left hand, and a tempo a shade calmer can then be introduced. The tempo resumes with the smooth phrasing of the syncopation of measure 134.

The higher register and the limpid key of C major lend a magical touch to the ensuing theme, while the slower accompaniment figure emphasizes its dignified calm. The suggestions for measures 33–43 can be applied to measures 143–153. The expressive subject (beginning at measure 153) has an important extension from measure 163 on with many harmonic suspensions. The significant rising-fourth steps of the soprano may be enhanced by a slight delay of the second quarter note in the middle voice; this delay also emphasizes the important role of the alto. An expressive legato and good voice leading are needed for the right-hand part in measures 167–170. "Calando" implies both ritardando and diminuendo. The tempo resumes with the last quarter note of measure 170. The variant of the main subject at measure 179 contains an easily overblown crescendo—especially if the left hand cannot be confined to its accompanying role.

The coda opens with a rhythmic problem: the triplets have to be played strictly in time over the eighth-note accompaniment. Distortion in the following manner should be avoided:

measure 182

It may be helpful to practice first in the following way:

measure 182

The triplet figure should have an important dynamic drive to the ensuing sforzando. The fortissimo chords are to be played with the fingers prepared on the surface of the keys and with a sudden, quick raising of the wrists, as if the chords were to be pulled out from the keyboard. In measures 189–192, the metrical evenness of the triplets has to be impeccable, in spite of the increases in the skips between the first and second triplet notes on the downbeats and in the middles of the measures. The left-hand chords are best "pulled out" as in measure 185.

A full outburst of fury is reached at measure 192. Left- and right-hand sforzandos seem to chase each other relentlessly. In opposition to the powerful sforzandos, the downbeat of each measure has to remain sufficiently light. A broadening of the tempo from measure 198 on—along with the appearance of the Neapolitan sixth—will enhance the ensuing modulation to A flat major. Only a short silence is needed after the dramatic fermata in measure 202.

It is difficult and almost unnecessary to enforce the tempo primo for the ensuing fragments of the main subject; however a too-sluggish tempo would be just as unsuitable. Nevertheless even in a tempo a shade slower, the rhythm should be kept immaculate. The slurs in measures 206–208 make the downbeats of the measures light. If the tempo is slackened, only tempo primo (and not a faster one) should be adopted at measure 208 with the sudden explosion of the fortissimo.

Performances of the Rondo usually transgress the classic law of unity of tempo in one movement. A too-fast tempo may lend brilliance to the triplet part, but it is not suitable for the first subject, with its elaborate melodic line, or for the middle episode. But breaking away from the unity of tempo at those points in order to accommodate the changing character of the music is totally unacceptable.

The other danger lurks in the pedaling. Whereas the first two movements have few pedaling problems, the Rondo may be tastelessly overpedaled or may sound, equally tastelessly, dry. If the main subject needs only light pedaling, the lyrical sections of the first and second episodes deserve a clean but generous use of the pedal.

BEETHOVEN

Sonata, Op. 27, No. 2

Without a doubt, this sonata—its first movement, especially—enjoys greater popularity than any of its thirty-one companions. Composed during the winter of 1801–1802, it was published in the fall of 1802. Beethoven's designation *Sonata quasi una fantasia* (which is less evocative than the familiar *Moonlight Sonata*) refers to the absence of the customary allegro opening movement and to the intensely improvisatory character of the first movement, Adagio sostenuto.

Adagio sostenuto

M.M. ♩ = 54–60

Form: Two themes with elements of development and recapitulation

	MEASURES
Introduction	1 – 5
First theme	5 – 15
Second theme	15 – 24
Elements of development	24 – 42
First theme, recapitulation	42 – 51
Second theme, recapitulation	51 – 60
Coda	60 – 69

The inscription at the beginning of the movement, "Si deve suonare tutto questo pezzo delicatissimamente e senza sordino," means: "The whole piece to be played very delicately and without dampers." The instruction "very delicately" is further confirmed by "sempre pp," which places strict limitations on all crescendos. "Senza sordino" is often understood (erroneously) as a prohibition against using the left pedal. Beethoven always referred to the "soft" pedal as "una corda" or "due corde." *Senza sordini* means "with raised dampers," that is, using the right pedal; *con sordini* means "with dampers on the strings," that is, without pedal. Needless to say, while a pedal held throughout an entire piece may have sounded very well on the weak-toned pianos of Beethoven's time, it would be unthinkable on our modern pianos.

There are two main difficulties in this movement. One is maintaining a refined tonal balance among the layers of sound within the limits of "delicatissimamente" and

113

''sempre pp.'' The melody played by the fifth finger should be in the foreground, the bass on the second plane, and the triplets in the background. The role of the right hand is particularly difficult. The melody, intensely focused but still pianissimo, floats on the underlying triplet motion, which is kept triple piano yet with every note intelligible. This triplet motion has the further responsibility of emphasizing the harmonic changes by a slight prolongation of the first note of each group at the changing points. If they are kept absolutely even, the triplets will impart an unwelcome mechanical uniformity to the performance. On the other hand, excessive prolongation will overromanticize the piece.

The other difficulty concerns the simultaneous performance of a dotted eighth-and-sixteenth rhythm and a triplet rhythm in the same hand. Even the slightest deviation from accurate dotting will become evident in the slow tempo at which this movement unfolds. Performers are too frequently satisfied if the duration of their sixteenth notes is half that of the triplet notes; this execution produces a sharp dotting that is unsuitable to the character of the piece.

The four opening measures have to be played in a particularly delicate manner so as to allow the top voice to enter in measure 5 pianissimo and still sound like melody. In measure 8, the interval to be played simultaneously is a ninth—a difficult one even for large hands in the required delicate tonal balance. An early release of the preceding melodic note (F sharp, which is held anyway by the pedal) allows time to prepare the hand for the large interval. The solution

measure 8

is acceptable only if a simultaneous attack on the ninth is totally impossible. In that case, the bass note has to be sustained by the pedal throughout the second half of the measure; the pedal also sustains the two melodic notes involved in a barely tolerable way. Even the slightest possible breaking up of the interval of the ninth is out of the question.

A similar difficulty is encountered in the second theme, in measures 16 and 18. The solution of a left-hand crossover must be discarded at these points because it would result in the loss of the overhanging bass octaves. While the level of the melody may be raised here to piano, the expressive swells of measures 16 and 18 concern mainly the bass line, and their proportions should be kept small.

In measure 23, the rising broken arpeggio should be played without the often-heard accents caused by a heavy thumb. The crescendo-decrescendo in measures 25–27 is a most effective shaping device for the melody. Measures 28–31 are inspired by chamber-music texture: the violin and cello answer each other while the pianist plays the accompanying triplets; then, suddenly left alone in measure 32, the pianist hesitantly makes the accompaniment figure more interesting by improvising rising and falling arpeggios. Although the triplets belong to the softest level of sound, their curling up to higher regions invites a light swelling in the sound to show the shape. The sound falls back to the softest level in measure 37 to allow the cello to make his reentry off the beat.

measure 37

Throughout the rising-arpeggio passage, the harmonic changes have to be emphasized through slight prolongations. A minimal broadening at the end of measure 35 makes the dynamic swell appear more expressive.

A small ritardando in measure 41 should prepare for the recapitulation of the main theme. A similar broadening in measure 59 and the prolongation of the downbeat of measure 60 distinctly mark the passage to the coda. Measures 63 and 65 include a fine part-playing problem for the right hand on their last beats. The last four measures die away with a carefully graduated diminuendo. The last two beats of measure 67 should have separate pedaling. Consummate tonal control of the closing chords is extremely difficult because under no circumstances should they sound louder than the preceding arpeggio. The indication at the end of the movement, "Attacca subito il seguente," requires proceeding—after a generous fermata on the closing chord and a short silence—to the Allegretto.

Allegretto

M.M. ♩. = 69

Form: Da capo, with trio

	MEASURES
First part	1 – 36
Trio	36 – 60
Repeat of first part	1 – 36

Part playing, along with correct articulation and tonal balance, is the main difficulty of this brief piece. From the beginning, the contrast between the legato first phrase and the following staccatos has to be rendered with clarity and charm. Specifically the staccatos should not be played too short, thereby preventing the top line from being sensed as a line. The second statement of the subject, with its syncopated suspensions in the soprano, is a severe test of part-playing ability. This section (measures 8–16) has to be practiced with the right hand alone to secure the precise articulation of the voices. Especially difficult is a natural rendering of the slur relations in the soprano, patterned after the human voice. If slur endings are played too short, they will impede the spontaneous unfolding of the melody line.

The left hand's articulation, which is different from the right hand's throughout the section, has to be correctly carried through. The next section, measures 16–24, shows a longer, more expressive legato line. The articulation and phrasing of both hands coincide most of the time. An exception is measure 22, where the right hand breathes after the sforzando and then plays the syncopated third beat with a slighter but still distinct emphasis. The returning main subject (measures 24–36) combines the various part-playing problems previously experienced. The crescendo toward the sforzando (measures 32–34) should not be overlooked; the piano in measure 35 is sudden and needs careful tonal balancing in favor of the soprano.

Keeping the phrase endings and staccatos smooth is the main difficulty of the Trio. The sforzandos on the frequent syncopations of the right hand are meant to be executed in the prevailing piano dynamic; the fortepiano of the left hand is also to be interpreted as a moderate sforzando in piano. The second half of the trio, in sharp contrast, opens in a mysterious pianissimo. The sadly descending chromatic harmony has to be pedaled flawlessly, while the octaves in the right hand are to be played as legato as possible. "Allegretto da capo" (the repetition of the first part) is an absolute must in performance, but the repetition of measures 16–36 is omitted the second time.

Presto agitato

M.M. ♩ = 144–152

Form: Sonata

	MEASURES
Exposition	1 – 65
First subject	1 – 21
Second subject	21 – 43
Closing subject	43 – 65
Development	65 – 101
Recapitulation	102 – 166
Coda	167 – 200

The rising broken arpeggios represent one of the principal difficulties of the movement. Their execution is often spoiled by unevenness. The thumb has the prime responsibility for a metrically even rendering: it should not remain on the key where it is used too long but instead should move under the palm immediately, in preparation for its next use. Moreover the fingering of the arpeggios has to be correct and in accordance with the classic rules of arpeggio fingering. (This remark pertains to the use of the third or the fourth finger in arpeggio figures. The general rule is that the right hand uses 1-2-3-5 in all root positions and 1-2-4-5 in the two inversions. The left hand uses 5-4-2-1 in root position and in the first inversion, and 5-3-2-1 on the second inversion. Exceptions to this rule are the arpeggios from D major to F# major (using the circle of fifths) where the left hand uses 5-3-2-1 in root position.)

A new difficulty is encountered in measures 7 and 8, where proper positioning of the thumb is even more important because it is going to be used on keys the fifth finger has just occupied. Another difficulty of the main subject lies in securing faultless execution of the sudden sforzando chords at the end of each arpeggio without preparing for them with a crescendo. Only the first chord in each pair is sforzando; the second is less loud, though not quite piano. The crackle of the left hand's eighth notes, if they are played perfectly evenly, may keep the right hand from rushing. For the first eight measures, according to Beethoven's direction, the pedal should be used only on the chords, thus adding to the sudden ferocity of the sforzandos.

In measures 9–14, the tremololike figure of the right hand with the melodic line in its lower notes often sounds clumsy and stiff. A small rotation on the level of the forearm is recommended, as well as an emphasis on the melody in the lower notes. The suggested fingering is:

measures 9-10

The use of rotation rather than finger articulation is particularly important when alternating between the fourth and fifth fingers. In measure 13, distinct left-hand staccatos should bring out the harmony.

The fermata in measure 14 increases the dramatic tension, if it is held generously. The subsequent arpeggios are increasingly difficult, due to their uncomfortable positions, especially the one in measures 19–20, where a crescendo indication appears for the first time. A slight easing of the tempo, with a slight decrescendo, at the end of measure 20 prepares for the entrance of the second subject, which begins on the second beat of measure 21—an important clue to the interpretation of the same subject at its recurrences.

Over an apparently simple Alberti bass, the passionate melody leads to a grandiose buildup. The evenness of the Alberti bass is dependent to a large extent upon minimal finger articulation, especially in wider positions such as those of measures 36 and 41. The right hand has the difficult responsibility of the melodic line, in which the dotted rhythm of measures 22–24 has to fit in smoothly. Special care has to be given to the last sixteenth notes of these measures: playing them somewhat softer than the eighth and quarter notes will blend them perfectly into the line. The grace-note slide printed in front of the downbeat in measure 22 has to be connected to the preceding sixteenth note and executed "on the bar line," where the left hand yields an almost imperceptible amount of time to allow for completion of the ornament in a gentle manner.

In the restatement of the subject (measures 25–28), the octaves should be guided by the thumb to insure better legato and to avoid inaccuracies in the course of the passionate crescendo. Measures 28 and 30 include difficult trills. The recommended fingering is:

measure 30

(Five notes are sufficient for this "melodic" trill, and holding on to the low note is not imperative.) The fortissimo on the downbeat of measure 33 is best prepared for by a slight broadening of the tempo in the second half of the preceding measure along with a moderate crescendo in the Alberti bass. The recommended fingering for measure 34 is:

measure 34

Despite their passionate character, the left-hand chords in measures 34–35 and 38–39 are subordinate to the right-hand part. Coordination between the hands is the major difficulty in measure 36, inasmuch as the trill in the right hand often interferes with the regular speed of the Alberti bass. The syncopation of the chords in measures 38 and 39 involves quarter notes and eighth notes; their respective durations have to be clearly rendered.

The rising-scale melody of measure 40 is often spoiled when a heavy or stiff arm makes finger work impossible. The conclusion of the intensely passionate section needs a good-sized ritardando in the second half of measure 42 and a prolongation of the downbeat of measure 43. For the sake of the melody line, the double notes and chords of the closing section have to be closer to portamento than to staccato. The fingers are kept on the surface of the keys, or at least as close to the keys as possible;

the double notes and chords are played by a slight motion of the forearm with the wrist kept loose. Beethoven's notation—separate stems for the downbeats of the measures and later for the first and fifth eighth notes of the measures—implies a break in the phrasing along with a slight prolongation of the notes.

In measures 47–48 and 53–56, the slurs have to be played expressively and without undue haste; in particular, the second half of measure 55 may be slightly broadened. An uncomfortably wide Alberti bass in piano appears from measure 57 on. Small hands are seriously tested in measure 58 and similar passages elsewhere. In measure 58, the right-hand chord also includes an interval of a ninth. If a simultaneous attack is impossible, a quick, skillful breaking of the chord is acceptable. The grace notes in measures 61–62 are to be played as quick broken chords, the top note coinciding with the beat. The pedaling is particularly difficult in these measures: an inadvertent mixing of the tonic and dominant harmonies is unacceptable.

No new difficulty occurs in the development before measure 75, where the second subject appears in the left hand and the Alberti figure appears in the right. Accents due to a heavy right thumb may ruin the left-hand melody as well as the Alberti figure. Only fingers kept on (or as close as possible to) the surface of the keys are able to execute an even Alberti bass free from any accent. The principal difficulty of the melody in the left hand lies in blending the sixteenth notes into the melodic line.

Measure 78 includes a prominent crescendo to the forte downbeat of measure 79 followed by a noticeable break in the phrasing to mark the sudden piano opening of the next phrase. The Alberti figure grows increasingly difficult in measures 83–86; measure 84 is especially difficult to play with perfect regularity. Pulling the hand slightly outward just when playing the interval of the fifth (which is played by the second and fourth fingers) helps evenness and the simultaneous attack on the interval. The sforzandos of the left hand appearing in measures 83, 85, and 86 should not make the staccato ridiculously short. Often the ensuing eighth note gets (erroneously) a second emphasis almost the size of the preceding sforzandos.

The long octave-tremolo passage (measures 87–99) severely taxes the endurance of even the most experienced player. The tremolo has to remain soft and be kept well in tempo throughout: that is, each note (or chord) of the right hand has to coincide with the left hand's fifth finger. For practicing this passage, reducing the left-hand tremolo to a single eighth-note pulsation on the fifth finger and playing this together with the full right-hand text is recommended. Once the coordination between the left hand's fifth finger and the right hand is established, the full tremolo may be reinstated. A relaxed hand and a slight rotation of the forearm are more suitable for octave tremolos than finger articulation alone.

The recapitulation does not reveal any new difficulty. The compression at measures 133–134 has been erroneously "corrected" by some editions to make these measures similar to measures 38–40.

At measures 163–166, the broken-arpeggio figure appears in a new form close to that of dramatically rolled chords. The rhythmic components of these measures have to be well observed, with each hand beginning its arpeggio one eighth note after the main beat. Special attention has to be given to the difference between the thirty-second notes of measure 164 and the sixteenths of measure 166, both of which are played in broadened tempo as the fermata is approached. The fermata in measure 166 should be followed by a dramatic silence.

The tempo adopted for the last appearance of the second subject (measure 167) may be slightly slower than the general tempo has been; full Tempo I will be approached with the crescendo of measures 175–176 and firmly established at measure 177. It is essential to make an audible distinction, in measure 167, between the first note of the left hand (a simple bass note) and the second note (the entrance of the second subject). The same distinction has to be made in the right hand between the chord on the downbeat of measure 171 and the ensuing octave. Slurs and staccatos in measures 175–176 have to be clearly articulated, with the slurs outdoing each other in expression as the crescendo grows.

The emotional climax of the movement is reached in the subsequent measures (177–189). The arpeggios raging through the keyboard are often the victims of forcing the sound beyond reasonable limits, especially if excessive fingerwork is involved. Helping out with the left hand in measure 184 should be considered only as a last resort. The expression of vehement rage vested in measures 185–186 makes the chromatic scale difficult in every respect; here finger articulation is essential. Curved fingers will minimize the difference in position between black and white keys.

The trill of measure 187 should be started on the main note and played with strong fingers, such as the thumb and the third finger. The declamatory cadenza in small print (which bears a striking resemblance to measures 308–313 in the first movement of the *Kreutzer Sonata,* Op. 47) is to be understood in the following way:

measure 187

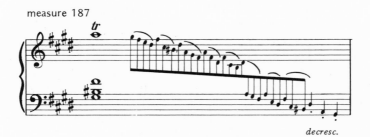

decresc.

The added slurs are to be understood as grouping and not as phrasing. They will emphasize the expressive descending fourths in each group.

The octaves in measures 188–189 have no fermatas; they last for four beats of a slow (adagio) tempo. The first sixteenth note on the downbeat of measure 190 needs a sizable prolongation—to make it seem as if Tempo 1 will only come back reluctantly. The difficulties of this wide Alberti bass have been discussed previously. In measure 196, only a very small delay between the chord on the downbeat and the first note of the arpeggio is acceptable. The left hand has to change position at lightning speed. Each note of the arpeggio has to be perfectly synchronized. The closing chords are to be played with the greatest ardor, strictly in tempo, and with a short pedal on each one.

The performance of this movement is often the victim of a too-fast tempo chosen in consideration of the stormy first theme and unsuitable for the more lyrical subjects. Besides the tempo, dynamics have to be planned with care. The passionate character of the Presto agitato often compels a performer to play everything loud. A genuine piano wherever it is required will not reduce the passion: on the contrary, strong contrasts will only strengthen the drama and passion of the movement.

BEETHOVEN
Sonata, Op. 28

~~~~~~

The noble, peaceful character of this work (written in 1801 and published in 1802) evoked the inappropriate subtitle *Pastoral,* which suggests a meaningless comparison with the sixth symphony. The only parallel between the sonata and the symphony that can be sustained is the incessant and clear suggestion of orchestral effects throughout the sonata. As opposed to the more usual short motives in Beethoven's works, the themes in opus 28 are generally long melodies.

Allegro

M.M. $\downarrow$. = about 66

Form: Sonata

	MEASURES
Exposition	1 – 163
First subject	1 – 39
Transition	40 – 62
Second subject	63 – 135
Closing subject	135 – 162
Development	162 – 268
Recapitulation	269 – 437
Coda	438 – 461

Difficulties of maintaining legato and tonal balance are evident in the main subject. The left hand's repeated D pedal point, kept soft throughout, should not be entrusted to a finger alone: it has to be helped out by a slight motion of the forearm while the finger involved constantly remains on the surface of the key. The fingering of the right-hand part should include substitutions to insure the best possible legato in the top voice. The lower voices have to be played at the level of an accompaniment, well below the level of the top voice. Special attention has to be given to the smoothness of the eighth notes in the soprano. This is especially true in measures 9 and 10, where they move in thirds with the accompanying voice. Playing these thirds legato and with the lightness required for phrase endings taxes even the most experienced performer. The recommended fingering is:

The second statement of the first phrase (which is an octave higher than the first statement) distinctly suggests a change in tone color, under which the countermelody appears in the tenor on the second plane. Both statements of the first phrase (measures 1–20) unfold in absolute serenity. From measure 21 on, crescendos and sforzandos introduce a more personal tone. A singing legato should remain the performer's principal preoccupation throughout the passage. The nimble *fioriture* (blossoming) of measures 27–28 should be sensitively brought out. The crescendo in measures 29–30 and the sforzando in measure 31 should outdo their previous occurrence in measures 21–23; subsequent sforzandos falling on the third beats of measures will be less sonorous. The section ends with a conclusive forte.

Maintenance of good tonal balance is also the source of the transition section's difficulties. The fortepianos from which the phrases gracefully unfold have to be played with expressive depth. The variant of the same phrase from measure 48 on encompasses serious part-playing difficulties requiring veritable finger twisting to insure legato and good voice leading. Turning the hand slightly outward eases the unavoidable overlapping fingering. To make possible compliance with the decrescendo at measure 60, a crescendo is suggested from measure 56 on. The solitary E conclusion (measures 61–62) has to be a full two measures long.

The subsequent pianissimo phrase also contains the difficulty of maintaining good tonal balance. The melody line should emerge as a legato and finger substitutions in the soprano are recommended. If the pedal is used at all, it should be employed very skillfully in order to avoid changing the pizzicato character of the left hand. A deliberate rhythmic character—yet still in pianissimo—has to be given to the staccatos in the left hand to make them sound like pizzicatos. A very slight emphasis on the diminished-seventh chord in measure 67 will help to hold the line together.

Smooth phrasing after the downbeat of measure 70 is difficult. Covering the considerable leap between the downbeat and the following note may cause an abrupt break. Although the bass in measures 71–76 is not marked staccato, it should be played pizzicato to correspond with its previous occurrence. The phrase here has a driving crescendo leading to a subito piano at measure 77, where a new texture, also involving tonal balance difficulties, appears. The top line, entrusted to the outer fingers (and later on, to the fifth finger alone), has to be played in a singing legato tone. The bass line, in parallel motion with the soprano, is on the second level while the busy, tremololike accompaniment is on the softest level, even though it is played with the strong fingers. The required tonal balance can be achieved only if the tremololike figure of gentle eighth notes is played without raising the fingers from the surface of the keys.

A new difficulty appears from measure 91 on: an unusually large stretch is required between the second and fifth fingers—one that is difficult enough even for large hands. In the melodic line, which is played from this point exclusively with the fifth finger, a legato execution can only be secured through calm hands and arms that are ready to glide smoothly and without tension from one key to the next. Relaxed hands and arms are even more needed when the crescendo of measure 98 raises the sound to forte. The sforzandos need an especially full sound without harshness, brutality, or drama.

The ensuing scale passages severely test the ability of the player. Besides the usual difficulty of passages containing thumb crossovers, this passage has problems that are created by the rhythmic notation. To play two triplet groups and one group of five sixteenth notes in the three beats of the measure without accents on the beats is a delicate task that calls for a good sense of timing. The accuracy of the sforzando in measure 105 is often spoiled by a precipitate handling of the leap. The hand should be stretched suddenly at the moment the thumb is used at the end of the scale, thus bringing the fifth finger closer to its target. The same stretching is recommended between measures 106 and 107 and at all the occurrences of similar leaps. The frequent sforzandos between measures 121 and 125 should be executed in the same manner as the ones in measures 101–103—they need a full sound without harshness.

The rhythmic components of the left-hand scale in measures 131–132 (like those in the right-hand passage at measure 104) have to be clearly rendered, but without accents on the beats. The conclusion of the section, measures 134–135, may have a very slight ritardando; the tempo then resumes on the last beat of measure 135, showing clearly that the closing subject begins ahead of the beat. The graceful character of this theme lies in gently rendered slurs and staccatos; meanwhile the left-hand chords have to be played with jovial elegance. This same mood has to be preserved for the second statement (measures 143–159), where rough octaves and abrupt phrase endings should be avoided despite the crescendo and forte. The A octave of the left hand in measure 159 may be slightly prolonged since it closes the exposition. The articulation of the right hand changes meaningfully in measure 160 to an expressive portamento that leads to the development—or to the repeat, if the player so decides.

The principal difficulty of the development lies in the eighth-note figuration that is a counterpoint to the main subject. Here the performer's first task should be choosing an appropriate fingering. There are several possible ways to finger the passage in both the right and left hands, and the selection of one or another fingering should take into account the personal characteristics of the performer. Once chosen, any fingering has to be adhered to at every execution of the passage. The irregularities and zigzagging of the line sometimes lead to surprising inventions in the domain of fingering that critically jeopardize accurate performance. Throughout the development, the motives of the main subject should stand out, regardless of whether they appear in the right hand or the left.

The piano in measure 199 is sudden. The tail motive of the main subject appearing here should be devoid of accent at its conclusion (on the downbeats of measures

200, 202, and so on). The sforzandos from measure 209 on have to be carefully gradated, until the fortissimo is reached at measure 216. Each motive (or measure) of the passage (measures 208–218) has to be skillfully separated by a slight break in the phrasing on each bar line. From measure 219 on, the successive sforzandos in the left and right hands seem to chase each other relentlessly, in a paroxysm of passion. In spite of the large gap between the hands and the sforzandos in fortissimo, the left hand should not overpower the right.

The piano at measure 227 should enter without preparation; the sforzandos in measures 228–229 (in many editions these markings do not appear) are to be interpreted, if at all, strictly in piano. The section comprising measures 230–256 is to be played with the utmost simplicity and smoothness and with good tonal balance by favoring the right hand. From measure 240 on, the cascading top notes of the right-hand chords are to be brought out lightly, while the size of the crescendo in measure 247 is to be kept minimal. After a generous fermata and silence, the unassuming closing motive—its appearances in major and minor modes separated by meaningful fermata rests—is a real test of imaginative performance. The ultimate gentle question of the Adagio is especially difficult to render with unaffected charm. Though the fermata at measure 268 is very long, it needs to be followed by breathing time only, and not by a long silence, before Tempo 1 resumes.

The recapitulation has no new difficulties. In the coda, only the sforzandos of measure 449 have not been heard previously. They have to be carefully gradated in the required crescendo, and they may reach the level of a light forte in measure 455; the tail motive of the main subject participates only moderately in the crescendo. The graceful character of the closing pianissimo chords calls for a short pedal even though the chords are staccato.

The difficulty in performing this movement lies in the length of the subjects and in the lack of contrast between them. To perform long themes successfully, the performer needs a sense of proportion, the ability to focus on the melodic line, and a good, singing legato. The lack of contrast between the subjects is best compensated for by applying to the study of this movement a keen sensibility that is able to discover and bring out the faintest suggestion in the score of subtle changes of dynamics, phrasing, and orchestral coloring.

Andante

M.M. ♪ = 80–88

Form: Ternary, da capo

	MEASURES
A	1 – 22
B (trio)	23 – 38
A	38 – 82
Coda	83 – 99

Once again, maintaining a smooth, singing legato is the principal difficulty of the first phrase. The task is complicated by the pizzicato character of the left-hand accompaniment, which prohibits a generous use of the pedal. To prevent interruptions of the melodic line, rapid finger substitutions on the top notes of chords are recommended where needed or possible, together with a half-pedal effect on each chord. In spite of the word *half,* when half pedal is used, the right pedal is not depressed half the distance to the bottom but only slightly—just enough to raise the dampers almost imperceptibly from the strings. In this position, the strings of the lower register usually remain under the control of the dampers while the upper strings can vibrate almost as much as with full pedal. The use of the half pedal will thus allow a good legato in the melodic line without impairing the deliberate pizzicato of the accompaniment.

In addition to rhythmic accuracy, the dotted rhythm of measure 2 has to have a natural flow to show the curve of the ending motive. The crescendo applied to the chords underlines the increase of emotion from one harmony to another and leads to the sudden piano on the downbeat of measure 4, which may be delayed slightly. The second half of the phrase (measures 5–8) unfolds similarly. The legato bass in the first and second endings has to be brought out expressively. Repeats should be taken as indicated throughout the movement to preserve the equilibrium of the form between the first part and its recapitulation (which is a variation on the first part).

It is somewhat easier to play the melody legato in the next section, measures 9–16. No sensitive interpreter will miss the poignant dissonances between the pedal point and the harmony, which are stressed further by the syncopations of measures 10, 12, and 13. The execution of the repeated-note pedal point, like the one in the first movement, should not be entrusted to finger articulation; the notes should be played with a slight downward motion of the forearm coupled with a free wrist while the finger does not leave the surface of the key. For the right hand, strict obedience to the detailed dynamic markings, along with a singing legato, will unravel all the emotion contained in the phrase. The quarter notes of measures 15 and 16 are often misread and played as eighth notes.

The half-pedal solution may be used at the reappearance of the opening idea, which is presented in octaves this time. An additional difficulty attends the faultless execution of the frequently occurring dotted rhythm: clumsy thumbs will land with an unacceptable accent on the second beat of the measure, following the thirty-second note, thus not only making a serious musical error but also jeopardizing the expressive sforzando on the last eighth notes of the measure. A slight broadening of the tempo in measure 21 underlines the end of the first part.

The playful, mildly humorous mood of part 2 presents a welcome contrast to the expressive first part. The difficulties of this section lie in the faultless execution of both the dotted rhythm and the required articulation. The downbeat dotted sixteenth has to be played as a short staccato with a slight accent. The other two chords will use this accent to bounce off while the wrist remains free and flexible. Heaviness and inadvertent accents on the concluding chords of the dotted rhythm should be avoided. The upbeat to the jovially staccato sixteenth-note triplets must have the accurate short duration of a thirty-second note: under no circumstance should it sound like another triplet sixteenth note. Furthermore it has to be bound, legato, to the first triplet note. An often-heard mistake consists in playing this section in the pulse of 4/8 instead of the required 2/4, thus dangerously multiplying heavy beats.

The small accent following the second beat in measure 26 reveals a refinement in the phrasing between the third and the following scale motive, rather than a real accent. The forte for the dotted rhythm in measures 28, 31, and 32 should not occasion heaviness; rather it enhances the nervous energy of the rhythm. In measures 29 and in measures 30a and 30b (the first and second endings), correct slurring brings out the irresistible charm of the phrase endings. The crescendo-decrescendo of measures 32–34 makes the middle section's only legato line emerge more clearly. The second ending of the middle section (measure 38b) needs a sizable ritardando. For a sensitive interpreter, the change in key signature will occur before the last eighth note. It will suggest, along with taking time for the end of the phrase, a change of color for the A, the upbeat to the reappearance of the minor key.

The recapitulation of the A section includes repeats of the themes in variational form with an embellished thirty-second-note line. Interestingly the accompaniment to the variations gives up the deliberate pizzicatos for a less conspicuous legato in measure 51. In the right hand, a singing legato tone should be maintained throughout the variational repeats, thus treating the thirty-seconds as an embellished melody. Hence excessive finger articulation is to be avoided in these passages. The embellishment of the second half of the recapitulation (measures 69–83) includes many poignant dissonances between the embellishments, harmonies, and pedal points (see measures 72, 73, and 74). The downbeat of measure 77 may be played as an octave in the left hand, allowing a better positioning of the right thumb on the second thirty-second note. The articulation of the second beat of measure 81 and the first beat of measure 82, together with the dissonant frictions between soprano and bass and the impending conclusion of the section, call for considerable broadening of the tempo. A substantial break in the phrasing is needed after the tonic chord on the second beat of measure 82; the ensuing thirty-seconds (with a decrescendo) lead to the highly improvisatory coda.

Tonal balance is easier to maintain during the simple choralelike reappearance of the main subject than it was in the preceding passage. A prominent crescendo is needed in measures 85 and 87; it should be followed by a slightly delayed sudden piano chord topped by a meditative fermata. Be careful to keep the reappearance of the joyful middle part in measure 89 soft in order to allow the prescribed crescendo to grow to the forte in measure 91. The triplet sixteenth notes have to be phrased with witty accuracy. Measures 92 and 93 have to be completely devoid of unwelcome grouping accents; in particular, the transition from triplet sixteenths to ordinary sixteenths in measure 93 has to be managed without accents. Meanwhile a sizable crescendo prepares the listener for the two successive sforzandos of measure 94 that result in a well-balanced minor third. The ensuing thirty-second notes of the bass are to be played almost piano, matching the decayed sound of the minor third and avoiding a heavy landing on the downbeat of measure 95. In measures 96–97, the submissive sighs of the right hand have to be played with the utmost delicacy. The ornament of measure 98, laid out calmly, leads to a very moderate, expressive sforzando. Maintaining good tonal balance in the last four measures is difficult, considering the large gap between the hands.

The main difficulty in performance lies in finding a suitable tempo for the movement. Usually a too-fast tempo adopted for the first part transforms the recapitulation into a brilliant demonstration of finger dexterity. The recommended tempo is suitable for rendering both the first part and its recapitulation in the expressive mood of a ballad.

Scherzo: Allegro vivace

M.M. ♩. = 92–96; trio, ♩. = 88

Form: Scherzo, trio, scherzo

	MEASURES
Scherzo	1 – 70
Trio	71 – 94
Scherzo	1 – 70

The four motionless initial measures have to be strictly in tempo. The motive of measures 5–8 usually is played with complicated, overlapping fingerings to emphasize the interruption between slur endings and staccato—an interruption that most probably was not intended by Beethoven. The phrasing presumably refers to the bowing of a stringed instrument; it indicates a gentle change in the direction of the bow rather than a hard interruption or—even worse—a transformation of the two eighth notes into two jerked sixteenth notes. The simplest fingering, 4–2–1, is perfectly adequate at this point. A slight dynamic swell on the subdominant harmony in measure 6 will hold the four-measure period (measures 5–8) together. The same slight swell is recommended at every upcoming recurrence of this four-measure period. The accompanying chords, which resemble light foot stamping, remain distinct throughout.

The fortes of measures 17–20 and 25–28 are explosions of good humor that do not affect the whimsical piano of measures 21–24 and 29–32, despite the addition of the right thumb to the texture. (The fingering for the soprano is 5–4–2.)

The second part of the Scherzo ingeniously combines the full-measure notes with the foot-stamping motive. The sharp but soft staccato chords of the right hand contrast strongly with the sustained legato of the left. The crescendo marked at measure 39 blooms mainly from measure 41 on, though its size has to be kept small; the decrescendo happens rather quickly in measure 46, and it is accompanied by a considerable ritardando as the fermata is approached. Only a short breath will separate measure 48 from measure 49. The explosion of the fortissimo in measure 57 should supervene as a complete surprise. The chord in measure 59 is best entrusted to the right hand.

The driving crescendo should not spoil the metrical accuracy of the foot-stamping measures, either by extending or by shortening the rests on the last beats of the measures. In spite of the humor, the forte of measure 68 should remain effortlessly elegant. The double octave of measure 69 has to have a pedal to avoid dryness, and the following one-measure rest is to be strictly observed.

The principal difficulty of the trio is the left-hand accompaniment figure, which contains an abundance of broken octaves combined with exacting leaps. Perfect evenness in the left hand must be maintained to accommodate the right-hand melody. A faultless solution requires long and patient work. The left hand should first be practiced separately, with a relaxed hand and the fingers on the surface of the keys avoiding high articulation. It is especially important in the broken-octave passages that the fifth finger glide into its next position rather than move into it from a raised position high above the keys. No rotation may be used here to help the broken octaves, since the forearm has the responsibility of moving the octave position of the fifth finger and thumb up and down the keyboard. This motion has to be felt as continuous and capable of merging the broken octaves into one uninterrupted line.

The fact that measures 79–83 are often uneven is due to a sudden outburst of excessive finger activity. Measures 84 and 86 include the difficult leaps, among the broken octaves. Without contracting the arm muscles, the forearm has to bring the hand quickly but smoothly into the new position while the fingers glide over the surface of the keys. When the right hand is added to the accompaniment, new obstacles to perfect synchronization of the hands are created. The dotted rhythm of measure 72 and similar measures has to fit in with the even eighth notes of the left hand. The grace note to the downbeat of the measure is to be played short. Only the first measure of each four-measure period may be felt as a true downbeat; the measures between remain light. Finally the dynamic markings should be literally observed, with a sizable stress on the sforzando of measure 91.

It is hard to miss the rather coarse humor of the Scherzo. The danger lies in exuberant exaggerations—especially of the dynamic contrasts. The really hard problem is the trio: its solution requires a prolonged and well-focused effort.

Rondo: Allegro, ma non troppo

M.M. ♩. = about 84

Più allegro, ♩ = about 100

Form: Sonata rondo

	MEASURES
A	1 – 16
Transition	16 – 28
B	28 – 51
A	51 – 67
C	67 – 113
A	113 – 129
Transition	129 – 144
B	144 – 167
Transition	168 – 192
Coda	192 – 210

Faultless part playing, perfect rhythm, and precise articulation pose the principal difficulties of the Rondo. An impeccable rendering of the bagpipe figure in the left hand requires a strong rhythmic sense. The eighth note of the figure should be neither lengthened nor shortened: it should be exactly half the duration of the preceding quarter note. Furthermore it should fit perfectly into the even eighth-note figure of the right hand at measure 3. In the right-hand part, a clumsy thumb can easily impair the tonal balance. The slurs and staccatos of measure 4 have to be played with grace and wit. Tonal balance is particularly difficult to achieve in the short motives of the right hand from measure 9 on because the thumb (which is still relegated to the soft level) has to bring out the alternation of dominant and tonic harmonies. The intervals of the ninth and tenth appearing in the middles of measures 9–11 should not trouble players with small hands: the thumb may be released when the A is played (it should be played with the fifth finger). The varied form of the same motive needs a good rhythmic sense and light finger work for the sixteenth notes.

The broken arpeggios of the transition contain many difficulties. Even just plain learning the notes is often troublesome, especially if the player fails to recognize the descending diatonic scale (hidden by the frequent changes between lower and higher registers) in the fifth finger of the left hand. But the major difficulty lies in the perfect synchronization of the hands. A good way to surmount the rhythmic difficulty of the passage is to reduce the left-hand figure to its first two sixteenth notes and then to join to this figure the full text of the right hand; this preliminary exercise is effective in establishing perfect evenness in the uninterrupted sixteenths motion. If the right hand treats its arpeggio portion as a broken chord, without appropriate finger articulation, a nervous jerking of the arpeggio will take over, impairing the evenness of the passage. When the remaining two notes of the left hand are added, they should also be played with finger articulation and should fit metrically into the right-hand arpeggio.

The right hand in measure 20 has to be played with light finger articulation; the staccatos on the double notes include a slight accentuation. The crescendo begins only at measure 21 and raises the level to an elegant forte in measure 26, where heaviness in the left hand has to be avoided for the sake of tonal balance. A fluent legato is needed for the exposition of the theme of the first episode (measures 28–32). The imitative entrances suggest the sound of a string quartet or an orchestra. In the varied form of the motive (measures 32–35), the sixteenth notes have to be rhythmically precise, in tempo, and without nervous jerking. The sforzandos on the last eighth notes of measures 36, 38, 39, and 40 should stand out clearly, yet without brutality, as they grow more and more enthusiastic up to the forte in measure 41. The trill of measure 42 is best played with the fingering 5–3, and it needs a tail.

The arpeggio opening of the closing section (measures 43–50) needs rhythmic clarity, not just a nervous twitch. The broken octaves have to be played principally with forearm rotation and a slightly raised wrist while the line of the thumb (which is in parallel motion with the bass) is handled melodically. The double octaves of measures 49 and 50 are often spoiled by a harsh, unbalanced sound that is due to stiff arms and hands or to an excess of enthusiasm. The only novelty in the reappearing first theme is the introduction of a sixteenth-note motive in measures 56 and 57. As has been pointed out, its execution should be governed by rhythmic accuracy.

The middle episode begins in jovial mood. Its humor should be underlined by the deliberate pizzicatos of the left hand. Measures 75–76 and 77–78 have prominent dynamic swells. At the end of measure 78, the sound level should drop to prepare for the pianissimo of measure 79, where the fugato begins. The difficulty of the fugato is not in the part playing or in the few awkward leaps. The real problem here lies in conceiving a colorful, imaginative interpretation. A merely correct execution of the voice leading can be transcended by applying distinctive tone colors to the individual voices. The first dotted quarter note of the fugato motive (soprano, measure 79; alto, measure 83; tenor, measure 87; bass, measure 95, with upbeat) should have a distinctly different sound at each entrance; the nature of the sound is governed by the imagination of the performer. The general layout of the fugato alone will achieve the crescendo beginning at measure 91: with no special effort, the sound increases naturally to reach the fortissimo at measure 95. A slight broadening of the tempo here will allow a better focusing on the bass line. The brilliant scale passage is best played with the right hand in measures 109–111; the left hand takes it over on the downbeat of measure 112. The approach of the fermata requires a considerable broadening of measure 112. The ensuing recapitulation includes no new difficulties.

The transition to the coda begins in a carefree mood. The right-hand staccatos (measures 169–176) have to be played as deliberate pizzicatos. The expressive crescendo at measure 175 leads to a sudden piano on the downbeat of measure 177. The ensuing long legato passage needs careful fingering and a smooth execution. The following fingering is recommended:

measures 177-181

In the forte passage (measures 183–186), the hemiolas produced by the minute slurs of the right hand should be clearly rendered, without pushing the general tempo ahead. The next section, measures 187–192, has to be played with metrical evenness; yet the obviously improvisatory character of the passage has to be made evident by a slight ritardando in the course of the diminuendo.

The ensuing Più allegro quasi presto is often taken at a breakneck speed in which both note-perfect accuracy and precise left-hand rhythm are impossible. The rhythmic precision of the octaves is absolutely essential: it is this consideration that the choice of tempo should be based on. The accuracy of the passage may be improved by focusing carefully on the thumb. In the right hand, light, distinct finger work is needed along with sudden elastic extensions when the fifth finger is used. The frequently recurring arpeggio figures should be kept light and in strict tempo. The repetition of the same note in the middle of measures 194 and 198 requires the use of two different fingers (1 and 3) on the same key. The synchronization of the hands should be faultless, since the slightest deviation from it may be disastrous. From measure 204 on, the difficulties are augmented. The interval of the tenth at the end of measures 204 and 205 is difficult to handle. A smooth but quick lateral motion of the hand together with an elastic extension is advisable. The zigzag arpeggio in measure 206 is often the victim of a heavy thumb or of a lack of elasticity in the hand.

The Rondo is the most exacting movement of this sonata. It taxes, not only technique, but also imagination and artistry. The irresistible liveliness of the movement should not foster dangerous excesses in tempo or in dynamics, both of which would ruin the relaxed, jovial mood that prevails throughout.

Franz Peter Schubert

Born 1797, Vienna; died 1828, Vienna

It is generally recognized that of all the composers for the piano, it was Schubert who created the musical miniature—a work that is lyrical in content and confidential in nature. In this regard, he was the forerunner of Schumann. Spontaneity is the most striking quality of Schubert's music. The natural flow of his melody is unsophisticated to such a degree that it makes all other music—sometimes even Schumann's—appear artificial.

Schubert's natural predisposition toward beautiful, long melodic lines may not be the ideal equipment with which to create a sonata in full "Beethovenian" style, with striking, concentrated subjects and heroic gestures. Long melodies are not ideal for developments. However the Schubert sonatas have been criticized far too much on this point, and their acceptance as an authentic part of the piano literature has prevailed only in fairly recent times.

Schubert was not a performing pianist on the level of Mozart or Beethoven. His performances took place within a private circle of friends and acquaintances (at "Schubertiads"), and were closer to informal improvisation than to predetermined programs. His piano writing does not differ from that of his predecessors and contemporaries. It includes the usual chords, arpeggios, scales, Alberti bases, and many triplet figures. The difference is in the way he uses these musical tools.

The first striking fact is that Schubert constantly uses the piano to evoke the sound of the orchestra. Appearances of motives now in the lower, then in the higher register provide clear clues to the orchestration. The many instances of repeated chords appearing in his piano music are distinctly of orchestral origin. It is therefore only reasonable to expect that the performer should have a good knowledge of orchestral sound—especially the sound of the Schubert orchestra—before undertaking the performance of a Schubert sonata.

In addition to the orchestral sound, a difficulty lies in the constantly changing mood of Schubert's distinctive subjects. The infinite variety of expression in his music ranges from subtle refinement to popular humor. The true challenge for the interpreter is in the sensitive rendering of these delicate changes.

SCHUBERT

Sonata in A Major, Op. 120 (D. V. 664)

~~~~~~

Most probably composed during Schubert's 1819 visit to Steyr, this sonata is among his shortest and most concise. The material used is simple and charming, like the countryside that inspired it. Yet it contains a great number of technical prerequisites for a good performance, such as a singing legato tone, a flexible left hand that can stretch easily for the accompaniment figures, and swift finger technique.

Allegro moderato

M.M. ♩ = 120

Form: Sonata

	MEASURES
Exposition	1 – 47
First subject	1 – 20
Second subject	20 – 42
Closing subject	42 – 47
Development	47 – 79
Recapitulation	79 – 126
Coda	127 – 133

The chord on the first beat of the first measure often poses insuperable difficulties, especially for those with small hands. Even with an adequate span in the hand, this chord may sound heavy and clumsy, and it may be the cause of a chopped-up melodic line. The difficulty begins in the upbeat to measure 1: the chord on the first beat is preceded by the sixteenth note of the dotted rhythm. The only available help may come from the thumb reaching as far as possible (yet without strain) toward the C sharp of the chord while the top fingers are playing the upbeat.

It must be admitted that the opening of the sonata is difficult to perform. It belongs to the category of "floating" starts, where the listener should have the impression that the performance has begun even before the first note is struck. In the course of this sonata, Schubert calls for a wide span of the hand many times; for example, in the middle of measure 3, the accompanying interval of a second in the lower part of the right hand has to be released in order to deal safely with the melody. Long and patient work is needed to establish a singing legato line for the melody, which is played with the top fingers of the right hand, without making inadvertent accents on notes struck together with accompanying chords.

Throughout the first subject group, the player has to keep his right arm as quiet as possible. The accompaniment in the left hand should be played evenly legato despite the fact that some of the distances involved between the first and second eighth notes (for example, those at the beginning of measure 3) are rather large. The recommended fingering is:

measure 3

For most performers the chord in the middle of measure 7 is impossible to play without arpeggiating. The recommended execution is:

measure 7

The dynamics, in the first eight measures (and in measures 13–20) are quite simple: there is only one crescendo-decrescendo, in measures 5 and 6; and the rest is to be played piano.

The middle part of the main subject (measures 8–12) intimates a change in tone by adding the darker color of the lower octave to the melody. The soprano and bass proceed by imitation, with very important dynamic changes. The last beat of measure 12 is to be treated as an upbeat to the returning main subject. The chord on the first beat of measure 13 is easier to play here than in measure 1 because the thumb has been resting on the crucial C sharp through the whole length of measure 12.

At the close of the main subject (the first beat of measure 20), the A-major chord has to be prolonged slightly to delineate the end of a section; the scale in triplets is begun after a slight delay. An easy, singing legato is hard to maintain in this scale because the fingering has some complications: the player has to work out a smooth passage of the thumb following the use of the fifth finger on the C sharp. From measure 21 on, special attention has to be given to the left hand because it is easy to make a false accent with the thumb on the second and fourth beat of each measure. (Only the thumb can be used on the second and fourth beat [first notes of triplet groups] of these measures. The fourth finger is indicated for the first beat.) The melody has to be sustained by long-enough portamento notes that are very close to legato. Furthermore the slurred ending of every measure needs sensitive treatment: the last eighth note of each measure is to be played light. The two-note slurring of the melody is even more important from measure 25 on; it is also more complicated to execute because it occurs between octaves.

Measure 28 contains an important ending for which the tempo has to be broadened. The resolution to E major (in the middle of the measure) has to be slightly prolonged in the left hand in order to provide the time needed to reach for the ensuing accompaniment figure one octave higher. The tormented chromatically falling sequence (measures 30–31) calls for especially expressive playing. The performer should listen with special attentiveness for the correct rendering of the two eighth-note octaves, which should be undisturbed rhythmically by the underlying triplet accompaniment.

The first note of measure 30, which closes the preceding section, has to be slightly extended; then the left hand should play with the expressivity of a cello. Beginning in measure 34, the second subject presents itself in the bass—this time in minor. The accompaniment figure in the right hand is uncomfortable and often overpowers the melody of the left hand. Measures 38–39 comprise the already mentioned chromatic sequence, with repeated chords in the right hand: it should be played espressivo, just as before, and the eighth notes of the left hand should be metrically exact.

In the closing subject, the portamentos have to be played as long as possible. The sforzandos on the quarter notes should be accents in piano or pianissimo. The closing motive (the first three beats of measure 47) has to be broadened. At this point, either the repeat of the exposition section or the beginning of the development should be slightly delayed: the a tempo starts with the upbeat of either part.

The development section starts out with a difficult imitation between the soprano and the bass. Its execution is often marred by a heavy, overplayed bass line. An elegant dotted rhythm is especially difficult to achieve because of the clumsiness of the octaves in the left hand. Two explosive chords (measure 56) in crescendo introduce the unexpected development, which is based on the transition scale (measure 20). Brilliant, easy virtuosity is needed for this passage: the octaves in both hands should be forte, but they should not have the hard sound of a stiff arm or wrist. The metrical difference between the triplets and the eighths should be accurate. Only the chords in the right hand have sforzando indications.

The following passage (measures 65–79), which leads to the recapitulation, is built on repeated portamento eighth notes; they should be played almost legato, as they were previously. The slurs, especially those in measure 68, should be clearly rendered, with light eighth notes. Sensitive performers won't miss the teasing charm of the motive in imitation between soprano and bass in measures 69–70 and 75–76. A broadening of the tempo is necessary in measure 79 to prepare for the recapitulation, which begins on the last beat of the measure.

Only a few novelties are to be found in the recapitulation. One is the strengthening of the melody by the octaves in measures 83–87 and 95–99, which makes accurate rendering of the dotted rhythm more difficult. The underlying accompaniment is also changed at times. The rest between the end of the recapitulation and the coda should be generously timed, thus preparing for the slower tempo that should be adopted from this point on. The coda treats the main motive in a pensive mood; it is the final reconsideration.

The main difficulty of the movement lies in insuring a good legato. On this point, the first subject is particularly troublesome, because of its broad accompanying chords under the melody. The necessary fluency between the first and second eighth notes of the left-hand figure is often difficult to obtain. The tone should be mainly lyrical, and harshness in the more dramatic section of the development should be avoided.

Andante

M.M. ♩ = 60

        Form: Sonata

	MEASURES
First theme	1 – 15
Second theme	15 – 32
Development, first theme	33 – 49
First theme	50 – 59
Second theme	60 – 69
Coda	70 – 75

The intimate slow movement requires sensitive, singing tone. The performance should have the flexibility of an improvisation.

An acute sense for sound is needed right away with the first chord: the small accent, in pianissimo, should sustain its sound. The ensuing A and chordal ending of the motive (including the downbeat of the second measure) should match perfectly the decayed sound of the initial B. The three eighth notes of measure 2 climb back with a slight crescendo to the level of the first accent. The phrase is to be played as if it is being sung by the human voice, by giving the impression that the piano is able to sustian the sound without dying away.

From measure 5 on, the shorter motives require an accent on every downbeat. It is particularly difficult to sustain the line in measure 7, where the dotted eighths have to be played loud enough to accommodate the ensuing thirty-seconds in the melody. (Notice the interesting irregularity of the phrase: the first four measures, which contain a two-measure motive played twice, are balanced by a three-measure motive.) The definite crescendo at measure 11 reaches forte at measure 13 and is followed by an unprepared piano in measure 14. A slight extension of the first sixteenth note of the right hand in measure 15 will bring the main subject to a calm ending.

In a very expressive way, the transition prepares for the great anxiety revealed in the second subject. Measures 16–17 and 18–19 are pressing questions, posed with ardor first in the major and then in the minor key. The answer comes with a longer, sad phrase (measures 20–22 and 23–26). The even, singing flow of the melody can be easily disturbed by a heavy left hand, especially on the double notes. Yet the left hand —and more specifically the double notes upholding the harmony—have to be played with clarity, but they should remain in the second plane of the tonal balance. Furthermore the contrary motion between soprano and bass adds to the expressivity of the phrase.

The ornament of measure 22 is to be played as follows:

measure 22

The following bridge passage (measures 26–32) meditates over the main motive in imitation between soprano and tenor. A slight crescendo-decrescendo accompanies the modulation toward G major that appears here like pale sunshine piercing through gray clouds. The pace of the development section beginning at this point seems faster than the preceding sections because of the triplet division used in the accompaniment figure; this figure is the main difficulty of the section. The left hand should smoothly connect the distant notes of the figure. Elaborate fingerings to connect the notes will only be of little value; it is better for the performer to rely on smooth lateral shifts of the hand on the keyboard.

The crescendo of measure 41 leads to a vehement dramatic climax in measures 42 and 43. The octave imitation of the left hand in measure 43 should not be overplayed. Little by little the ardor dies away (measures 44–49) and gives way to the intimate feeling of the opening.

The recapitulation, which contains imitation between the hands (more precisely, between the soprano and tenor), brings about some complications: while one hand is playing a chord with an accent, the other is playing a light chord. Keen ears are needed for a good rendering of this imitation. In measures 55 and 56, small hands will have problems in playing the broad chords without impairing the lyrical tone. The repeat of the cadence measures (measures 58–59), which are in minor and played pianissimo, should chill the listener and pave the way for the desperate questions that reappear here without transition. Notice that the order of the major and minor keys is reversed here. The answer comes in minor (measures 64–66), then suddenly it appears in major (measures 67), thus conveying comfort and encouragement and ending the movement on a positive note. The ornament of measure 66 should be played as follows:

measure 66

The coda uses the main motive. The unexpected appearance of the minor sub-dominant chord in measure 73 is like a reminiscence of sad events.

The performance of this movement should be modeled after the interpretation of a Schubert Lied. The task is somewhat more difficult here, for the words of a Lied can elucidate the music. The pianist, who is not dealing with words and instead is relying only on his own sensibility, has to consider the smallest detail of the melody and harmony in order to detect the refined changes in mood and expression. It is useful to point out once more the necessity for good ears with which to match the decayed tone of the longer notes.

Allegro

M.M. ♩. = 80

Form: Sonata

	MEASURES
Exposition	1 – 84
First subject	1 – 19
Transition	19 – 34
Second subject	35 – 61
Closing subject	61 – 84
Development	84 – 121
Recapitulation	121 – 203
Coda	204 – 216

After the serious, intimate slow movement, the Allegro is like an explosion of joy—a joy obscured only temporarily, in the development section. The performance requires, not only good finger technique and sound arpeggio playing, but also chord technique and a disposition to handle big leaps.

The lighthearted, dancing mood prevails from the outset of the movement. In the first measure, the three C sharps have to be played clearly staccato, taking good care with the third, which is often inadvertently slurred to the ensuing legato motive. Constant attention must be given to maintaining an accurate speed in the scales in sixteenth notes, which are sometimes played with undue haste, faster than the tempo requires. The dotted rhythm can occasion some problems too: if the sixteenth note is played too short, it cannot be heard as part of the melodic line.

A little hesitation in the tempo in the first half of measure 8 will enhance the charm of the reappearance of the opening phrase. Intervals of a tenth occurring in the accompaniment in measures 11 and 12 may be quickly arpeggiated if the performer is not equipped to strike the two notes simultaneously. In this event, the bass note should be played slightly ahead.

At measure 15, the resolution A (the first eighth note of the right hand) should be played as a phrase ending, without accent, and the ensuing break in the phrasing should be smooth. Notice the difference between this measure and measure 19, where the first note is part of the new section and is emphasized with a sudden forte. In the section following the arpeggios (measures 21–23), there are difficult leaps for the left hand. The following division between the hands eliminates the leaps and the possible entangling of the hands:

measure 21

A similar solution is suggested for the recurrences of the passage.

Measure 24, which is often unduly shortened, should be given its full time value. The captivating rhythm of measure 25 will play an important role later in the movement: it has to be rendered with nonchalant Schubertian charm by using flexibility in the tempo. In measure 26, the scale can be more securely started by using the right hand at first and letting the left hand take over on the last two sixteenth notes of the measure.

measures 26-27

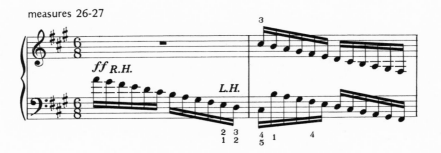

Measure 33, with its vivacious rhythm, can be somewhat enlarged to introduce the one-measure rest, which has to be given its due generously.

The second subject contains a very difficult ornament; it has to be executed on the beat with the "weak" fingers without crashing on the last note of the mordent or altering the dotted rhythm immediately following it. The performer hasn't much choice in the fingering of the mordent; the two possibilities are 3-5-4 and 3-5-3. In the latter case, the fourth finger has to be substituted for the third to insure legato for the dotted figure. The fortepiano chord following the staccato chord in measure 36, should be delayed in a winsome manner, and its length (a measure and a half) should be accurate. Throughout the second subject, the slur endings are to be played staccato. In measure 42, the mordent in the left hand and the rhythmic dissociation between the hands are troublesome.

The second exposition turns the subject into a charming Viennese waltz with a jumping accompaniment figure that is so difficult that it is only seldom performed with perfect accuracy. The difficulty consists in the fact that the performer has to use his fifth finger on the bass note and on the lower note of the ensuing interval as well, thus increasing the possibility of wrong notes. Further complications may arise from the staccato indication: the performer may easily miss one note of the double notes if he plays them too short. Exhaustive practice of this section is recommended; first each note or interval of the left hand should be played twice, and then one or the other note of the interval should be held down in the following way:

measure 44

Only later can the performer practice with the two hands together, and then he should constantly have his eyes on the left hand. Often the tempo tends to accelerate unduly during this section since the jumps in the left hand get more and more animated and speed up the pace considerably. The tempo is to be adhered to rigorously throughout this section.

Measure 52 has a sudden forte that should not be overdone. A heavy left arm can ruin the passage beginning at this point: the charm of the waltz is to be maintained in spite of the forte. The right hand should participate in the shaping with a coloring crescendo-decrescendo. Measure 56 is particularly difficult for the right hand. The recommended fingering is:

measure 56

The last two sixteenth notes of each group of six are often played too fast, like nervous jerks. The left hand should assume the responsibility for the tempo here.

From measure 57 on, the figure of the right hand is further complicated by an arpeggio in which the thumb has to be used on a black key. The sudden change to piano in measure 61 brings the legato touch back into the scales. Good tonal balance should keep the left-hand chords soft. A swift change to an animated fortissimo occurs in measure 65 with a scale that leads to long, singing sforzando chords that contain contrary motion between the voice played by the second finger of the right hand and the bass.

The waltz, with its difficult accompaniment figure, reappears in measure 69. At measure 72, the leap imposed upon the right hand is very large. To avoid excessive risk, playing the first two sixteenth notes of the scale only with the left hand and letting the right hand join in on the third note is recommended.

To render the dotted rhythm of measures 74–75 perfectly, the dotted chord and octave are to be played short—almost staccato—with pedal; the ensuing sixteenth and eighth notes should bounce weightlessly off the keys. The character of these measures (like that of measures 67–68) is overflowing gaiety and not serious drama; it is followed in measures 69–71 and 76–78 by an expression of elegance.

Once more the fortissimo explosion in measure 79 takes place without heaviness. The final confirmation of the key (measures 81–82) may include a small broadening of the tempo; the ensuing sixteenth-note figure leading to the development (or repeat) should be in tempo.

Right from the opening, the development communicates a feeling of insecurity. The strongly emphasized minor mode lends a different, fearful character to the main subject. At measure 92, the anxiety of the nervous scales in imitation seems to grow with the modulations. The scales have to be treated throughout as legato melodies. The first note of each scale in measures 92 and 93 clashes with the harmony; the sorrowful dissonance has to be brought out. At measure 98, the anxiety yields to passion with the sudden outbreak of the forte.

From measure 100 on, the space between the scales is filled out in each hand with staccato eighth notes, which strengthen the passionate progress toward the climax at measure 102. The right hand's difficult figure is best fingered:

measures 102-103

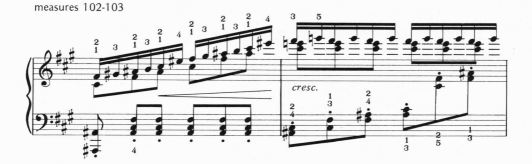

The descending scale immediately following the climax introduces a playful passage where the hands joyously imitate each other in rising arpeggios. The touch should be a light nonlegato. Even the more serious chords related to the minor mode, such as those in measures 112 and 113, won't suggest any more fear or drama; they leave the peaceful virtuosity of the passage undisturbed. It is strongly recommended that the performer use changes of finger on the repeated notes occurring at the end of each arpeggio in the following way:

measures 106-107

The long chord in measure 112 has to be sustained for the full length of the measure.

The legato returns to the right hand's figure at measure 118, preparing the way for the recapitulation with a slight easing of the tempo. The recapitulation takes place in D major, the subdominant key. This is a simplified recapitulation procedure in which the composer can pass through the modulations already established in the exposition and end up in the tonic key without much labor. However there is an unexpected modulation in the recapitulation to the remote key of F major in measure 145.

Recommendations given for the division of the notes between the hands for the exposition can be used for measures 142, 147, 186, and 193. The coda uses the motive of the main subject. An essential change occurs in measure 209, where the melody makes an upsurge for the first time. In measure 211 it levitates into thinner regions, and in measure 213, it introduces a sorrowful minor turn. Two full-orchestra chords put an end to the sonata.

The performance of this movement has to be able to do justice to its cheerful animation and its exhilarating virtuosity, as well as to the fearful anxiety and rising passion it expresses. The interpretation of the Allegro is the easiest of all the movements but at the same time the Allegro is the most arduous technically. Difficult figures and arpeggios and chords and leaps in uncomfortable keys abound. The sound should be brilliant and witty, and devoid of any kind of heaviness.

SCHUBERT

Sonata in A Minor, Op. 164 (D. V. 537)

~~~~~~

    Well balanced in form, this sonata is among the most compact piano sonatas of Schubert. The attractive material is used throughout in a very imaginative way. While it presents only limited technical challenges to most performers, the real difficulty of the sonata lies in the ever-changing, refined expression it demands.

Allegro ma non troppo

M.M. ♩. = 76–80

Form: Sonata

	MEASURES
Exposition	1 – 65
First subject	1 – 27
Second subject	28 – 53
Closing subject	53 – 65
Development	65 – 121
Recapitulation	121 – 186
Coda	187 – 196

    The passion contained in the opening motive reminds us of the first measures of Beethoven's Sonata, Op. 90. The accuracy of the dotted rhythm in a perfect legato line should be the main concern of the interpreter. The staccato eighth notes in measures 2–3 and 7–8 are not to be played sharply, and the indicated crescendo must be well managed in order to release the accumulation of energy on the forte chords in measure 3 (and 8); smaller hands may pass the left-hand chord's top note to the right hand.

    The ensuing measures (4 and 5), with their crepitant diminished-seventh figure, increase the passion to desperation. The following two fingering possibilities are available—the upper for larger and the lower for narrower hands:

measures 4-5

After the restatement of the main motive, measure 8 contains in its last eighth note a very sensitive modulation that should be displayed by means of a diminuendo; thus the diminished-seventh figure in measures 9 and 10 begins softer and grows to the forte at measure 11. The piano appearing at the end of measure 12 is a suggestion for the tone color.

At the end of measure 13, slurs appear for the first time over the motive of two sixteenth notes. A perfect rendering of these slurs with a small interruption of sound before the ensuing heavier quarter note is of the utmost importance every time this motive appears. A slight upward motion of the wrist for the sixteenth notes followed by a slight downward motion with the quarter note will insure suppleness of the hand. (The left wrist follows the motion of the right—slightly up for the staccato eighths and down for the quarter note.) The crescendo included in the passage culminates in the sforzando at the end of measure 15; then suddenly the dotted rhythm of the opening appears in piano, like a light-footed waltz with proper accompaniment. The slurs over the half-measure motives lighten the last eighth note, which is to be played short. Notice that in the melody there is only one accent per measure; thus beware of heaviness on the second beat of the measure. The accents appearing in the left hand are small: their function is only to punctuate the waltz accompaniment. The fingering for the accompaniment is:

measure 16

At measure 20, as a result of the crescendo, a happy forte is reached. The accents on the second beat of the measure appearing at this point should be only moderate so that the impression of a second downbeat in the measure can be avoided. The excitement is still growing toward the sforzando of measure 24, which should be sonorous yet not too loud in the left hand; then the phrase gradually calms down and comes to a standstill on the full-measure rest, which should be generously counted. The only fingering possible in measures 24 and 25 is the successive use of the thumb on the lower part of the sixth chords. The performer needs a light thumb to avoid heaviness and maintain the dotted rhythm accurately.

The second subject, which appears at this point, has the only real technical difficulty of the movement: it is the part-playing problem contained in the left hand. Extensive slow practice is needed to solve this intricate difficulty. The fifth finger on the repeated notes should not be articulated but helped with a slight motion of the hand, while the thumb holds on to the top notes without exerting excessive heavy pressure on the key. The inner voice is a melody that has to be played as legato as possible, using a sliding second finger most of the time.

The task of the left hand is further complicated in measures 39 and 41 when the thumb of the right hand has to play (twice) the F onto which the left thumb is supposed to be holding. The execution of these measures is:

measure 39

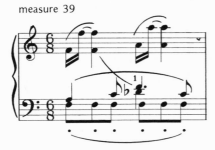

The theme itself floats along in octaves in the right hand. From measure 33 on, a more serious note is struck. The part playing of the left hand remains difficult: the recommended fingering is:

measure 33

The accents following the slurred sixteenths grow insistently. The rendering of the ornaments in measures 34 and 35 is:

measure 34

The grace note of measure 36 is part of the melodic line and is to be played in an expressive way. The unexpectedness of the turn of the unison line toward the C sharp will not escape the attention of a sensitive performer.

After the new statement of the second subject, the music takes a different turn at measure 44. The accents grow more and more insistent as the music modulates, and near desperation is reached with the repeated chords in measures 48–49. The climax on the first chord of measure 50 is to be introduced by stretching the tempo slightly; afterwards the tension is dissolved in the falling arpeggio.

The closing subject floats between major and minor. The performance needs to bring to life the sorrowful dissonances between the soprano and tenor at the beginnings of measures 54 and 57. The passage ends with a particularly expressive sigh motive in measure 56 that will play an important role throughout the development. The repeated low note of the left hand is to be entrusted, as it was previously, to the hand rather than to the fifth finger alone. From measure 61 through the first or second ending, the repeated notes should be played with changes of finger: 3-2-1 should be used throughout.

The aura of mystery achieved after the second ending (with the modulation to G flat major) is dispelled by a surprise fortissimo that superimposes the key of E major upon the prevailing key of G flat major. The accents are on the quarter notes, while the slurs lighten the eighth notes to the extent that they should be barely audible.

After the seeming standstill of the preceding mysterious passage, the music suddenly becomes full of energy again. The sound for measures 73–74 is that of a lively brass section. The rising arpeggio motive should be played without accents or divisions; even the ending quarter note is weightless.

From measure 85 on, the musical importance is concentrated in the left hand. In particular, measure 86 (and similar ones) should be brought to life as if a dramatic question were contained in the eighth notes and the ensuing sigh motive. The chords of the right hand should not be struck heavily: they are destined only to sustain the accompanying harmony. The last dramatic question of measure 90 is followed by a no-less dramatic full-measure rest; then the question is repeated twice without its previous assurance, first in piano and then in pianissimo, and the section is brought to a complete halt. Notice that the full-measure rest at measure 95 has a fermata.

At this point, resuming the tempo only reluctantly, the repeated E flats (like horns in the orchestra) introduce a waltz theme related to the main subject. Its main feature is the dissonance arising between the soprano and the bass every other measure (measures 97, 99, 101, 103, and so on). The calm, legato accompaniment figure lends a dreamy character to the phrase. At its second exposition (measure 105), the accompaniment chords contain motion contrary to the melody's, thus lending more vigor to the music. The ensuing diminished-seventh arpeggios in groups of seven notes may be accommodated approximately as follows:

measure 106

The enharmonic modulation of measure 109 needs a sensitive stretching; the tempo will resume at measure 110.

The tension begins to build up from measure 114 on as the contrary motion between melody and harmony seems to strike deeper and deeper. The dynamic progression (measures 114–119) is often ruined by poor tonal balance, with the repeated chords of the left hand totally covering the motive of the right hand. Though there is no large gap between the hands, it is very easy to overplay the left hand at this point.

The progression climaxes in the forceful outcry of measure 120. The grace-note arpeggios of this measure are an important part of the violent outbreak contained here; therefore they should not be played at an inarticulate speed. The suggested metrical division of the measure is:

measure 120

Except for the fact that it opens in the subdominant key, the recapitulation shows no change from the exposition.

The passionate exclamation that is made in three separate statements in the coda is built on a motive of the main subject (measures 189–191). In addition to the important dynamic progression, the increasing passion also calls for a ritardando as the fermata is approached. The answer comes softly and full of resignation, ending the movement on a sorrowful note.

There is no taxing difficulty in the first movement of this sonata except for the part playing of the accompaniment to the second subject. The challenge to the performer is more in the often-changing expression and in the quality of the tone, which is able to accommodate both the dreamy second subject and the elegant waltz as well as the dramatic outbursts of the development.

Allegretto quasi andantino

M.M. ♩ = 66–72

Form: Rondo

	MEASURES
A	1 – 16
B	17 – 42
A	43 – 58
C	59 – 96
Transition	96 – 114
A	115 – 130
Coda	131 – 144

Schubert is at his best in his slow movements, where he is free from the strain of writing a movement in sonata form (especially its development section). Beautiful themes come to his mind in profusion. This particular movement emphasizes strongly the mediant relationship between the keys of the different episodes.

To convincingly perform the enchanting A subject, the performer needs to rely on his natural musical sense more than on affectation or sophistication. The theme itself, seemingly the very essence of Schubert's musical language, has its germ in the popular song. The problem of this Lied is that it has to be "sung" on the piano. How close the pianist can get to the human voice when playing the legato octaves determines his success. To insure good legato octaves, one has to avoid abrupt motions of the forearm and hand. In this movement in particular, the use of the fourth (or third) finger on black keys is strongly recommended. When this fingering is used, the hand is turned slightly outward, and the fourth finger falls naturally on the neighboring black key when the fifth is used on a white key. Meanwhile the arm and elbow are relaxed.

Measure 7 contains a difficult change of finger (from the fourth to the third on the F sharp) that enables the hand to cope with the ensuing sixteenth-note octaves. The thumb should remain light throughout.

In measures 13 and 15, the dotted rhythm needs to be performed accurately and with ease, while the hand and wrist are kept relaxed. It is important that the downbeat following the dotted rhythm is played lightly, without undue accent. Patient work is needed in order to secure a round, relaxed sound for the staccato in the left hand of this section. To avoid abruptness, every note should be conceived as being within a continuous motion, like the steps of someone taking a stroll. Whenever the accompaniment changes to a legato touch (as it does in measures 4, 8, and so on), it carries some important additions to the melody. Good part playing is essential in those measures.

The execution of this accompaniment raises another controversial issue—the use of the pedal. It is a widely shared belief that staccato notes should be executed without pedal. However the ideal execution of this subject requires the use of the pedal; without it the phrase will turn out unbearably dry. The recommended pedaling is:

Franz Peter Schubert

measures 1-16

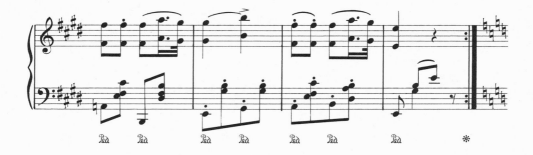

The first episode begins in a Schumannesque way—a sort of story telling. The mezzo forte indication immediately followed by a diminuendo points to an expressive prolongation of the first sixteenth note of the right hand, clearly displaying the octave step in the melody. A singing legato is a must for all the sixteenth notes: the fingering for measures 18 and 19 should be chosen with this in mind. In the left hand, the middle voice carries a souvenir of the main subject that has to be brought out as a complement to the right hand's main melody.

The smiling mood raises the sound to forte in measues 21 and 22, in which the hands cheerfully imitate each other. Excessive felicity strifles the sound with a sudden piano at measure 23. The slurring of the descending sixteenths is most important for the expressivity of these two measures. The left hand plays a sustained legato.

The first sixteenth notes of measures 25 and 26 need a slight extension to underline the important diminished-seventh harmony. The separate stem for the first sixteenth note of the left hand at the beginning of measure 28 means a generous break in the phrasing. From this point on for four measures, the left hand has the main role, which is like a cello solo.

At measures 36 and 38, the first sixteenth note is further emphasized by a forte, this time it requires even more extension of the note than it did previously. Measure 38 needs an especially convincing prolongation because it has to confirm the suddenly imposed new key of F major at this point. The three measures preceding the double bar calm down the atmosphere and lead to the second exposition of the main subject, which is in F major here.

The left hand is given a new difficulty here: the first sixteenth note of each group lies far away from the other three notes. The separate stem for this first sixteenth and the staccato dot indicate a separation and a subtle delay between the first and second sixteenth note. Another difficulty arises from the staccato indications, which in performance degenerate too readily into undue accents. It may be helpful for the performer to imagine this accompaniment figure as shared between the cello (pizzicato) and the viola. A further difficulty begins in measure 51 with the introduction of double notes to the figure. The danger is that the hand with the double note will be set down heavily, producing an undue accent. Also the evenness of the figure may suffer so much from this new difficulty that it may become increasingly troublesome to keep the two hands together. Practicing this section (measures 43–59) with the left hand alone is strongly recommended: it should be played slowly at first, without tension in the hand or arm, and the sound and evenness should constantly be controlled; then the speed should be increased gradually until the desired rate is reached.

The only complication for the right-hand octaves lies in the choice of the key: because of the many more white notes in F major, a good legato is more difficult to maintain. Hands with a wider span have a definite advantage at this point.

There is something visionary in the second episode, at measure 59. It gives the impression of a terrifying legend or popular ballad. Here again the left-hand accompaniment has to be dealt with first, in detail. Continuous motion is also preferred here to abrupt, separate movements. The parallel thirds moving in the lower part of the chords should be enunciated with great clarity. Fragments indicated as legato, like measure 68, are of particular importance. The right hand states the subject without warmth or tonal shading. The crescendo beginning in measure 63 remains small and is followed by an icy pianissimo at measure 67. The crescendo at measure 73 should begin the same way, then suddenly increase to a wicked forte, and then—almost afraid of its own effect—fade to pianissimo.

The refinement of this episode lies in the difference of touch between the hands. Well performed, this section will provoke an icy shiver in the listener.

The transition is immediately permeated with more warmth as both hands play legato. The expressive sixths need a fingering suitable for the required legato. The slur endings have to be played smoothly, without picking up the hand. The left hand enunciates the dotted rhythm like a distant menace; then, at measure 105, it adds an expressive contrary motion to the melody of the right hand. From this measure on, the phrasing should become even smoother, and the syncopated character of the top voice should be brought out.

At measure 109, the motive is shortened to a two-note, weeping slur. Its heavy first part is a dissonant chord that is to be played with a sorrowful accent. The light resolution should be played very softly in spite of the heavy beat and the accompanying octave. The slurs lose their sorrowfulness little by little from measure 111 on and slide back to the main subject almost unnoticed.

In the final recapitulation of the main subject, the left hand has to deal with new difficulties. Once more patient, slow practice is recommended until complete mastery of the accompaniment is achieved. The difficulties involved here are multiple; the first one involves the ability to produce a light, lateral movement of the hand to distant regions of the keyboard. The second difficulty consists in playing the figure in thirds without undue accents, either on the first or the last third. Another difficulty involves slurring certain chords (see measures 116 and 120) without excessive heaviness on the first chord. There are also part-playing difficulties in measure 118, where the fingering should be:

measure 118

Especially difficult is measure 125, with its descending sixths. The position of the body in the higher area of the keyboard is such that it is difficult to play the first chord with the required fingering. Leaning the torso slightly to the right will allow more space for the left hand. Still, heaviness is a real danger in this measure.

Last but not least is the difficulty of playing each chord complete and with perfect accuracy. Many otherwise acceptable or even appealing performances have been ruined at this recapitulation. In addition to the persisting difficulty of the accompaniment, the coda has also an uncomfortable finger change, which occurs first in measure 133. The finger alone should be involved in the execution, without the weight of the arm.

This ravishing slow movement is the strongest part of the sonata. It requires good singing legato octaves, natural musicianship in shaping the melodic line, a good sense for timing and smooth phrasings, and the ability to render varied expression through subtle changes. One difficulty is the choice of the tempo. "Allegretto quasi andantino" suggests that one is dealing here with a borderline case. A tempo that is too slow would be just as detrimental as one that is too fast.

M.M. ♩ = 66–72 seems right.

Allegro vivace

M.M. ♩. = 84–88

Form: Rondo

	MEASURES
A	1 – 58
B	59 – 163
A	164 – 229
B	230 – 309
Coda	310 – 367

This lively rondo, using themes greatly varied in character, has a clear tendency to modulate into the key of the Neapolitan sixth. The form is exceptional in that there is no middle episode—a lack that brings this rondo closer to sonata form without development.

The first section of the main subject breaks down into three parts—measures 1–9, measures 10–21, and measures 22–30—each of which explores a different key. The first part remains in the main key, the second explores the Neapolitan area, and the third takes the direction of the more smiling major key. The fact that each one of these parts contains a violent contrast between its component motives is self-evident. However the interpretation of the frequently occurring fermatas needs close consideration. It is most probable that assigning all fermatas the same length would not do justice to the music and that they have to be considered seperately from the point of view of their function.

The fermatas at the ends of the violently rising unison scales serve as transitions between loud and soft. Some editions erroneously indicate accents (>) at these points; they should be read as short diminuendo signs: ▷──── . The length of the fermata should allow a natural transition from the forte to the ensuing piano. The fermatas at measures 9 and 21 conclude the first two parts of the main subject. They have to be approached with a rallentando. The count should be suspended on the rests over which they appear; however the time for the rest should not be simply doubled because this lengthening would disrupt the continuity of the subject. Notice that there is no fermata on the rest at measure 18; therefore there is no need for a rallentando in the preceding measures.

Measures 19–20 should slow down for the reasons just explained. Measure 30 may be slightly prolonged because it occurs at the end of the entire A section. The attention of the performer also needs to be drawn to the differences in length of the downbeat notes in the violently rising scale motives. In performing this section, maintaining the accuracy of these different lengths is an absolute must.

The second section of the main subject is in a happy, dancing mood. Some difficulty may be experienced when playing the top line in measures 31 and 32, since only the weaker fingers are involved in the figure. The left hand should be very light, allowing the right hand to play with ease. The descending line (measures 35–38), in which the notes are slurred by twos, takes the fingering 3–2 throughout.

The character of the music becomes more serious at measure 39, with the sudden piano. The melody is a short, yearning motive. Tonal balance here is very important. The left-hand accompanying chords should not cover the right-hand notes, though the changes of harmony from the dominant to the diminished-seventh chord and vice versa should be enunciated with perfect clarity.

The sound is increased to forte at measure 47, where a desperate mood prevails. It is difficult to finger these four measures (measures 47–50) in the right hand so as to satisfy the legato indication. To avoid abrupt changes in hand position, the following fingering is recommended:

measures 47–50

The fortissimo explodes in measure 51 with a vehement question, repeated in piano. Measure 59 brings a complete change of character with the introduction of a charming ländler that totally ignores the preceding violent outbreak. The theme is regularly constructed of four-measure motives. In each of the first three motives, it shows a stress on the third measure that is underlined by an important chord (see measures 61, 65, and 69). The main difficulty of the subject lies in a smooth execution of the grace notes. They should, of course, be played short, and on the beat, as measure 64 indicates:

measure 64

The left hand holds onto the bass notes, each of which indicates a change of the pedal.

At measure 71, without preparation, the dominant of A major is superimposed over the key of D major. The dominant chord does not resolve as expected but leads to another unprepared superposition, this time to the chord of F major; once more the Neapolitan sixth relation is stressed. The latter superposition is introduced by a diminuendo: the pianissimo at measure 79 should be interpreted as the confession of an intimate secret. The coloring of measures 79–94 should be most subtle, and the performance may be tinted by the hesitation between the tonic and the dominant of F major. Finally, by enharmonic means, E major gleams like the end of a dark tunnel. Hesitation is still part of the music, which falters between the higher and lower registers and between major and minor, giving important clues to the interpretation.

At measure 111, the closing virtuoso part explodes. The rising broken-third passage is quite difficult to deal with. Only one fingering is possible:

measures 111-112

Throughout the section, the left hand has to be kept light. In the left hand, the distinct articulation of staccato and tenuto is needed.

At the height of the excitement (measure 127), the music stops and the Ländler reappears as a reminiscence. The entire virtuosic section is repeated at this point; the reminiscent Ländler leaves the section unresolved, like an open question, and it approaches the fermata of measure 163 with a rallentando.

The recapitulation of the A subject is in E minor; it passes through the same nuances in key and mood as it did in the exposition. The important modulation toward the original tonic key takes place at measure 221, where the vehement question of the repeated chords is restated a semitone higher, thus reaching the key of G major for the Ländler subject. There is no other alteration in the recapitulation, except that the explosive virtuoso section (measures 282–306) is not merely reproduced from the exposition; here it has repeat marks that should be obeyed for the sake of formal balance.

The coda starts off with the main subject, but this time the final question—left open up to here—is answered in measure 330 by a deceptive cadence that changes the key abruptly to F major. The repeated chords, alternating between tonic and dominant, in fortissimo and piano, are to be played like vehement questions and timid answers. This section is the dramatic climax of the movement. Suddenly at measure 347, the rising arpeggio gets transformed into a cascading one: the following A octaves need a slight stretching to underline the home key of A major, which is reached at measure 350. The mood is one of complete resignation from this point on. The repeated octaves, reminiscent of the vehement questions, recede farther and farther into the distance.

Of all the movements in this sonata, the rondo is the most exacting technically. But in addition to physical skill, the movement also requires sensitivity to follow the capriciously transitory moods. Beauty of tone should be a constant concern, especially in the vehement passages. Still the most important trait of the movement is the frequent use of the fermata. The interpretation of these holds will determine the natural flow of the movement and consequently the flow of the entire performance.

Robert Schumann

Born 1810, Zwickau; died 1856, Endenich

Combining passion with delicate sensibility, Schumann's works are among the most beautiful creations of Romanticism. Following the path of Schubert, Schumann developed further a new branch of music literature, the miniature. His short character pieces show a great deal of refined nuance expressed in concentrated and concise forms.

The first years of Schumann's production were almost entirely devoted to the piano, and most of his acknowledged masterpieces were written in this early stage. They are unique in that they are the creations of his one and only master, the imagination.

Schumann's music often carries within it literary or mystic allusions, such as musical themes formed from the letters of the alphabet that are the names of musical pitches. In *Variations on the Name "Abegg,"* A–B (flat)–E–G–G is the opening phrase of the theme; *Carnaval* is built on the four notes A–Es (E flat)–C–H (B natural), the name of a small town where one of Schumann's girlfriends, Ernestine von Fricken, lived. Other nonmusical suggestions allude to the "Davidsbündler," an imaginary association of Schumann's friends, fighting against the "Philistines," a sort of musical petite bourgeoisie depicted by a musical motive called "Grossvatertanz," which appears in the finales of both *Papillons* and *Carnaval.*

For Schumann, these suggestions express, not only wittiness, but a sort of mystic relationship of people or phenomena as well. The miniatures forming the large, cyclic works are sometimes signed with the initial "E" or "F"; these initials refer to Eusebius and Florestan, imaginary characters that represent Schumann's peaceful and passionate selves, respectively. This deliberate splitting of his personality may be an early sign of the mental illness that later paralyzed Schumann's creative powers and eventually killed him.

Variations on the Name of "Abegg," Papillons, Davidsbündlertänze, Toccata, Carnaval, the three sonatas, *Phantasiestücke, Symphonic Études, Kinderszenen, Fantasie in C Major, Kreisleriana,* and *Faschingsschwank aus Wien* are his most important works for the piano. They contain technical difficulties that are quite different from the ones encountered in the works of the other Romantic composers. Schumann believed that the piano was the most eloquent and attractive instrument to write for and that it offered unlimited possibilities for the expression of his delicate sensibility. As a result, Schumann's music is taxing on the imagination and the sensitivity of the performer just as it is on his finger dexterity.

SCHUMANN
Papillons, Op. 2

~~~~~~

Directly inspired by *Flegeljahre,* a novel by "Jean Paul" (J. F. Richter), Schumann's opus 2 is a Romantic suite consisting of an introduction and twelve pieces. Schumann's idea of the suite was very different from that of the Baroque composers. In *Papillons* there is no common key or connection of musical materials between the movements. Like so many different personalities, the movements unfold in different tempi and in different rhythms. The use of the material of the first movement in the last movement is the only attempt at unification, and it is limited to lending some perspective to the work instead of really unifying it.

Some of the movements are in a sort of ternary form; others show binary forms or even consist of only two statements of two different thoughts, which sometimes even end in a different key from that in which they began (see numbers 2 and 7).

Introduction: Moderato

M.M. ♩ = about 138–144

In a very typical epic mood, the introduction is a sort of double question. The entire motive springs forth from the first D, which should be played by freely dropping the hands and arms, yet be well balanced in sound. The motive advances freely with a slight acceleration to the G sharp of the third measure. There the question mark curls up, and it is then softly and dreamily repeated. A grand pause follows.

No. 1

M.M. ♩ = about 138

The waltz rhythm of the opening movement is significant because it sets the stage for the whole work in a ballroom. The first piece begins with a longingly rising legato motive in octaves that requires the third and fourth fingers to alternate on the top of the octave line in order to insure a singing legato. In the left hand, the simple waltz accompaniment turns into part playing from measure 5 on. The different articulations of the right hand in measures 9–10 and 11–12 have to be well brought out, and there should be a slight ritardando in measure 12 where a G suddenly appears in the middle of the left-hand part and is held for three measures. Here the only possible fingering (a constant substitution of the fifth finger for the thumb and vice versa) often slows the tempo down unacceptably.

A well-punctuated staccato and a slightly delayed long note will bring charm and wit to measures 8, 9, 10, and 16.

No. 2: Prestissimo

M.M. $\quad \downarrow$ = 120

The first four measures are often the victims of inaccuracy, especially in the octaves section. One of the difficulties of these alternate octaves lies in the fact that the left hand hides from view the key that the thumb of the right hand plays immediately following the left-hand octave. The passage has to be practiced first with the thumbs only, to establish coordination between them as well as to learn their respective places on the keyboard. The left hand, used only on black keys, has to stay *sopra* (over the right hand) throughout. Even after much work, achieving the promptness to perform this passage remains a problem for many performers. Even the second half of the piece contains the problem of rhythmic coordination between the hands. The left hand has to be kept down to an accompanying tone, while the right plays the melody. A clear distinction has to be made between the melody interrupted by rests and the continuous line.

No. 3

M.M. $\quad \downarrow.$ = 50

The clumsily advancing octaves depict the intrusion of a grotesque character into the ballroom. The quarter-note octaves are to be played with a separate tenuto touch, the eighth-note octaves can be legato, and the half-note octaves have solid sforzandos on them. At the second ending (measure 8b), the F-sharp octave in the left hand has to be released in time to make room for the E octave of the right hand. The accompanying full-measure octaves in the left hand add even more clumsiness to the music in the second section (measures 9–16). The recapitulation of the first statement is in canon; even so the left hand should not be overplayed. In measures 24–26, the right hand keeps the F-sharp octave down; consequently the middle voice is uncomfortable to finger.

No. 4: Presto

M.M. $\quad \downarrow.$ = 92–100

Rhythm is the essential element of the first statement. The sudden shiver of passion represented by the crescendo in the second measure accelerates the tempo toward the sforzando of measure 3, where the "stolen" time is paid back. The passionato gives way to teasing staccatos, in tempo, from measure 5 on. At measure 9, the crescendo grows even more longing, produces a long line, and reaches the forte with an easing of the tempo. The three even eighth notes shared by the hands in the middle section need constant attention. The left-hand part, a sort of pizzicato, should not be part of the melodic line. The slurs of the right hand indicate that the third eighth note of the measure is heavier than the subsequent downbeat. From measure 30 to measure 32, an expressive horn passage in the left hand doubles the melody, which slows down as it approaches the fermata. The variant of the main subject in measure 35 (G sharp instead of F sharp) has to be well brought out; it is also doubled in the tenor (in the thumb of the left hand).

No. 5

M.M. ♩ = 76–80

One of Schumann's warmest, most lyrical phrases begins this movement. The melody is in the soprano: the "basso cantando" indication does not mean that the bass should be played in the first plane. The held bass notes often make the repeated intervals in the top part of the left hand sound loud and heavy, overpowering the poetic melody line. The basic rhythm of the piece is that of a polonaise, though the character constantly remains lyrical and essentially feminine.

In measures 3 and 4, the melody is split into two voices. The beautiful counterpoint transforms these two measures into a real *duetto*. Measures 6 and 7 have difficult broken chords that should sound rich and mellow, without undue haste or dryness. The recommended fingering for the left hand is:

measures 6-7

The triplets of the left hand in measure 8 are to be played meaningfully, in a very relaxed tempo, and without interference from the dotted rhythm in the right hand.

The sforzandos at the beginnings of measures 9, 10, and 11 are like loud exclamations. The tempo can be eased in measure 12, thus delaying the downbeat of measure 13 and making the sudden key change even more audible. The polonaise rhythm appears clearly in measures 13 and 14. From measure 15 on, the phrase gets more and more expressive as it divides again into three voices. The return of the main subject at measure 19 may be introduced with a rallentando on the preceding three eighth-note chords, bringing the chromatic contrary motion in their middle voices out well. There is much sadness in the subdominant modulation of measure 23. The last two measures should have a small but very expressive crescendo-decrescendo.

No. 6

M.M. $\quad \downarrow$ $\cdot$ = 60–69

An angry character is quite evident in the opening statement. The slurred chords with the sforzandos draw all the weight to the third beat of each measure to such an extent that the listener really feels the downbeat on them. Feeling the measure this way causes a strange, irregular four-beat bar to be sensed around the end of the phrase. The simple bass note between the chords has to be played short and relatively lightly. In order to play the eighth-note octaves in the fourth measure with ease, the player has to begin them with a swing of the arm, let the hand bounce freely on each octave, and use only $\frac{5}{1}$ as the fingering.

The following pianissimo section contrasts with the violent character of the opening. The chords should be played almost legato; their recommended fingering is:

measures 7-8

The return of the violent statement has a more difficult double-octave scale in measure 18: the performer has to swing both arms. In measures 20–22, it is difficult to repeat the thirds in the right hand effortlessly in pianissimo; only the hand should be involved in the light bouncing. At measure 25, a new idea is opposed to the angry motive in the form of a nonchalant waltz. The tempo can be slightly slower here. A slight prolongation of the sforzando broken chords will add to the coquettish charm of the phrase. The second ending (measure 32b) has the same hornlike reinforcement of the melody that appears in No. 4 at measures 30–32. The angry phrase returns for the ending and exits slamming the door with the last two chords.

No. 7: Semplice

M.M. $\quad \downarrow$ $\cdot$ = 54–58

The character indication "semplice" is the key to this piece. The unsophisticated first phrase is in the style of a folksong. It is important to notice the articulation of the left hand—a light eighth note in the first measure, a heavier dotted quarter note in the second measure that is to be held and slurred to the third measure, which is light again. Thus heavy measures of the melody coincide with light measures of the accompaniment, lending the phrase a touch of unreality. The chords in the left hand have to be rolled gently ahead of the beat, and the bass notes have to be kept down as required by the tie. If doing this is impossible for small hands, the key of the bass note has to be struck again silently before the second chord is played and the pedal changed.

The ending diminished-seventh chord leaves the phrase open, like a glance into infinity. A warm, singing tone is needed for the second idea in the top of the right-hand part; the lower part is to be played in a very different accompanying tone. The first note of the left hand has to be kept down as long as possible throughout the second idea, and there should be a pedal change at every bar line. Great intimacy is the prevailing character of the movement: it is a sort of confession.

No. 8

M.M. $\downarrow$ = 54–60

This effervescent waltz is a drastic contrast to the intimate simplicity of the preceding movement. Overwhelming good humor is revealed in the difficult repeated chords, which should be played with a freely bouncing hand kept very close to the keys. The quarter-note chords are legato, with the fourth and fifth fingers alternating on the top line. From measure 5 on, the chord on the third beat is slurred to the following downbeat, enhancing the general cheerfulness even more.

The waltz motive has an accent on the third beat of every other measure. Notice that wherever the accent appears in the music, there is no staccato mark; the sforzando chords have to be held for their full value. At measure 17, the "ritenuto" marking means that a slower tempo should be adopted as far as measure 25, allowing the second eighth-note chord in measures 17–19 to be gently rolled. The ritenuto can increase along with the crescendo; the tempo primo starts almost reluctantly at measure 25. Small hands are definitely handicapped at the two last measures; the G flat of the right hand can be taken into the left hand, if need be.

measures 31-32

No. 9: Prestissimo

M.M. $\downarrow$ = 104–112

The first statement is a fast passionate phrase in which the interval on the second beat in the left hand has to be brought out in every measure as an answer to the sforzando on the first beat in the right hand. The second idea, with its staccato intervals and chords in both hands, shows many imitations in the four voices. The fingers should be very relaxed and kept close to the keys; the intervals are played by a slight vibration of the forearm while the wrist is constantly relaxed. The melody line has to emerge throughout. The rests of measures 22 and 23 have to be of exact length, as do those in measures 38 and 39. The more expressive character of the third section, measures 25–32, can be underlined by longing crescendos heading toward the sforzandos. At the ending, the personage evoked in the movement vanishes in the manner of Puck.

No. 10: Vivo

M.M. ♩. = 96

Più lento

M.M. ♩ = 152

A change of character is evident here, in spite of the fact that the pianissimo indication is carried over from the preceding number. The first statement, with its light, jumpy rhythm, seems to be setting the scene for a more important happening to come. Perfect repetition of the full chords is fairly difficult in measures 3 and 5, if the player takes the pianissimo seriously. From the upbeat of measure 9 on, the contrary motion between soprano and bass has to be brought out. The haphazard modulation leads to an ending in E minor.

The next statement (measures 17–24) has already been heard in No. 6. This time it is presented in a self-assured, majestic fortissimo. The positions for the middle fingers in the chords have to be well established, using the classical arpeggio fingerings:

measures 17-18

The last and most important part of the movement consists of a slow waltz beginning at measure 25, the pulse for this section is M.M. ♩ = 152. The right hand has the singing melody and *the* typical part of the waltz accompaniment usually given to the second violins and violas. The accents on the third beats are consistent. The left hand has an arpeggio accompaniment that is legato for two consecutive measures; the legato will be made possible by the following fingering:

measures 25-28

After the repeat, the phrase is interrupted at measure 41 by a free fantasia, like a double question that wavers between major and minor. Then, at the double bar, the waltz begins again. The fingering for the left hand at measures 55–56 is:

measures 55-56

At measure 57, the volume is increased to mezzo forte, and more intensity is lent to the phrase by the doubling of the melody in octaves from measure 59 on. There is a new interruption at measure 65, this time by some noisy company. The waltz returns at measure 70 as a reminiscence and dies away in triple piano. The low C is the only note to play in the last measure.

No. 11

M.M. ♩ = 112

In this number, the gaiety of the ball resumes with a noisy polonaise. The introduction (first three measures) is in the style of an orchestral tutti. The chords should be played with sharp rhythm, and they should be fully repeated. Measure 3 slows down in charming expectation of the main melody. Its entrance is further enhanced by the broken interval at the beginning of measure 4. The left hand has the difficulty of dealing with the bouncing fifths in sharp rhythm and without obtrusiveness. Measures 6 and 7 again bring a doubling of the melody by the horns. The line is inflated by a crescendo-decrescendo. The sudden arrhythmia of measure 10 has to be well brought out with sharp accents.

Following the longing motive, which is repeated once (measures 12–13), measure 15 presents a real problem in making the zigzag arpeggios accurate. The recommended fingering is:

measures 15-16

These arpeggios lead to an evanescent short motive in the right hand that is to be played staccato with short, coloring grace notes. The pianissimo indication belongs mainly to the left hand: the rising five-note scale has no crescendo.

A triumphant forte is back at measure 20, and it leads to the fortissimo at measure 22, where the alternation of hands is to be played with passion. The section ends in a strange, arrhythmic manner, in spite of the fact that measures 29 and 30 clearly fall into three 2/4 measures. There should be some hesitation on the first two beats of measure 29; then, suddenly, on the last beat, a new idea begins in tempo or even faster. It reminds one of a conversation with someone who interrupts his own sentence and changes the subject.

The rest in measure 31 should be held for the exact length of time specified. The way the idea of the middle section is shared between the hands gives a strange impression of limping, because of the successive accents on the second and third sixteenth notes of every group of four. The second note in each group (which is played in the left hand) has an especially important harmonic function. The whole section is to be played with physical and mental quietude.

The noisy interruption of the polonaise rhythm at measure 40 pushes the tempo slightly faster; then calm returns at measure 42, where the grace notes are to be played gently, in the manner of slides of the human voice. The grace notes on the top notes of the octaves in measures 44–46 are very difficult to play in the soft manner required. Using the fourth finger on the grace notes (the only fingering possible) stiffens smaller hands to such an extent that there is no possibility left for legato or controlled tone. The only way to keep the hand relaxed is to keep the fourth finger relaxed. A slight forward motion will open up the relaxed hand into a fan-shaped position and allow the fourth finger to play the grace note ahead of the octave with ease.

The lively polonaise is only partly recapitulated; its only novelty here is a different figure in measures 50 and 51, that leads to the evanescent motive. The interruption at the end of the number should have a great deal of vivacity and wit.

No. 12: Finale

M.M. $\quad$ = 60; $\quad$ = 60

The ''Grossvatertanz'' (''dance of the grandpapa'') makes its appearance here orchestrated for woodwinds doubled by horns. Used in the Finale of *Carnaval* as well, this subject ridicules the "Philistines," musical conservatives and enemies of the "Davids-bündler" (as mentioned in the introduction to Schumann's works). The "Gross-vatertanz," written in 3/4, is followed by a polka in 2/4: a measure of the first tempo should be the same duration as a measure of the new tempo, as the recommended metronome settings indicate.

At measure 22, the "Grossvatertanz" fades out, giving way temporarily to the theme of the first number; it comes back again at measure 31, and the two themes are combined. Real difficulties in maintaining the independence of the two motives arise from this combination—for example, in measure 35, where the dotted rhythm of the left hand should live its own independent life without interference from the right hand's rhythm.

From measure 47 on, according to Schumann's instruction, the pedal should be kept down without interruption to the end of measure 73. Although such pedaling was probably tolerable on Schumann's instrument, it is not allowable on our pianos. The performer can safely use the middle (sostenuto) pedal here to keep the low D sounding for the required time.

Important as it seems at first glance, the resonance of the pedal point is only a small problem. The real difficulty lies, as before, in the independent handling of the motives without rhythmic interference between the hands, at least through measures 47–56. Especially difficult are the measures where the right hand has syncopated rhythms, such as measures 50–52 and measure 54. Only a determined separation of the motives in the mind can lead to a successful performance at this point.

From measure 56 on, the role of the right hand is progressively reduced. Then, at measure 62, the clock begins to chime 6 A.M. The chime should enter with a sonorous mezzo piano and should not follow the diminuendo indication intended for the lower voices. The coda beginning at measure 74 is the postlude to the whole work. The pizzicato chords have liveliness, and their harmonic importance should be brought forward. From measure 86 on, the chords vanish with the rallentando. The arpeggio of measure 89 is like a broken chord from which the performer has to release the notes one after another. The final "throwaway" cadence is again in a vivacious, witty tempo.

Sensitivity and imagination should guide the performer in the performance of *Papillons,* where only five of the twelve movements and the introduction bear a tempo or character indication. Furthermore, because most of the pieces are very short, the performer has to be able to switch from one character to a diametrically opposite one in a split second.

It is hard to assign a definite program to *Papillons.* Yet the performance should give the impression of a crowd of different character types in a ballroom, where the story takes place. The technical difficulties, though important, seem less so in comparison with the task of a simple, unsophisticated musical approach. Simplicity and spontaneity are the most precious qualities for the performer who plays these delicate miniatures. Lastly here is one piece of practical advice to the pianist: in the course of performance all repeat marks have to be obeyed.

SCHUMANN
Phantasiestücke, Op. 12

~~~~~~

Some cycles by Schumann require performance in full; it is unthinkable to select a number of pieces from *Carnaval* or *Papillons* and play them in a program isolated from the rest of the work. Other cycles, such as *Phantasiestücke* ("Fantasy Pieces"), Op. 12, allow this procedure. There is no unifying musical motive or compositional method tying the eight pieces together. The titles they bear discourage any further research to find a unifying mystique or literary program. Only the last piece *Ende vom Lied* ("The End of the Song") should never be isolated from the rest and should be performed only when the cycle is played in full.

No. 1: Des Abends ("Evening")

Form: Two parts (repeated) and coda

	MEASURES
A	1 – 16
B	17 – 38
A	39 – 54
B	55 – 77
Coda	78 – 88

The indication *sehr innig zu spielen* ("to be played very intimately") says enough about the character of this sublime nocturne. Over an even triplet motion, the long line of an ethereal melody floats in cross rhythm. It is self-evident that the thumb of the right hand should be weightless and avoid thumping in order to keep the melody afloat. The other difficulty of the piece is in maintaining the perfect togetherness of the hands. Usually the left hand has a large gap to fly over and on this account may arrive late (or too loudly) on the second note of the triplet. Both hands use the thumb on this note throughout the piece; the player has to take good care to synchronize them and to melt the sounds they produce into the accompaniment.

In measure 3 (and later, in measure 41), the second note of the left hand comes in as the third triplet note of the measure and carries the melody. Only a keen ear can direct the thumb of the left hand in the fulfillment of its role at this point. At measure 6, the grace-note ornament has to be perfectly melted into the ethereal line of the melody. It should be played ahead of the beat in the manner of a melisma.

From measure 9 on, the melody gains more intensity; also the bass gives up the D-flat pedal point. The curling upward of the melody has a small crescendo: the tempo hesitates slightly in measure 12 before the final crescendo-decrescendo begins in measure 13. From this point on, the togetherness of the hands should be of particular concern, for the left hand has a large gap to fly over. In measure 16, beware of playing the last note of the left hand bumpily or too loud.

The new section begins with a lingering motive that contains a particularly sensitive turn in measure 18. From measure 21 on, the melody appears off the beat below an upper pedal point. The sudden change to a remote key by means of enharmonic modulation, which appears at measure 25, needs sensitive rendering. The tempo should be slowed down in measure 24 and the pedal changed on the last triplet note of the measure, which is the upbeat to the E-major section. The C flat of measure 24 will thus be transformed into a B natural for sensitive ears.

After the statement of the lingering motive (this time in E major), more chromaticism appears from measure 32 on, reducing the length of the motive to one measure. Notice that the left hand omits the bass note from this point on. The rests appearing on the beats have to be obeyed by both the hand and the pedal, which has to be changed with each melodic note. Particularly important is the half-measure rest at measure 36. The entrance of the left hand with a sforzando on the second beat of the measure has the character of syncopation. In this measure, the same transfiguration takes place as in measure 24; only here it is in the opposite direction: the F sharp of the left hand becomes G flat, while the D sharp of the right hand is held in the next measure as E flat.

The lead back to the recapitulation of section A is achieved by a recitativelike scale in the left hand that begins hesitantly after a prolongation of the first triplet note, gains speed with the crescendo, and slows down finally on the last triplet group of measure 38. After a restatement of sections A and B without change, the coda at measure 77 breaks the long line of the melody into shorter, two-measure motives. The melodic notes appear sometimes in the upper part of the right hand and sometimes in the lower part—in measures 83–84, the melody even appears in the upper part of the left hand, suggesting a different color for each register. The concluding phrase (measures 85–88) has two lines: one is in the top part of the right-hand part; the other begins in measure 86 with the B flat in the top part of the left hand. This phrase should sound like the most intimate confession; the last note of the right hand should sound like a distant bell.

The technical difficulties of this simple piece are quickly overcome. The real challenge of *Des Abends* is in employing the imagination and freedom of the performer, in poetic, smooth phrasing, in subtle contrasts, and in the omnipresent demand for sensitivity.

No. 2: Aufschwung ("Soaring")

A great many technical and musical difficulties are present in this popular piece. It demands good octave, chord, and figure playing in uncomfortable positions, together with lyrical tone and imagination.

Form: Sonata rondo

		MEASURES
A		1 - 16
B		16 - 40
A		40 - 52
C		53 - 114
A		114 - 122
B		122 - 146
A		146 - 154

The tempo indication *sehr rasch* ("very fast"), coupled with the many fortes and crescendos in the first section may easily mislead the performer. He might play as fast and as loud as possible through the first sixteen measures of the piece and then find he cannot deal adequately with the new section that appears in sixteenth notes. Miscalculating the tempo can have a disastrous effect on the clarity of the dotted rhythm and on the control of tone in general. A tempo of ♩. = 92–100 seems appropriate.

The upbeat to the first measure is an early forewarning of the difficulties involved for small hands. At this point, it is possible to circumvent the problem by using the left hand for the lower notes of the right hand up to the last two eighth notes of measure 1, where the right hand has to take over in order to allow the left to prepare for the entrance of the bass in measure 2. The dotted rhythm of this main motive should be metrically perfect and the slur on it obeyed, while the eighth-note chords have to be short, aggressive staccatos, attracted by the climactic, deep sforzandos at the beginning of measure 2. The left hand fingering for the three Cs of this measure is 5-1-2. At this point, the left hand is again ready to play the low notes of the right-hand part on the upbeat eighth-note chords, though the jump to the octave in the bass is somewhat risky.

At measure 5, the legato melody virtually "takes off" and is kept in the air by the accompaniment figure of the left hand. The last sixteenth note of measure 6 is followed by a grace note at the same pitch, which is to be played ahead of time. A finger change on the same key is necessary:

measure 6

An often-heard mistake consists in holding the first chord of measure 16 for a full measure; this error is the result of misunderstanding the double bar drawn in the middle of the measure, the sole reason for which is the change of key signature. A slight prolongation of the chord is justified, for the first idea ends at this point; but it should not be misleadingly executed. The section beginning at measure 16 is often a victim of stiffness due to the tiring stretched position of the right hand. The strain may be reduced if the thumb can be relaxed while the upper fingers play the figure. The melody is at the top of the figure; yet it should be played without excessive weight on the fifth finger. Notice that the dynamic mark is piano and that there is a soaring crescendo-decrescendo. The tenor (first finger of the left hand) adds some color to the harmony.

At measure 24, the figure appears with different articulation, without the melody line on the top, and with staccatos on the low notes. The second half of the phrase is particularly difficult at measures 26–27 and 30–31. At this point, the melody reappears at the top of the figure, but its doubling in the tenor (top part of left hand) does not have the same rhythm. The correct, smooth execution of these measures is difficult.

The initial phrase of section B is restated, after a ritardando, at measure 32. The left hand has an additional difficulty with the leaping basses. The use of the fifth finger should be restricted here exclusively to the low bass note. The fingering is:

measures 32-34

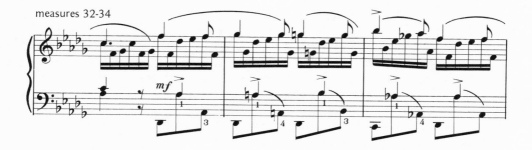

The phrase is now played mezzo forte; therefore the danger of stiffness or tiredness is even greater. The two-handed solution for the recapitulation of the main subject may be used in measures 40–41, but the left hand is, practically speaking, no help in measure 43 because the quick jumping down and up can seriously upset the rhythm. Still this is the only way out for small hands. From measure 45 on, the subject appears in B flat minor, and the left hand adds some commentary in canon to the phrase, thus further complicating the rhythmic difficulties—especially in measures 46 and 48, where the right-hand sforzando on the second eighth note coincides with the dot of the dotted rhythm of the left. The articulation is also very difficult at this point: the right hand plays the first eighth note of the measure staccato and the second tenuto with the syncopating sforzando, while the left hand slurs through the dotted rhythm. Another difficulty of measure 48 is the interval of a tenth involved in the left-hand chord. The right hand cannot pay the left hand back for the services it has so generously provided in the course of the piece. For small hands, the only solution is a swift arpeggio. The flying motive, this time in octaves (measures 49–52), has even more impetus.

The middle episode has a calmer character. The choralelike melody floats over the eighth-note accompaniment figure borrowed from the flying motive. Gentle accents in the course of the phrase (in measure 54 in the right hand and in measure 55 in the left hand) are slurred over to the next measure and are in fact syncopations. Despite the sharp dotting in measure 59, the calm that has prevailed during the whole phrase should be preserved.

From measure 61 on, the low voice of the right hand is uncomfortable to finger. Although the piano is difficult to maintain, it has to be kept throughout the passage. The difficulty is increased from measure 65 on, with more motion in the melody and position changes in the left hand. The phrase dissolves into two arpeggios (measures 67–68 and 69–70) that arise like meaningful questions. The rising octave step is to be played in an especially sensitive way. Measure 70 slows down and gives way to a new, scherzando idea in measure 71. The motive begins with a moderate sforzando. The grace-note ornament should be played ahead of time, like a tremble: it introduces the comic staccatos over the pedal point of the left hand.

Finally the staccatos lead to another meaningful question in measure 73, with the same rising octave step heard on previous occasions. The phrase is repeated, modulating chromatically. This section is the freest part of the piece and needs an imaginative performance. The moderate sforzando note at the beginning of the phrase should be prolonged and the tempo picked up only reluctantly. The staccato notes lead (with a small acceleration of the tempo) to the expressive octave step, where the tempo becomes slower again.

A more important rallentando from measure 83 onward prepares the return of the B subject at measure 85. After this the most interesting part of the piece is reached with the transition section, measures 93–114. Over the mysterious scales of the left hand, chords reminiscent of the chorale melody are held for a full measure. The scales should be perfectly even in execution, the fingerings established and well learned. The register of the right-hand chords may remind us of the sound of trombones. The dominant chord of C major appearing in measure 103 has to be played with extreme sensitivity.

From this point on, fragments of the main subject appear over the indefatigable scales, emerging from a gloomy pianissimo into clearer regions until the triumphant entrance of the full main subject occurs. Wider gaps open up between the last and first notes of the scales in the left hand. Despite the gaps, the rhythmic flow of the scales has to be maintained to allow the right hand to play the precise rhythm at measure 111. This section is one of the most effective passages of the piece. The long crescendo brings the fragments of the motive closer at every appearance and increases the feeling of expectation.

At the recapitulation, the difficult octaves prevent the left hand from assisting the right in the task of playing the intervals of the tenth and ninth. Smaller hands have to adopt the following text here:

measures 114-115

The tempo for measure 115 may be slightly slower, underlining the grandiose octaves of the left hand doubling the melody. Aside from the different key used for the B section, there is no change in the recapitulation before the surprise ending, where for the first time the motive concludes (with the piece) strikingly and almost as a surprise in the key of F minor.

Aufschwung is one of many works contradicting the generally accepted idea that Schumann's compositions are technically easier than those of Liszt and Chopin. As a matter of fact, this piece may appear easier at first glance, but the insistence of Schumann on certain types of technical difficulty quickly convinces the performer of the contrary. Here the length of the B section seriously taxes the endurance of the performer. Smaller hands have problems keeping the playing mechanism supple throughout the piece. Besides technique there are also musical difficulties, such as handling the scherzando section imaginatively and maintaining a sense of proportion in the transition section. *Aufschwung* is an exhilarating virtuoso piece that is most effective in qualified hands.

No. 3: Warum? ("Why?")

Subtle nuances in the rendering of the voices, as well as a good sense of rubato, are needed throughout for the performance of this refined piece.

Form: Lied

	MEASURES
A	1 – 16
B	17 – 30
Variation on A	31 – 42

The regular four-measure-long questions are reduced only once to two measures (measures 29–30) in the course of the piece.

The melody floats over a syncopated accompaniment, leaving the ends of the four-measure periods open in expectation of an answer that never comes. The dotted rhythm on the second beat of each question is a typical feature of the subject. It should not be nervously overdotted, and it should have the flow of the human voice. The second question, beginning in the alto (low part of the right hand) in measure 5, lasts four measures like the other questions; the soprano (top part of the right hand) in measures 7 and 8, though only a countermelody, draws attention away from it almost completely. It does so even more at measures 11 and 12.

In measure 7, the dotted rhythm should not be upset by the grace note on the same pitch. Its execution is as follows:

measures 7-8

In measure 10, the two grace notes are to be played ahead of time as well, in a soft, melismatic manner. The tempo slows down in measure 12 to emphasize the harmonic subtlety and to allow the left hand to play the arpeggiolike grace notes of measure 13 ahead of time, in such a way that the main note falls on the downbeat together with the right-hand octave. The arpeggio should sound ethereal, like a softly broken chord on the harp. The grace note of the right hand coincides with the last grace note of the left.

measures 12-13

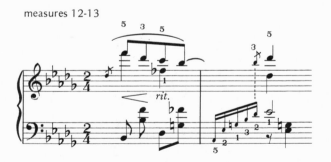

When the initial question appears at this point, it almost has the calm of a submissive answer.

At the double bar, the alto and bass share the questions in dialogue. For measures 19–20 and 23–24, the right hand can cross over the left to play the bass part from the second beat on. It is just as appropriate to handle the bass line with the left hand: in this case, the right hand plays the top part written in the bass clef, of course. The two syncopated chords of measures 20 and 24 have to be played very meaningfully. The volume increases to the forte in measure 23 as the questions become more and more pressing, and the character of the music becomes frankly passionate. The many grace notes are to be handled as it was suggested they be handled in measure 7—almost completely melted into the line, in the manner of a melisma. Notice the difference between the last chords (which are often misread) in measures 26 and 28.

In measure 30, a large ritardando not only allows a smooth execution of the arpeggiolike grace notes but also helps in regaining the initial meditative tone after the passionate section. At measure 33, the imitative entrance of the alto is to be played in the most expressive manner. In particular, the harmonic implications of the C flat on the first beat of measure 34 have to be shown. The character of the music is more and more submissive as the end is approached. The syncopations of measures 41 and 42 are like heartthrobs after strong emotion. The repeat marks have to be obeyed, and the final conclusion should be played with an extensive rallentando.

Sensitivity is an absolute must for the performance of this delicate miniature. Besides refined tone colors, it needs a good sense for rubato and for drama in the emotionally pressing questions. The performer should be reminded, however, that *Warum?* can be ruined by too-violent emotion just as well as by inexpressive playing. Simplicity of expression alone will guide the performer to a balanced performance.

No. 4: Grillen ("Whims")

Good chord playing and, consequently, large hands are required for the performance of this capricious, funny piece—a real whirlwind of ideas and good humor.

Form: Sonata rondo

	MEASURES
A	1 – 16
B	16 – 44
A	44 – 60
C	60 – 96
A	96 – 112
B	112 – 140
A	140 – 156

The upbeat to the first measure already displays humor, if the downbeat is slightly delayed. Despite the shortness of the staccato chords, their top line should constitute an easy-to-follow melody for the listener. The line should grow in volume toward the important sforzandos in measure 3, which should be humorously delayed, and the last beat of the measure should have a slightly smaller accent in the lower voices of the right hand. From this point, the melody has more line, and the accents on the second beats of measures 5 and 6 are strong enough to make the subsequent downbeats seem light. Then, in measure 7, a capricious jump of the staccato chords leads to the conclusion of the phrase (measure 8) one octave higher.

The second appearance of the subject has larger chords, occasioning problems of clarity in the middle voices. The following fingering should be solidly established and learned:

measures 8-11

Measure 15 seems to cause insuperable problems for some pianists, with its fast succession of three chords (not two chords, a fact that is often overlooked). A full understanding that the middle voices of the chords remain unchanged throughout the difficult succession is of main importance in the chords' execution: only the extremities of the chords move, in octaves. One slight swing of the forearm for the three successive chords and a loose wrist give the only assurance of successful execution; in addition to giving the passage the correct speed, this motion will allow every chord to be played fully, without missing notes.

The eighth notes appearing on the second beat of the measure from measure 17 on in either hand shed humor on the entire phrase. They should be played fairly short, almost staccato. The grace notes of the left hand complete the harmony and make up intervals with their respective main notes. It is difficult to keep the eighth-note motive on the second beat at an accompaniment level with the appearance of a new, waltzlike idea from measure 25 on. A heavy fall of the hands on the second beat has to be avoided, and the melody should be played in the foreground, with slight accents on the third beats slurred to the lighter downbeats. A more reflective mood is reached at measure 33 with the imitation of the octave step between the two voices of the right hand. A slight ritardando lasting into measure 36 is in order; then, at the double bar, good humor takes over again as the initial subject of part B jumps in, ornamented by the quick grace note of measure 36.

The middle episode (measure 60) strikes up a calmer, more ponderous mood, in a tone color reminiscent of the brass choir. The melody should stand out without exaggeration, while the bass, moving with elegance, should be brought out on a lower level of importance. The accents on the third beat from measure 66 on occasion a change of the time signature at measure 68. The rest on the first beat of measure 69 should be impeccably correct in length in order to regain the feel of the returning 3/4 time signature. An important crescendo goes along with this rhythmic fancy, raising the volume to fortissimo at the phrase ending.

The second half of the C section begins piano (measure 72). The expressive portamento that appears in measures 74–75 has to be played with a relaxed wrist. From measure 76 on, the performer has to observe the slurs between the dominant chords and their subsequent resolutions. This is particularly difficult here because the grace notes can make the resolutions too heavy, thus robbing the slur relation of its natural dynamics from heavy to light. Besides being light, the resolutions should be short and lend prickling humor to the phrase. By a sudden caprice, measures 78–80 introduce a longer motive that disappears, pianissimo, in a puckish manner. The restatement of subject C at measure 80 suggests the sound of the woodwinds, while the full orchestra gives the answer at measure 84.

The grace notes in measure 87 are to be played as a slowly rolled chord; their execution should fill out the length of the last beat of the measure in ritardando. The suggested fingering for measure 87 is: 5–2–1–3–2| ① . The pedal should prolong the grace notes for the full length of the ensuing fermata. This stop suggests an outburst of emotion, a sort of outcry of longing for love.

After the fermata, the initial humorous mood returns with the comical slurs and prickling staccatos. The second ending of section C (measure 96b) contains one note on its second beat that does not belong to the ending of section C (which is no longer in G-flat major) but does not belong to subject A either, because this subject has only one upbeat. From this point on, the recapitulation of sections A and B does not show any difference from the first exposition, except for the key of the B section. The last two measures (measures 155–156) should be played with a considerable easing of the tempo to underline the ending.

Beyond the main technical difficulty of well-balanced chord playing, and sometimes of chords in quick succession, the performer has to demonstrate his ability to detect and elucidate the many different ideas and moods that show up in even quicker succession than the chords in the course of this piece. Every single detail needs attention in order to do justice to the variety of the humor. An imaginative performance is greatly dependent upon the colorfulness of the touch.

Frédéric Chopin

Born 1810, Zelazowa Wola; died 1849, Paris

The music of Chopin is among the most original and personal body of works, not only in the Romantic period, but in the whole of music history. He did not use any of the existing forms (with the exception of the impromptu, the concerto, and the sonata) for the form's sake, but rather found original forms for his miraculous melodic and harmonic inventions. He composed—with few exceptions—exclusively for the piano: two concertos, three sonatas, four scherzos, four ballades, four impromptus, polonaises, waltzes, mazurkas, preludes, études, a barcarolle, a berceuse, and a fantasia.

What makes Chopin one of the most popular of composers is his long melodic lines, which are easy to recognize and to follow. However a long melody does not lead naturally to a "development," and Chopin has often been criticized for his lack of developments. His music also abounds in improvisatory elements that influence the musical forms he adopts.

Chopin was the great inventor of the modern piano technique. At the first lesson, his students had to become familiar with a new hand position: the hand was put on the keyboard and turned slightly outward, with the fingers on the keys of E, F sharp, G sharp, A sharp, and B. In comparison with the usual exercises on white keys in C major, this was a revolutionary approach to piano playing. It also had important further consequences. While the white-key approach makes the third finger the pivoting center of the hand, Chopin's approach gives this role to the second finger. Most of his figurations (even including the chords, which are more "full" at the top most of the time) are patterned after this hand position. This hand position also leads to large, arpeggiated chords, to legato octaves alternating the third, fourth, and fifth fingers, and to the passing of the third or fourth finger over the fifth finger, as is done in the Etude, Op. 10, No. 2. Particularly for the left hand, this new position resulted in wide, extended Alberti basses.

But Chopin's new ideas did not stop at the level of the hand. In disagreement with most of his contemporaries, he also required a relaxed forearm and upper arm.

Still the essential difference between his ideas and the innumerable "new" piano methods of his time lies in the fact that Chopin's ideas were not self-serving. They were not invented for the technique's sake. Their only purpose was to provide the means for beautiful tone.

Besides the relaxed playing mechanism, the music of Chopin by its very nature requires a great deal of freedom and artistic imagination. *Rubato* is the name of the rhythmic freedom almost constantly used in the performance of Chopin. It means that certain important notes in the measure can be extended beyond their true value on the condition that the other notes in the measure give up a small fraction of their value in order that the total length of the measure may remain unchanged. It is a refined and complicated process that calls for musicianship and especially for good taste in determining the proportions of the "give and take." Most of the major offenses against Chopin works come from the use of the rubato as a pretext for all sorts of extravagances.

The traditions of interpreting Chopin were not set during his lifetime, partly because his students (who were generally of mediocre talent) were unable to transmit them to the next generation. However, if one were to condense the likes and dislikes of Chopin, it would be safe to say that Chopin hated excesses or sentimentality and liked a well-controlled, balanced performance.

CHOPIN
Etude in F Minor, Op. 25, No. 2

~~~~~~

This étude, which is not technically difficult for anyone trained on Cramer or Clementi, constitutes an excellent introduction to the Chopin études. It needs a light, precise, and even *jeu perlé* touch (i.e., without raising the fingers high above the keys) in the right hand and a flexible wrist for the left hand.

Form: Three parts and coda

	MEASURES
A	1 – 34
B	35 – 50
A	51 – 66
Coda	66 – 69

The fingering plays an unusual role in the learning process for this étude. Most of the figures are repetitive and often confusing. Their fluency depends largely on a well-established and solidly memorized fingering. What fingerings should actually be adopted can be debated, but the final decisions will be determined by the hand of the performer.

The fingering suggested for the first two measures varies widely from edition to edition. The fingering on the bottom line may be uncomfortable for narrow hands; yet this simple fingering secures a kind of natural approach. A more sophisticated fingering for the same measures is given on the top line:

measures 1-2

Between measures 4 and 5, the left hand has a wide jump, introducing the second difficulty of the étude—synchronization of the hands. Here the left hand needs more than the allowed time to reach the lower bass note, and it generally arrives late, thus confusing the right hand. A similar inaccuracy could have happened earlier in the performance, but there it would have been less important, and the performer might not even notice it. The right hand never has a leap at the bar line, and consequently it can reach the downbeat of the next measure without delay. The performer has to deal with the gaps in the left hand constantly by flying over large distances very quickly, in order to be in time. A laterally flexible wrist will be of great help in doing so.

The performance of the diminished-seventh arpeggio of measure 7 is often jerky if the player keeps all of the four fingers needed to play the arpeggio stiffly in position. Measure 11 perfectly illustrates the preliminary remark on how the fingering can be of help in learning the different turns. In measure 3, the third finger was used on the E natural; in measure 11, the E flat is to be played with the second finger. The use of one finger instead of the other should switch the performance onto the right track. The fingering of measure 11 also offers several possibilities:

measure 11

The augmented sixth degree in the left hand has a sorrowful accent in measures 16–17 (this is also true of measures 35–36 and 39–40). After an unchanged restatement of the A section (measures 20–34), a new technical difficulty appears with the B section at measure 35. It is impossible to avoid the use of the outer fingers in such measures as 38 and 42: the performer has to keep his forearm from rotating to "help" the fifth finger. These figures have to be played using only a small, even finger articulation.

measures 37-38

measures 41-42

A *forte* should be reached in measure 43—the only *forte* in the étude. It is the result of a crescendo that began in measure 36 and imparted some passion to the frequent modulations of the middle section. The forte vanishes quickly: measure 45 is already piano. The two measures preceding the recapitulation (measures 49 and 50) can have a considerable easing of the tempo.

The reappearing A section shows some differences from its previous versions. One is the portamento touch in measure 57, which has a ravishing effect if the tempo is slightly eased. The new turn of measure 62 is to be learned solidly. The arpeggio of measure 63 is to be fingered the following way:

measure 63

The section ends on the first triplet of measure 66. A little time is to be taken for ending the phrase here. The coda begins on the top C and dies away with a ritardando. The execution of the grace notes on the last beat of measure 67 is as follows:

measure 67

If this étude does not seem challenging at first to the technically well-prepared performer, very soon its real challenge will appear—the inseparable connection between technical and musical difficulties. The usual noisy finger articulation or any other athletic approach will not do justice to this piece. The performance should be ethereal and light; the main goal is effortlessness. This is the essential meaning of the molto legato indication appearing in the first measure.

The original pedal indications by Chopin unfortunately cannot be followed on our more sonorous instrument. One pedal for a full measure is more than the ear can take. Two pedal changes per measure will allow the design of the right hand's pattern to emerge clearly. Even more frequent pedaling is needed in measures 16–17, 35–36, and 39–40, where the pedal should be changed on the last quarter-note triplet of the left hand in each measure in order to make the dominant harmony clear. The dynamics prescribed by Chopin are to be followed rigorously: there is only one forte in the étude.

CHOPIN

Etude in F Minor, Op. 10, No. 9

Extension and looseness of the wrist in the left hand and singing tone and poetic expression in the right hand are the principal goals of this étude, which is also a study in subtle differences in expression applied to the same motive.

Form: Three parts

	MEASURES
A	1 - 16
B	17 - 36
A	37 - 64
Coda	65 - 67

The first concern of the player should be to render this piece with ease in the left hand. The fingering indicated by Chopin (fourth finger on the C) was probably intended to make each C light by using the weakest finger on it. Unfortunately this fingering puts too much strain on even the largest hand. It is advisable to use the third finger following the fifth, like this:

measure 1

Here one has to use the typical hand position of Chopin: four fingers of the left hand pointing left and the thumb pointing right. The third finger will be used as a pivot in this position, and the fifth and first fingers will be brought into position by lateral motions of the wrist. The first exercise for this follows (the third finger depresses the key without sound):

The legatissimo indication in the first measure undoubtedly belongs to the left hand and means the exclusion of finger articulation. Normal-size hands usually overcome the difficulty fairly quickly and become able to produce a soft, refined and even-sounding accompaniment.

Once this goal is achieved, full attention has to be given to the right hand. The touch is portamento, the tone expressive, and the shaping of the phrase poetic. A loose wrist is the requirement for a good portamento touch. In the first eight measures of the subject, crescendos and "con forza" indicate a passionate interpretation and this mood is further enhanced by the sforzandos in measures 4 and 8. Measure 8 has the typical motive , which appears several times during the piece and needs different expression at every single appearance. This time the expression is that of an interrogation governed by the ritardando.

The next eight measures (9–16) should be in a contrasting sotto voce; only small, coloring crescendos should be used, and even the sforzandos (measures 12 and 16) are weakened.

In the middle part, the tone rises to a more intense declamation, and the expression is more pathetic than lyric. The crescendo and stretto (measures 25–28) end with the typical motive ♭♭♭, which this time sounds like a dramatic exclamation. The left-hand fingering changes; in certain positions, the second finger takes over the role of the third, as it does in measures 20 and 22 (first group of sixteenth notes):

measure 20

The four measures 25 through 28 need special care in the left hand. The fingering should be the one just suggested. The accurate placing of the fifth finger has to be worked out well so as to allow a clear rendering of the harmonic progression. Measure 25 is especially difficult where the fifth finger moves from a white key to a black one.

The following section (measures 29–36) is a study in contrasting expressions applied to the same motive. The forte measures have indications like "stretto" and "appassionato" also; the pianissimo measures should be in a contrasting, pensive mood. Insufficient independence of the hands can easily mar measures 33–36. Instead of attempting a mathematical division of the group of five, the player has to bring an expressive freedom to it. The left hand has to be practiced alone at first, while the player imagines or sings the right-hand notes or just taps the right-hand rhythm. Notice that in measures 33 and 34 the group of five has an inherent crescendo toward the middle of the measure, while in measures 35 and 36 the group has a diminuendo that has a calming effect on the phrase.

The recapitulation completes the main subject with nervous little ornaments, to be played lightly and on the beat, filling out the eighth note with an even triplet:

measure 38

At measure 45, octaves appear in the subject, thus adding to the intensity of the theme's soaring toward the climax at measure 56. The left hand is particularly difficult in measure 50 because of the distance between the fifth and third fingers. This gap obliges the performer to shift his hand without raising it, quickly and on the surface of the keys.

In measure 52, the interval is enlarged to a tenth. Usually even if the sound is under good control up to here, it suddenly gets clumsy because of the unbearable stretching of the hand. In order to insure the continuous elegance and ease of the sound, dividing this figure between the hands is recommended, as follows:

measure 52

This solution will also allow the final crescendo and accelerando to be begun without stiffness or fatigue.

The typical motive appears in its most dramatic form at measure 56. The half note was to be held for its full value, and time must be taken before the piano entrance at the end of the measure. The next four measures (measures 57–60) have the most subtle contrasts in expression: the dynamics vary only between piano and pianissimo. The following four measures bring the forte-piano contrast back and even push it to the extreme—fortissimo-pianissimo coupled with a ritenuto. Notice the new rhythmic outlook of the groups of five. The inherent crescendo or decrescendo remains the same. In measure 64, the autograph includes a grace note that is not reproduced in some editions:

measure 64

The silvery coda is in hemiola—3/4 for both hands. The basic pulse should remain the same, with a rallentando to the conclusion. If the leggierissimo and smorzando are well played, they can lend to these almost impressionistic measures a beautiful effect.

Pedaling is necessary throughout the étude, with changes every time the left-hand fifth finger is used. These changes are recommended even when the harmony does not change (for example, in measure 20) to keep the notes from unnecessarily blurring. The pedaling of measures 27 and 28 is also changed on the fifth finger, even though it appears in cross rhythm. The coda (measures 65–67) should be kept within one pedal and changed on the last note.

Opus 10, No. 9 is the perfect example of what an étude can become in the hands of such a composer as Chopin. The technical difficulty is hidden under a poetic content. A performance that sounds like an étude would be completely out of place here. The ideal interpretation lies closer to dramatic poetry or a ballade; the piece has to be approached in the most personal way, and the performer should be guided by sensitivity to the quality of sound, to freedom of tempo, and to contrasting expression. This goal can be achieved only if the technical element—here the accompanying figure of the left hand, in particular—is under control throughout and constantly serves the shaping of the phrases in the right hand.

CHOPIN

Etude, Op. 10, No. 12

The difficulty of this étude is generally described in a one-sided manner: most of the comments are limited to the left hand's problems and completely overlook the great difficulty of the right hand. In fact, everything is difficult here—the almost-continuous sixteenth-note motion of the left hand, with its sudden leaps and unusual fingerings, and the passion, declamation, and rhythmic freedom of the right hand.

The nickname of this piece, "Revolutionary Étude," refers to the revolution in Warsaw in 1831. It could also refer to the revolutionary treatment of the étude as such: the most useful technical study, in Chopin's hands, becomes a most impetuous and dramatic piece of music.

Form: Three parts

	MEASURES
Introduction	1 – 8
A	9 – 28
B	29 – 41
Introduction and A	41 – 84

The left-hand figure (in measures 1–6) is uncomfortable if the lateral motion of the second finger is not helped by a slight outward pulling of the hand. This pulling will facilitate the required accents on the second finger. Chopin indicates legatissimo here, meaning that excessive finger articulation should be avoided. In measures 7 and 8, the large gaps in the figure have to be emphasized and the notes grouped accordingly:

measures 7-8

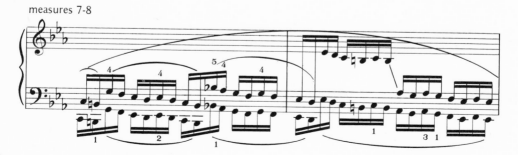

189

The passionate and noble interpretation of the right hand throughout the étude
depends mainly on the quality of the sound and on the impetuosity of the rhythm.
This is well illustrated in the second and fourth measures, where the nervous precision
of the rhythm should not be altered to accommodate the difficult jump. The sixteenth-
note octave and the following half-note chord should be conceived of as one swinging
motion of the forearm. The dot after the first chord has to be considered a rest that
allows the hand to be lifted slightly in preparation for the swinging motion.

At measure 9 in the left-hand arpeggio figure, it is of the utmost importance that
the top E flat in the middle of the measure is played with the second finger:

measure 9

If the player inadvertently uses 4–3, he brings his hand into a disadvantageous position. The wrist, which is in a normal position at the beginning of the measure, is
gradually raised higher for the highest note in the middle of the measure, and then
moves back to its initial position along with the descending figure.

In measure 10, once more the nervous precision of the dotted rhythm has to be
observed, while the difference between the forte and the piano should only be slight.

The left hand has a very difficult figure in measures 15 and 16: the range of the
figure makes for frequent use of the thumb, and there is a consequent danger of
extreme heaviness. The chromaticism in the fifth-finger line has to be displayed and
the middle of the measures well punctuated. The right hand increases the passion in
these measures; the nervous rhythm needs even more care here.

There is a very difficult chromatic run for the left hand in measure 17. The main
problem lies in the fingering: it is impossible to maintain the regular pattern established easily on the second beat of measure 17, and the irregularity has to be mastered
perfectly to allow fluency:

measures 17-18

Measure 25 contains severe difficulties for the left hand in the form of wide distances between certain notes. The solution is a loose wrist, moving laterally and bringing the fingers into the right position to perform their job. To keep the stretch in the hand is harmful: when the fifth finger plays, the thumb is almost under the hand; when the thumb plays, the fifth finger moves far away from the key where it was used. A good preliminary exercise for this passage consists of holding the third finger on the B flat and playing just the notes to be played by the fifth finger and the thumb, bringing these two fingers into position by a decisive lateral motion of the wrist (see example 169).

In measure 27, certain editions show a dotted figure that is probably in conformity with Chopin's intention:

measure 27

In measure 29, a new difficulty consisting of quick jumps between successive sixteenth notes involving distances of two octaves or more arises in the left hand. Meanwhile the right hand is presented with a longer line. The mood and dynamics become somewhat subdued to allow a crescendo in measures 34–36 that reaches *tutte le forze* in measure 37. The jumps in the left hand can be made somewhat easier if the hand is turned slightly outward and the thumb is stretched out before jumping, as if reaching for the note. The other difficulty of the passage is in measures 29 and 31, where the fifth finger has to be used frequently in the same hand position, regardless of whether it is to be used on a black or a white key. Special care has to be taken with these eight measures, probably the most difficult and tiring of the whole étude.

In measures 35 and 36, the left hand alone has to achieve a tremendous crescendo to reach the climax of the piece. A slight easing of the tempo in these two measures will facilitate the fulfillment of the crescendo. At the climax (measure 37), the right hand assists the left in achieving the fortissimo; in fact, from this measure on through the succeeding four measures, the left hand may ease the sound.

In measure 40, the use of the fifth finger (rather than the fourth) on the A flat is probably best:

measure 40

Especially difficult is the chord at the beginning of measure 45, even for a large hand. The only possible fingering is:

measure 45

The hand should be turned outward.

The recapitulation of the main subject (measures 50–64) increases the pathetic-declamatory character of the right hand with an almost free, speaking rhythm. Independence of the two hands has to be the main preoccupation of the player here. In particular, the fourth beats of the measures have to be treated freely to allow the articulation of the pathetic declamation in the right hand's dotted triplets. At first the left hand has to be played alone and the right-hand notes only played mentally. When the relative evenness of the left hand is no longer disturbed by the imaginary melodic line, one can add the right hand.

At measure 65, a new climax is reached. The performance of measure 66 is often marred by the left hand because most editions indicate an impossible fingering for the passage. The recommended fingering is:

measure 66

Sliding the thumb here is easy and puts the hand into the right position to finish the rest of the F minor scale.

The pace of the étude slows down from measure 69 on, as though exhausted by the continuous excitement. Measures 73 and 74 again contain another difficult chromatic run where the fingering pattern keeps changing.

measures 73-76

The tempo slows down in measure 80, and this slowing down is followed by a sudden explosion of fortissimo with the a tempo on the downbeat of measure 81 (some editions indicate the fortissimo and the a tempo starting only on the sixteenth-note figure of the measure). The unison sixteenth-note figure is to be played very violently; the two closing quarter-note chords should be dry (without pedal) and very short, but still well balanced in tone.

This piece is one of the most Beethovenian in character among Chopin's works. It requires vehement, passionate delivery. To achieve this goal, the player has to have total mastery of every single technical difficulty. This advice should be applied to any work, of course; but it is probably more appropriate in regard to such popular pieces as the *Revolutionary Etude.* Patient, humble practice and an acceptance of the indications of Chopin, whether dynamic or expressive, can restore grandeur and nobility to a piece much abused in performance.

CHOPIN
Impromptu No. 1 in A Flat, Op. 29

~~~~~~

The impromptu, as established by Schubert, has a large, three-part form. Usually the main parts have fast figurations, while the contrasting middle section shows a contrasting mood with a singing melody. The difference between the impromptu and other three-part forms lies in the highly improvisatory character of the impromptu. This definition puts it close to the fantasy. The material used is generally simple and unpretentious; consequently it requires a simple, straightforward handling.

Form: Ternary

	MEASURES
A	1 – 34
A$_1$	1 – 8
A$_2$	8 – 18
A$_3$	19 – 30
Close	30 – 34
B	35 – 82
B$_1$	35 – 50
B$_2$	51 – 82
A	83 – 119
Coda	119 – 127

Besides the elegance and ease of the *jeu perlé* for the right hand, the main technical problem of this impromptu lies in maintaining smoothness and flexibility in the left hand, for which some preliminary practice is needed. Use the third finger as a pivot on an E flat and reach for the low and high notes by twisting the wrist laterally. Neither the fifth finger nor the thumb should be kept stretched out. Mere finger articulation without flexibility of the wrist will not bring results. In some measures, such as measures 7 and 8, the bass note lies quite far away from the center of activity of the left hand. The player has to reach these notes without wasting time—for the right hand cannot wait—and without a heavy bump. The jump, reduced to the minimum by twisting the wrist, has to be horizontal more than vertical.

The right hand's elegance will be insured through the use of a light hand and the avoidance of excessive finger articulation. In particular, a heavy thumb should be avoided in passages where the ensuing note lies far away—for example, on the third beat of measures 1, 2, and 7. The piece opens with a mordent, which should be smooth and clearly played, but still fast enough to take the time of only one triplet. The two fingerings possible here (1–3–2 or 2–3–2) have their vices and virtues. Unquestionably the fingering 1–3–2 is faster; however it exposes one to the danger of jamming the mordent and producing the loud noise of an alarm clock. The other fingering, 2–3–2, is definitely smoother but can lack in clarity and also carries the danger of tensing up the hand. Rhythmically the execution should sound like this:

measure 1

To maintain the elegance of the melody, heaviness on the quarter notes in measures 1 and 2, as well as later, in measures 9 through 12, should be avoided.

Lyricism should not be forgotten when the grace notes of measures 10 and 12 are played. In this section, the bass note is held like a pedal, without involving any accent or obtrusive harshness. It is easy to rush the tempo in measures 13 and 14, where the melody has a particular chattering character and points ahead to the coda.

In measures 15 through 18, the right hand joins the left in holding the first notes of each group. Accents appear on the quarter notes, but accenting should not be overdone because the line is of utmost importance. In measure 18, a small rallentando is recommended, followed by a tempo in the next measure. The new section A is modulating and shows some complications later. The modulations begin in measure 20, where the second half of the measure is to be played very meaningfully to underline the new harmony. In measure 21, the bass notes lie far away from the rest of the notes and also have small accents on them. No extra time can be taken here by the left hand, for it would greatly impinge on the regular speed of the right hand. Also the crescendo that leads to the climax in measures 23 and 24 starts here. The melody is carried by the notes marked with accents, in cross rhythm. The tone should be singing fully here; even the tempo gives in (poco ritenuto in measure 24) and then picks up again (accelerando in measure 25) at the moment when the harmony comes to a standstill.

The small, repeated turns of measures 27 and 28 remind one of a top spinning around; then the top slows down and falls over before the charming short fermata of measure 30. Notice the quarter-note holds that appear from measure 29 on. The right hand is fairly difficult in measure 31 and the following measures. The hand should be perfectly relaxed and weightless. The forte in measure 34 should appear like an explosion, without preparation. The scale passage is uncomfortable because one note of the scale is missing. The player often compensates for the missing note by pressing heavily on the keys.

The two last quarter notes of measure 34 lead to the sostenuto, where a singing legato is the main requirement. Typical features of the line are the phrasing and the accents at measures 38 and 40, which should be played without exaggeration and with good taste. Also the dotted rhythm in measures 37 and 39 should be part of the melodic line, without being overdotted. Some editions indicate wedges on the bass notes almost throughout, instead of the more realistic staccato points. Whichever markings appear in your music, they mean a slight accentuation rather than excessive shortness. The singing, calm character of measures 35–50 is nevertheless disturbed by a sort of panting in the left hand, expressed by the rest at the beginning of every other measure.

A calmer, more nocturnelike mood establishes dominance only at measure 51. There are two gruppettos, or fiorituras, in these first sixteen measures. The gruppetto in measure 45 is in the best vocal tradition and is to be played:

measure 45

The fioritura in measure 48 is introduced by an important ritenuto (measures 46–47), underlining the modulation. The fioritura itself has to be played delicatissimo, without undue rushing. Time has to be taken on the last two quarter notes of the measure, with the last bass note falling together with the top B of the fioritura:

measure 48

The left hand needs attention in measures 49–50 for correct part playing. The middle voice has to be held.

The main feature of the ensuing section is the repetition of the initial statement in a different form with different expression (see measures 51–52 and 53–54, 59–60 and 61–62, and so on). The echo effect is the key to the performance of the first two occurrences, and there should be a great deal of the fantasia element in the repeat. In performance, the singing tone should be even more sustained in this part than before. The grouping for measure 61 is:

measure 61

The passion rises at this point: contrary motion makes the gap between the soprano and bass bigger, and the climax is reached in measure 64, where an audible rest on the second beat of the measure in the right hand is essential. Beware of rushing the measures containing trills. Players with an insufficient sense of timing often abridge trills because they cannot control the duration of the fast, unmeasured motion of the fingers.

From measure 66 on, the previously mentioned echo effect between the two statements of the first phrase disappears; rather, the tendency is toward crescendo. The fantasia elements remain, however. The grouping for measure 71 is:

measure 71

The ensuing "con forza" does not mean as loud as you can play; rather, it wipes out the preceding dolcissimo and refers to a declamatory sound. The trill in measure 75 is the shortest form of a trill—a mordent.

Measure 81 often receives a rough, fast treatment, and consequently it does not last nearly as long as it should. This measure contains only two more notes than measure 71. The difference lies in the sixteenths' notation, which should not induce the player into using excessive speed. The trills of the ensuing measures all begin on the main note and have to be given their full length, taking the ritardando into account. The recapitulation of the opening section does not show any alteration until measure 115 where the coda begins. It is made up of a chord sequence and the previously heard "chattering" subject. The chords have to sound unaffected, simple, and almost as if they have no melodic importance. In measure 119, a difficult broken chord, which should be played with ease and elegance, appears. From measure 121 on, instead of counting the rest, mentally playing the missing chords like an echo gives a much surer result. This way the calando (slowing down) will appear more natural. The piece vanishes rather than ends.

This impromptu is a light, captivating piece that requires fluent, even, well-controlled finger technique in the fast parts and good, singing legato in the middle part. Besides the technical requirements, there is a need for a fine artistic imagination that enhances the natural charm of the piece.

CHOPIN

Nocturne in F Sharp Major, Op. 15, No. 2

~~~~~~

Chopin's nocturnes are among the most important contributions Chopin made to Romantic music. He took the name, and also partly the form, from John Field. *Nocturne,* meaning "night piece," suggests feelings associated with nighttime experiences—beautiful dreams, frightening nightmares, tender serenades, and terrible storms. The form Chopin adopted for his nocturnes is usually A–B–A, with the middle section in a contrasting tempo and mood. The first and last sections of this particular nocturne are in the *bel canto* style; the melodic line is richly ornamented with fiorituras and runs. The agitated middle section blows up a passionate storm.

Form: Ternary

	MEASURES
A	1 – 24
B	25 – 48
A	48 – 58
Coda	58 – 62

It is evident that a good, singing legato is the most important requirement for the performance of the first and last sections of this nocturne. The sostenuto indication in the first measure also applies to the sound, which should be rich and well focused. Another important preliminary observation can be made about the synchronization of the hands throughout the nocturne. A very unfortunate but widespread practice is that of playing the bass notes, especially those on the beat, always slightly ahead of the right-hand notes. Such playing imprints a questionable musical taste on the performance and remains unacceptable.

The rhythm of the upbeat to the first measure should be filled with nobility. The thirty-second note has to be given its true value without being too short. The two portamento eighth notes in the second half of the first measure are to be played with great elegance and with a slight directional crescendo that prepares for the sforzando downbeat of the second measure; from here a light fioritura completes the first phrase in an elegant gesture. Small hands often get tense while executing this fioritura because their owners would like to play it with fingers prepared ahead on each key—an unnecessary preoccupation, as twisting the wrist sideways will bring the fingers into the right position.

After a second, more flowery version, the phrase begins a semitone higher (measure 4) and reaches the highest and most important note, F sharp, on the second eighth note of measure 6. The following measure has some difficulty in part playing for the left hand; if it is well executed, the succession of the harmonies colored by the overhanging notes together with the pedal point produces a magical effect.

The upbeat to the second half of the subject, at the end of measure 8, may be broken slowly, and generous time may be taken for this. In measure 11, the fioritura should be free and as independent from the left hand as possible. The ideal execution would avoid matching up any precise number of notes in the run to each left-hand note; however the last A sharp of the fioritura should coincide with the last eighth note of the left hand, and there should be a considerable rallentando because only six ornament notes have to be played in the time of one eighth note. If the performer lacks experience or does not command sufficient independence of the hands, he can (to begin with) divide the fioritura into sections by playing six notes against the first left-hand eighth note, nine against the second, nine against the third, and six against the last. If the left-hand notes do not occasion accents in the right hand, one can get by with this solution. In any case, the last eighth-note value of the measure can be conceived of as a rallentando, *senza rigore* (without strictness of tempo). As for the run proper, it should be played without any crescendo or decrescendo, thus insuring the maximum possible fluidity.

There is more warmth to the phrase reaching from measure 12 to the con forza at measure 14. In some performances, the downward arpeggio in thirty-seconds of measure 14 is played "freely," jamming all the notes together after the left hand's last chord. It is difficult to reconcile this pseudotradition with the fact that the thirty-seconds are part of the melody. The trill of measure 15 should be long enough to prepare a strong ending.

The new part of the section beginning with the upbeat to measure 17 needs a brighter, more sustained sound. The dolcissimo fioritura in measure 18 begins sufficiently late after the second chord that it may arrive on the quarter-note A natural simultaneously with the third eighth-note chord. As for the initial E sharp, the performer has to listen to it intently so as to be able to begin the fioritura printed in small notes *on* the same dynamic level as the decayed sound. The same remark applies to measure 20, where the looseness of the phrase is even more emphasized by a poco ritenuto.

From measure 21 on, the passion rises, reaching the con forza in measure 23 and stringendo in measure 24 and then calming down with the repeated A sharps before the doppio movimento. All ruggedness should be avoided in playing the broken chords in the left hand; they should not interfere with the melodic line.

The term *doppio movimento* means that the quarter note is now equal to the previous basic eighth note. The right hand has the intricate task of playing a good melodic line with the top fingers while the other fingers are busy with an accompaniment figure in which the third and fourth notes are held to sustain the harmony. The principal problem of the passage is the stretched hand position, and fatigue is felt quickly if the forearm is stiff. For the first eight measures, the right-hand figure is composed of groups of five notes; this irregular grouping makes the task of the left hand more complicated, since it must bring out the syncopations in such a way that the syncopated chords do not coincide with any note of the group of five. The sound, which should be sotto voce, is hard to produce in the stretched position of the right hand; the passage should be colored with passionate crescendos and decrescendos.

The technical ease necessary for the performance lies in the ability to relax the hand and forearm and in the avoidance of finger articulation in the low part of the figure. These two remarks should be constantly kept in mind. There is no choice of right-hand fingerings in this section; however the following fingering is recommended for measures 28 and 36:

measure 28

From measure 33 on, the groups of five make way for a stronger, more defined meter consisting of a dotted rhythm and a triplet. The dotted sixteenth sounds like more of a rubato prolongation and helps the melody to emerge more clearly than it ever could in the foggier preceding sotto voce part. Also the sound rises in an irresistible crescendo toward the climax of measure 41, passing through an intensely supplicatory motive (D natural, C sharp) that plays an important role in the subsequent diminuendo. It is particularly easy to overplay the bass in this part of the section, especially in measures 39–41. A heavily hammered octave would demolish the melody totally and transform its lyric passion into a shelling by heavy artillery. The fifth finger of the left hand should be used for the octaves only and never again on the chords or intervals. After the climax, the phrase quickly tires out, with the repeated supplication stepping an octave lower at each appearance. A long rest on the fermata will allow the peaceful sound of the beginning to reappear here.

In measure 51, the recapitulation, in shortened form, contains an embellishment figure even longer than its predecessor (measure 11); thus the left hand has to allow sufficient time and has to be elastic and free. The ideal solution is the independence already mentioned with reference to measure 11. If the run has to be divided, it should be into 9, 9, 10, and 12 notes per eighth note, and the last group should have an a piacere type of rallentando.

In measure 54, the con forza has a passionate brilliance. The three subsequent measures (55–57) increase the intensity by reaching into higher regions each time and by prolonging the trill at each occurrence. Measure 57 is to be played almost freely and very expressively, but it should still be without affectation. The slurred B natural between the two last groups of triplets in the soprano has a magical effect. It also slows down the pace of the phrase as needed to point out the final cadence of the piece, leading to the coda.

From here (measure 58) the calm is complete. The triplets are without nervousness: they should be laid out calmly. The correct execution of the left-hand chords in measure 59 can cause big problems for players with stiff arms. The repeated chords should in no way increase the volume and should have the ease of repeated single notes. Clumsiness here is often due to raising the hands too far away from the keys. The best result is obtained when the keys are struck again without letting them come up completely. In measures 60 and 61, a change of pedal on the last eighth note of each measure is necessary in order to make the harmony clear. The last C sharp of the right hand in measure 61 should have the special sound and prolongation of an upbeat to the ending note.

The peaceful calm of this nocturne is usually well rendered; the music has a strong character that is unmistakable for most performers. The real difficulty is in the sudden storm of the middle episode. Only seldom does one hear this section performed with ease and with good control of the sound up to the loudest forte. Even the slightest stiffness may cause deterioration of sound in those most difficult twenty-four measures and should be eliminated by patient practice. This nocturne is sometimes played too fast, probably out of deference to the metronome marking (♩ = 40) prescribed by Chopin. M. M. 40 is the slowest rate marked on the metronome: Chopin could not prescribe anything slower. Accordingly it may be advisable to take the eighth note as the pulse for the opening and closing A sections, at a speed of ♪ = 69–72.

CHOPIN
Waltz in A Flat Major, Op. 34, No. 1

Undoubtedly the most accessible works of Chopin are the waltzes. This popular dance form inspired him many times throughout his lifetime, probably more by its elegance than by the musical possibilities. At any rate, through much finesse in the details, the waltz, music for social dancing, becomes pure art form in Chopin's hands.

Form: Variant of rondo

	MEASURES
Introduction	1 – 16
A	17 – 48
B	49 – 80
C	80 – 144
B	144 – 176
A	176 – 209
B	209 – 245
Coda	245 – 305

This *Valse brillante* needs imaginative handling of the various motives, rhythmic accuracy, flexibility, precise finger technique, and effortless chord technique.

Performers unfamiliar with waltz accompaniments should begin to study the left hand first. The typical figure is a lone bass note (which may sometimes be doubled at the octave) followed by two chords or intervals. In order to secure the utmost accuracy in such figures, the use of the fifth finger should be reserved exclusively for the bass note wherever this is possible.

measures 16-20

The hand position resulting from this fingering will be similar to the "ideal" position of Chopin—the hand turned slightly outward and the fifth finger playing at an angle to rather than parallel with the key. This method of playing will bring the bass note a great deal closer to the upper chord or interval, making only a forearm motion necessary to bridge the distance between the keys.

In some measures, the use of the fifth finger on the upper chord or interval cannot be avoided (see measures 29 and 30); however the same at-an-angle-to-the-key approach has to be reserved for the bass note, to avoid the clumsiness that would result from a full-arm motion. Beware of playing such accompaniment figures exaggeratedly short, especially the bass note. The waltz accompaniment needs rhythmic solidity; its freedom, if any, is dictated by the melodic or harmonic turns.

The introduction starts with a real difficulty—the clear enunciation of the repeated notes. The fingering 1-3-2-1 is the only one able to cope with the difficulty; the first note bounces to allow a quick repetition of the same note. The phrase marking over the notes indicates the length of the phrase more than a legato. The sforzando bass is like a tympani beat, from where the chords spring forth with loose hand and wrist. In the second measure, the right hand should not stay in a stretched position; the downward motion of the hand will bring the fingers into position here, as well as in measures 11–16. Measures 13 through 16 are difficult in regard to the regularity of the run. Turning the hand outward so that the top fingers play at an angle to the keys will facilitate the approach of the fifth finger when it is closing in on the thumb. It is of the utmost importance that the fifth finger be able to play "alone," without the help of a rotation of the hand that will only emphasize the limping more. There is no way to help with the left hand, except in the following way in measure 16:

measure 16

The A subject has more intensity in the first two measures, and the main weight is on the second measure with its subdominant harmony. The period of eight measures is repeated in a more flowery version. The ornaments in measures 25 and 29 are close to triplets: they are on the beat and incorporated into the melodic line. The melody in continuous sixths is to be conceived as a singing, relaxed legato line. From the upbeat to measure 33 (which has to be separated from the preceding phrase ending, the character changes to a more playful and virtuoso one. Passing the thumb efficiently, without a downward motion of the hand, will insure evenness in the figure. The ornaments are always strictly on the beat and may be tighter (that is, faster) than previously.

At measure 39, the fifth finger of the right hand is used on the last G; turning the hand slightly outward facilitates the task of the fourth finger in reaching the A flat above it. The left hand's articulation needs good care throughout in order to bring the expressive slurs out clearly. The repeat is piano, and observing the sixteenth rests will underline the ethereal character.

Repeating the thirty-two measures that include the first subject is necessary to show the proportions of the work. After the double bar, measure 48 brings in the second subject, which is to appear one time more than the main subject. The second subject is the most characteristic subject of the waltz, and its appearance brings general animation every time. It begins with two successive syncopations. The weight remains on the first two measures of the phrase, as the two octave bass notes also demonstrate. After the preceding ethereal passage, the melody recaptures the full attention.

A modulation away from the tonic lends a real feeling of taking off to the phrase—a feeling also well emphasized by the introduction of double octaves and chords in the right hand. The excitement rises to real triumph at measure 61, where the accompaniment chords overflow into a two-measure wave without bass notes. From measure 60 on, the rhythmic preciseness of the melody demands differentiation between the eighth and sixteenth notes, but it should not be exaggerated.

The repeat of the subject includes a difficult, free scale in the right hand. Performances of this scale are often marred by a slow start, in such a way that the performer plays only two notes (G natural and A flat) on the last beat of measure 67 and consequently cannot cope with the remaining eleven notes in only two beats. Moreover sensitive ears can detect the wrong harmony when the D-flat bass note falls together with the B flat of the right hand. A suggested way to conceive of these two measures follows:

measures 67-68

(All the subsequent scales may be executed on this model.) Notice that the scale has no crescendo here: crescendos will appear only later.

The closing of the section, at measure 80, should be clearly understandable to the listener. From measure 81 on, both rhythmic and lyrical elements are present in the subject, making this section the most meditative one in the waltz. The clear enunciation of the rhythmic components throughout is important, especially with regard to the difference between eighth and sixteenth notes. The low part of the right hand in measure 110 can be brought out, thus contrasting with the interpretation of measure 94.

This middle episode can be conceived of as a quatrain, with the four lines each consisting of sixteen measures: the first line contains measures 81 to 96, the second line measures 97 to 112, the third line (where the phrase expands) measures 113 to 128, and the fourth line (a repeat of the first) measures 129 to 144. Looking upon the form this way will hold the middle episode together well, without breaking it into two parts at measure 113. The expression definitely changes at measure 113 with the appearance of the minor key, the sharper dissonances that are created between the bass and soprano, and the desperate insistence on the top G flat in both measure 113 and measure 121. This is a sad, intensely personal moment that darkens the atmosphere like the passage of a cloud.

Everything returns to the normal meditative mood with the fourth line, at measure 129. Aside from rhythmic precision, the legato in the consecutive sixths of the right hand is most important, especially in measure 127 with its gasping chromaticism. In general, legato sixths depend on the width of the hand: the 2-1 fingering forces the interval between the 2nd and 4th fingers up to the interval of a fifth—not easily negotiable for narrow hands. The rendering of measure 121 may easily be spoiled by an insensitive hammering of the repeated chords. A relaxed hand and wrist will help one find the required full, rich sound without harshness. Also, the dynamic setting can be as follows:

measure 121

Following the middle episode, the second subject appears as a refrain at measure 145. At the repeat (measure 161) the scales appear again, only this time the last chord is missing from the accompaniment. The last note of the scale is played alone, as the climax of a soaring crescendo.

The main subject returns at measure 177 without alteration and is followed by the second subject (as in the "exposition") at measure 209, unchanged until measure 237, when a succession of subdominant chords prepares for the coda. The sound grows thicker, and these eight measures become a sort of "built-in" dynamic climax of the work.

The coda begins at measure 245 and shows several interesting features. First the accompaniment figure changes in such a way that instead of a lone, low bass note, a chord situated in the higher region appears on the downbeat. This chord performs an important harmonic function. In the right hand, virtuosity takes over with a whirlwind figure that has a written-out mordent on the main beat. After the tempo broadens in measures 237–244, it becomes decisive to allow the virtuosity to show.

A more serious and expressive tone is reached at measure 261, where the line gains in melodic importance; this tone is aided by the expressive augmented fourth steps in every other measure coupled with chromatic modulations. This virtuoso section shows interesting fingering problems. To the unusual accompaniment figure (from measure 245 on) the already-mentioned principle of fingering is applicable, reserving the use of the fifth finger exclusively for the bass note. The fifth finger is used twice on the lower chords exclusively and cannot be used on the upper chord. In the right hand, there is a choice of fingering at the "whirlwind" passage (from measures 245 on):

measures 245-253

The fingering 3–5 on the augmented-fourth step is normally executed with a slight rotation of the hand in order to help the fifth finger. At measure 270, the simplest fingering is best:

measures 270-272

A more meditative part of the coda is reached at measure 277. The lively second subject, is presented here in a new light. It is like a regretful recollection of past events. The main difficulty is in the clear enunciation and correct rhythm of the repeated intervals. The presence of the left hand in the same region of the keyboard adds to the difficulty; therefore the player has to search for a right (and comfortable) way to establish the positioning of the hands, with one hand over the other. Most of the passage will be played with ease if the player possesses enough flexibility to change from one position to the other at the slightest hint of change in the texture. Here is the suggested way to play this passage:

measures 284-295

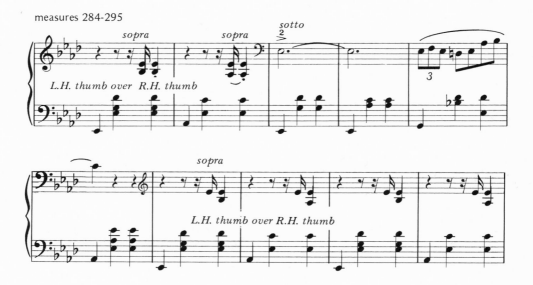

Measure 293 brings in the last portion of the coda, where fragments of the second subject rocket up like fireworks and vanish in the upper regions—before the two fortissimo chords set the final ending to the piece.

The simplicity of the music does not exclude good taste and imaginative handling by the performer, especially in sections like the reminiscent part of the coda and in the soaring lyricism of the transition to the coda. Beware of a too-fast tempo for the main subjects: their melodic, lyric character will not come across in a hurried tempo. The moto perpetuo parts, such as measures 33–48 and 245–276, may have a slightly more flowing tempo to allow the virtuosity of the player to shine through. The most important advice that can be given to the performer is a renewed warning about good taste. The simple material used is that of "salon music," and although Chopin never falls below his standards, a performance without distinctive taste will lower this music to the level of popular entertainment.

CHOPIN

Mazurka in A Minor, Op. 17, No. 4

The mazurka is a Polish popular dance that has its origins in three different dances: the *mazur,* an elegant, waltzlike dance with accents on the third beats of the measures; the *kujawiak,* a heavier, rather "peasant" dance; and the fast *oberek.* The form of Chopin's mazurkas is usually A–B–A, and section B is usually in a contrasting mood and a different key. The mazurkas sometimes have introductions, and the later mazurkas even have large-scale codas developing the previously heard material. Because of their rhythmic refinement and harmonic richness, Chopin's mazurkas belong among his most important creations. Their performance demands fine touch, great sensitivity, freedom of rhythm, and a sense of contrast.

Form: Ternary

	MEASURES
Introduction	1 – 4
A	5 – 60
A₁	5 – 36
A₂	37 – 44
A₃	45 – 60
B	61 – 92
A	93 – 108
Coda	109 – 132

The indication "lento ma non troppo" contains a warning against too slow a tempo. The basic tempo of ♩ = 152 seems well advised to the extent that a metronome figure can be applied to a mazurka requiring freedom of tempo, especially in the introductory measures. The performer should begin the chords slightly under the tempo; he should accelerate with the second measure and then slow down in the third, thus preparing for the triplet, which should be calm and expressive. The chords are sotto voce and should be well balanced; the middle voice carries the line, and the triplet should be played in such a way that it fits into this line. The main subject shows some contradiction: it has expressive yearning, but it also has casual manners. The difference between the dancing dotted rhythm on the first beat of measure 5 and the smoothly expressive eighths on the same beat of measure 7 offers a clue for refined contrasts. There are also harmonic subtleties to be found: measures 9 and 10 show a quite exeptional use of the third-degree chord for resolution after the preceding dominant-seventh chord. The slurs in these measures have dynamic consequences too:

measures 9-10

The ensuing measures (11–12) are in complete contrast: they are nonchalant and have a prickling rhythm. The sixteenth notes have a slight emphasis; they are played short and right on the beat, together with the left-hand chord. The second half of the subject is varied with fantasy elements, such as the triplets in measure 13 and the fioritura of measure 15. A free treatment of the latter measure seems self-evident; however this freedom is limited to the second beat of the measure, while the first and last beats are filled by regular sixteenths:

measure 15

The una corda adds to the charm of the fioritura.

Measures 17 and 18 display a new version of measures 9 and 10: instead of the expressive slurs, grace notes and chromatic fioritura embellish the main notes in a languido style. The contrast follows immediately: in the closing motive, the dance rhythm springs forth in tempo, with elegance. The mordent is to be played as a triplet in the time of a sixteenth note.

The second exposition of the subject contains more variants, such as the repeated notes in measure 29. These notes are to be played in a relaxed manner and without physical or rhythmic stiffness—almost a piacere. The fingering should be based on substitutions; one of the possibilities is:

measures 28-29

The fioritura of measure 31 will receive the same treatment as it did earlier: it should start and finish with regular, almost expressive sixteenth notes, and the freedom of the figure should be limited to the second beat. Note again the sudden awakening of the elegant dance rhythm in measure 35, following the two measures of languido.

The A₂ subject (measures 37–44) can be played in a slightly faster tempo. It has a more definite dancing character and less rubato; however the last beat of every other measure (measuers 38, 40, and 42) has the typical accents of the mazur and also carries a slight prolongation. The triplet in the melodic line is in the style of a slow mordent, except in measures 43 and 44; here the triplets inject passion. Measure 44 slows down considerably, in the manner of a sad question, and stops on the dominant. The G sharp in the right hand should be well sustained since its resonance is to be carried over into the next measure.

At the restatement of A₁, the subtle differences between this and the previous versions should be observed (compare measures 23 and 47, and measures 31 and 53). In measure 60, sudden warmth is radiated by the emergence of the major mood.

However the contrast here is limited to the major mood and to a certain peacefulness reflected in the longer uninterrupted lines. Yet the tone remains plaintive. The harmony is a simple drone bass, sustained (almost legato) exactly as in the preceding section. The only technical problems are the grace notes in every other measure of the subject. They have to be played ahead of the beat, without precipitateness or heavy accents on the ensuing double note. Furthermore the thumb has to keep its agility in order to play the repeated lower part without brusqueness or clumsiness. This is especially difficult where the repeated notes are transformed into triplets.

In measure 65, a slight excitement is conceivable with the crescendo, a moderate acceleration toward the top note at the beginning of measure 67. There the tempo resumes, and in measure 68 it slows down; a generous amount of time spent on the last beat in this measure emphasizes the harmonic refinement here. The meaning of each of the four similar measures at 73–76 is different: the march toward the tonic (measure 74, second beat) has something solemn about it.

From this point on, all meaningful details of the phrase call for extension in the tempo. In particular the top F sharp needs sensitive treatment. The crescendo in measures 89–91 takes on the proportions of a real revolt and reaches the dynamic and emotional climax of the mazurka in the dramatic rhythms of measures 91 and 92. Measure 92 also has a problem of tonal balance: the F in the left hand has to be played loud (because it should sound for the first three measures of the recapitulation), but it still should not overpower the right hand. The recapitulation of A₁ does not bring any novelty with it except that the usual fioritura is replaced here by apparently regular triplets (measure 103). However the touch used will be that of an embellishment.

The coda calls for even more nonchalant freedom. The persistence of the dancing rhythm throughout (the sixteenth note jumping toward the ensuing staccato eighth) only enhances the peaceful charm of measures 115 and 124, where expressive eighth notes close eight-measure periods. The charming rhythm is reinforced from measure 117 forward by the addition of a grace note before the last beat. Rhythmically the grace notes should be treated as sixteenth notes. The large distance between grace notes and ensuing main notes makes graceful execution difficult. The hand should be in open position and the thumb as close as possible to the main note without becoming stiff from considerable stretching.

The coda has a constant diminuendo that dies away until the melody disintegrates (measures 125–128) and the sound of the opening chords is reached. The chords' appearance here is absolutely magical; it is as if a window were opened on the infinite.

CHOPIN

Polonaise in C Sharp Minor, Op. 26, No. 1

The polonaise, like the mazurka, was a favorite form of nationalistic expression for Chopin. Powerful and chivalrous, the dance has a characteristic rhythm ♪♫♫ ♫ ♫ and usually goes in a majestic tempo. The form is a large A–B–A, and it often has an added coda. The polonaises of Chopin represent the very best of the genre, surpassing by far the productions of his predecessors as well as those of his contemporaries and followers.

Form: Ternary

	MEASURES
A	1 – 49
A₁	1 – 24
A₂	25 – 41
A₁	42 – 49
B	50 – 97
B₁	50 – 65
B₂	66 – 81
B₁	82 – 97
A (repeat)	1 – 49

The performer should be immediately warned against too fast a tempo, which the indication "allegro appassionato" could suggest. In the performer's mind, it should be completed, by "ma maestoso."

The first four measures have a somewhat introductory character; however they appear again with the repeat (measures 13–24). The thirty-second notes should be clearly played on the beat, taking the main accent and the weight. The small crescendo indications between the thirty-second notes and double-dotted eighth notes do not mean a real increase of sound on the longer notes: rather, they warn against an unwelcome diminuendo. The common image of Chopin as a weakling is shattered by the triple forte indication in measure 3. The simple dotting in this measure should be rigorously obeyed. The staccato chords are to be "pulled out" of the keyboard rather than played with heavy arm weight.

The subject (beginning of measure 5) is both chivalrous and lyrical. The typical polonaise rhythm appears in the accompaniment as well as in the melody. "Con anima'' means "with enthusiasm"; the tempo may be slightly more animated with the rising figure of ♪ ♫ up to the third beat of measure 6, where the lyrical character takes over, (once the polonaise rhythm has given up). The phrase gets to a half cadence in measure 8, where the music naturally slows down.

The next measure brings the polonaise rhythm back, but this time it is in piano. Its soaring is quickly stopped by the poco ritenuto in measure 10, where, in addition to the poco ritenuto, the large chords of the left hand need more time if they are to be arpeggiated without undue rushing (use the fingering $\frac{1}{4}{5}$ on the last broken chord).

The pianissimo appearing in measure 11 should be accompanied by an espressivo to convey the sensibility of the Neapolitan sixth chord. The part playing of measure 12 should be perfect: hang on to the B sharp in the right hand and to the G sharp in the left in order to have a full chord on the second beat of the measure.

From measure 25 on, the music seems motionless: there is hardly any melody, and the harmony and rhythm are repetitious. The only diversity comes from the troublesome embellishing runs in every other measure. At first glance, the question of when to start these runs arises. If the full time value were given to the preceding quarter notes, no time would be left in which to complete the runs, even with approximate, rubato timing. Therefore the time for the run has to be deducted from the preceding quarter note. Some editions give clear hints of where the low bass notes should be played in relation to the arpeggios. Though such extreme calculation seems unnecessary, it is important for the performer to realize where to take the time for the execution of the arpeggios. Also it is very important that the syncopations of measures 25 and 26 match each other perfectly. The arpeggios increase the volume little by little, and it reaches fortissimo at measure 32, where a delicate problem of tonal balance awaits. The D sharp of the soprano should be played sonorously but not hard: it should ring through the measure. The underlying harmony, with its four-voice texture, should not cover it even though it has the important duty of confirming the key of G sharp major.

The following syncopated D sharps are in a rallentando and diminuendo that prepares for the new subject that appears magically; it slides into E major by playing the B-natural bass at measure 34 meaningfully and in a somewhat delayed manner. The new phrase (measures 34–41) has an unsophisticated character, stemming from its repetitiousness.

Even this simple subject is not without its problems, like spacing out the group of seven in measure 37 and crossing the right hand over the left in measure 38 without making a bump on the first note. The melody in the low register presents more problems of good tonal balance. The preparation for the reappearance of A₁ takes place by means of a crescendo and rallentando. In spite of the trill's uncomfortable position, it should be played with apparant ease. The main subject is marked con forza this time. This term does not mean "play as loud as possible"; it does imply the forceful character that the subject takes on here, and the tone should be full but elegant.

The middle section, in D flat major, has quite a contrasting character. First the tempo slows down, "meno mosso." The tone becomes warmer and more lyrical. However the enthusiasm of the A section is still present: the expression marking at the beginning of the section is "con anima." The performer is immediately confronted with manifold problems of tonal balance and complications of rhythm. The tonal balance of the right hand should be settled first in a rhythmically uncomplicated measure like measure 52. It is useful to practice it in the following way:

measure 52

The rhythmic difficulty lies in managing the different rhythmic patterns of two voices in the same hand, as in measure 50. Again dissociating the voices by using different articulations and dynamics is preferable to a mathematical solution. Also the tonal balance can help to achieve a relaxed, expressive triplet if the eighth notes of the lower voice do not interfere with the melodic line.

In measure 51, one should give ample time to playing the embellishing gruppetto on the fourth eighth note. The tone should be soft and the execution much influenced by operatic practices.

The triplet sixteenths in measure 55 are very similar in character to the gruppettos, except that they are slower and therefore also more expressive. Note also the meaningful bass line in measure 55.

A laterally flexible right wrist is necessary for the rendering of measure 57. An unhurried presentation of the melisma in measure 58 calls for a good sense of timing. Sufficient time—that is, slight prolongations of the steps of the modulation in measures 59–60—will insure understanding on the part of the listener. Tonal balance is also very important here: especially good care has to be taken to make the B double flat of the soprano in measure 59 ring for the duration of two quarter notes because it becomes an A natural on the second quarter note and should not need to be played again.

The crescendo of measure 60 goes on for two measures and is followed by two measures of diminuendo. The ornament and the sixteenth triplet in measure 63 are quite troublesome. The tempo can relax here, as we approach the charming fermata on a thirty-second rest.

The cadence measures (measures 64–65) can be started a little under the tempo; then the dotted rhythm, finally can be accelerated, and, finally, some time can be taken on the closing dominant and tonic.

B₂ (measures 66–81) has the main melody in the left hand; however the countermelody in the right hand cannot be ignored. The harmony remains soft. The left-hand melody raises the tone to an intense supplication. Special care has to be taken with the dotted rhythm in the right hand at the end of measure 69. Again a generous timing of this third beat will give the necessary relaxed character to this rhythm.

There is some controversy about the first note of the soprano in measure 77. Some editions give a C flat here instead of a C natural (the C flat sounds quite justified). The left hand tries to regain importance with a chromatic scale drifting upward, and in fact the hands share in importance in the last three measures before the recapitulation of B_1. In many editions, the polonaise ends at measure 97 without indicating that section A should be repeated. To make the form balanced, the repeat of the first part is necessary: thus the polonaise will end at measure 49. Needless to say, the repeat indicated for measures 25–49 should be ignored when section A is played the second time.

Unjustly neglected in favor of the more popular polonaises, this work is eminently interesting from all points of view; it gives an excellent insight into the polonaise creations of Chopin. The study of this polonaise before turning to more complex works in the same genre, such as opus 44 and opus 61, is therefore highly recommended.

CHOPIN

Scherzo No. 2, Op. 31

~~~~~~

The word *scherzo* immediately brings to mind the scherzi of Beethoven. However there is but little resemblance between the sonata or symphony movement called *scherzo* by Beethoven and Chopin's four demonic examples of tone epics. The elements Beethoven's and Chopin's scherzi have in common can be reduced to the time signature 3/4 and the form: scherzo, trio, scherzo (A-B-A). This particular scherzo shows an exceptionally well-organized form, with a development included in the trio.

Form: Scherzo, trio, scherzo

	MEASURES
Scherzo	1 – 264
A	1 – 132
Repeat of A	133 – 264
Trio	265 – 583
B	265 – 365
Repeat of B	366 – 466
Development	467 – 583
Scherzo (A)	584 – 715
Coda	716 – 780

The scherzo opens with a question-and-answer type of dramatic contrast. Short chunks of motives are opposed in the most conspicuous way: the barely whispered question has a powerfully affirmative answer. Questions of tempo and rhythm are crucial for putting life into this dramatic dialogue. The tempo indication "presto" means here that the work is to be played with one beat to a bar. In Chopin's scherzi, it also suggests a structure in which a group of four measures should be regarded as the four beats of a 4/4 measure. Consequently there are "heavy" and "light" measures. If the motive is not long enough to fill out a four-measure structure, Chopin fills in several measures of rest, like measures 23 and 24 of this scherzo. In order to avoid any possible rhythmic misunderstanding in the very first measure of this scherzo, Chopin begins the motive on the beat with a half note. Everywhere else this motive starts with the triplet figure after a rest.

This first half note gives the performer a good chance to play a correct triplet on the last beat of the measure. Since the general pulse is one beat to the bar, the triplet often gets a rough, approximate treatment that promptly turns it into an inarticulate jerk. In spite of the sotto voce marking, the utmost clarity is needed here. Using the fingers (without excessive articulation) for the motive is strongly recommended, instead of a global motion of the hand that would definitely blur the outline of this most important motive. When practicing, take constant care that the rhythmic outline is correct.

The ensuing answer is fortissimo after a one-measure rest, should come as a surprise. The arms will be used for the chords; however hardness of tone is to be avoided, and the wrists should act as shock absorbers. The correct rhythmic outline is fairly difficult to maintain in measure 8 and similar measures, where the eighth-note chord often tends to become a sixteenth. The correct rhythm can be made easier to achieve by using the correct fingering on the chords. Using the fourth and fifth fingers alternately in measures 8, 16, 32, and 40 will contribute to the observance of the rhythm.

measures 8-9

(It helps in understanding this measure if one realizes that it is the fourth beat of the measure structure.)

The next fortissimo answer includes a difficult broken chord for the left hand in measure 14. The thumb of the left hand should be placed as close as possible to the D flat; in this case the chord can be arpeggiated in the time of a lightening flash.

Measures 20 to 25 present a problem of rhythm and interpretation. The duration of the F octave should be correct—two measures and a quarter note; the sforzando G flat should intervene brusquely on the second quarter of the measure, off the beat. The ensuing two measures of rest complete the measure structure, and the "downbeat" follows on the first beat of measure 25.

At measure 49, new material in D flat major appears. The gap between the two hands calls for prudence in tonal balance. The eighth-note run in the right hand lies well on the keyboard. The correct speed and good synchronization with the left hand shold be maintained. The fingering of the right hand should be:

measures 49-52

Some editions recommend 3 2 1 here. However, because the thumb is used on a black key, this fingering suddenly turns the hand out of its established position.

The contrast between the different motives remains violent: the dialogue is not yet over. In measures 54 and 56, the bass line of the left hand should be very expressive. The same idea in measures 61–64 appears in canon between the hands: two measures should be played with a slight crescendo and two measures with diminuendo. The expressive main part of the scherzo, with its long, passionate melody and very difficult accompaniment figure, constitutes the main difficulty of the first (or scherzo) section. It will be clear from the outset that this figure cannot be played by finger articulation alone because of the frequent extensions between the third and fifth fingers. A lateral movement of the wrist is needed to bring the individual fingers into position to play. At some points, the extensions are so great that a quick jump is needed—just on the surface of the keys, of course, without raising the hand into the air (see measures 90 and 106). Extensive work on the left hand is needed for results.

The right hand needs sensitivity and a good, singing legato to shape the phrase. The chords from measure 100 on need good tonal balance and a careful building up of the climax toward the end of the phrase.

The closing subject (measures 117–132) is difficult for both hands—particularly for the right because of the extension involved. A stretched position is to be avoided, and the thumb should move quickly toward the key where it is to be used next. Between the last note of the run (measure 118) and the ensuing sixth chord, a slight rotation of the forearm will allow the chord to be put down solidly. The low bass of measure 125 is like a big bell. The proposed distribution between the hands for measures 125–129 is shown on page 220.

measures 125-129

The length of the rest in the concluding two measures must be correct.

   Beginning at measure 133, section A is repeated in its entirety, with a few variants. First of all, the initial triplet motive begins without the half note. The correct feeling for the measure structure is still to be observed. At measure 148, an emotional group of five replaces the rhythm previously heard. It should be played almost freely, like an expressive recitative. The group of four in measure 172 should be played the same way. A new version, with a trill and a difficult leap, appears between measures 180 and 181. A well-known treatment of the end of the trill is played as follows:

measure 180

A new bouncing rhythm appears in the long melody at measure 233.

   The trio begins in a slower tempo with the expression marking "sostenuto." The melody is mysteriously hidden in the middle of the right-hand part, sotto voce. Good balance is needed in the right hand in order to isolate the melody from the rest of the chord. It is especially disturbing if the F-sharp octave in measure 266 (the second measure of the trio) is played loud as if it were melodic. The dreamy mood of this phrase should stand in sharp contrast to the dramatic or passionate character of the Scherzo proper.

   The ensuing nostalgic melody should have a more sustained sound. The grace notes are to be played ahead of the beat. The equally expressive succession of chords in the left hand is interrupted twice by rests that should be real rests, clear of pedal. The broken chord is best played the following way:

measure 281

delicatissimo

The use of the thumb on two successive notes will allow the slight separation needed between the chord and the filigree run, that has to be played delicatissimo. It is unnecessary to draw the attention of any sensitive performer to the beauty of this run and to the shimmering tone quality that can be applied to it.

The second exposition of the dreamy subject (measures 285–298 and also, in the repeat, meaures 387–400) presents us with an irregular measure structure: the last period, instead of having the usual four measures, has an additional fifth measure. Therefore the rest at measure 298 is a "heavy" beat; the C sharp comes in on the second beat and is held through the third, and the "slentando" ("hesitating") eighth notes are on the fourth. Is this irregularity a written-out rubato that underlines even more the dreamy quality of the phrase? It is hard to know. Anyhow the performer has to reveal the different length of this phrase in order not to confuse the rest of the trio.

Once more, attention must be directed to the differences in duration and also in tone quality between the C sharps at measures 277 and 299. The nostalgic figure at measure 299 begins with a slentando and gains in tempo on the way. The remarks formulated previously for the identical phrase at measure 277 can be applied here. The suggestion concerning the broken chord, measure 281 can be used in measure 306. The ensuing filigree is shorter here. Some editions correct the original text of Chopin and wrongly suggest a figure identical to that in measures 281–284.

A new, sad melody, which is stirred by a typical eighths-and-triplet motive in the middle voice, appears at measure 309. Every single voice of this section is independently expressive. To begin with, the main melody in the soprano should naturally be played with a singing legato. The alto has the difficult eighths-and-triplet motive, which needs a refined sense for rhythmic divisions. The tenor adds tension to the eighths-and-triplet motive, which needs a refined sense for rhythmic divisions. The tenor adds tension to the eighths-and-triplet figure, while the bass steps are in contrary motion with the soprano. It is obvious that the hands should be trained separately for faultless part playing before attempting to put them together. Special attention has to be focused, however, on the right hand. The importance of a rhythmically perfect eighths-and-triplet motive has already been pointed out. However a warning has to be added about the accent on the dotted half note in every other measure: it should be gentle, not violent. Correctly shaping the melody is essential; it should be done this way:

measures 309-312

espress.

legato

To render this shaping perfectly, the correct fingering is a must. The part playing of the left hand is equally important. Possible interruptions in the bass line are especially to be avoided.

The performance of this subject is difficult; it requires patient work. The possible mistakes that await the performer here are multiple and dangerous. But even more dangerous is a perfectly correct but musically unpoetic performance. Chopin left a lot here to the imagination of the performer, especially concerning the dynamics. The indication ''espressivo'' should guide the sensibility of the pianist toward achieving a well-balanced, poetic performance.

A virtuoso section in E major (measures 334–365) that is related to the D-flat virtuoso part of the scherzo proper (from measure 49 on) follows. It needs a leggiero touch—a light, easy right hand. The difficulty is somewhat lessened by the E major key that offers the hand a comfortable position on the keyboard. In measures 337–338, the correct fingering is

measures 337-338

Also beware of bumpiness in the closing run (measures 358–364) caused by too-flat third and fourth fingers and by clumsy passages of the thumb. The thumb should be brought into position in time, and it should play without a downward motion of the hand or arm.

The left hand has a part-playing problem: the bass line, which carries melodic importance (note the relation between the bass line and the soprano of the preceding part), has to be correctly played as indicated, legato or staccato. Special significance has to be brought to measures 340 and 341, where there is a sudden increase of speed in the melodic bass. In measures 352 and 356, the two octaves of the left hand are directly related to those in measure 22 of the opening and have to be played the same way. The correct duration of measures 364 and 365 has to be observed.

The ensuing repeat of the entire trio contains ravishing variants of the dreamy first theme. First the recapitulation begins forte, coloring the subject with exaltation. The tender feeling returns with the second presentation of the theme (measure 387 on), which contains a beautiful ''vocalise'' (measure 395) in which the performer can show most subtle imagination in tone color and rubato.

The rest of the repeat unfolds without change and leads us to the heart of this scherzo. The development section (measures 468–583) uses all subjects previously heard except the long, passionate melody of the scherzo section and the dreamy subject of the trio. This development is also the most exacting part, both technically and musically. The section opens with a run similar to the closing run of the preceding section. The thundering quality of the left-hand broken chord at measure 470 enhances the vigor of this passage.

Measures 476–491 present many problems. First the right hand needs a smooth passage of the thumb throughout. ''Skating,'' or moving the hand in and out on the keyboard, would make a bump every time the thumb was used. The fingers have to be used in a straight line on the keyboard, thus reducing the difference in position for black and white keys. Using the fifth finger consistently on the upward runs also helps in keeping a solid hand position. The suggested fingering is:

measures 476–491

(*cont.*)

measures 476–491 (*cont.*)

Each of these runs is to be played forte, but it should also be shaped with a crescendo-decrescendo. The left hand has menacing octaves that have melodic importance. The articulation of the octaves has to be observed, especially in the longer legato lines like those in measures 482–483 and 490–491.

The increasingly passionate runs lead to an agitato section (measures 492–516) developing the eighths-and-triplet motive of the trio. The agitato should not be interpreted as an invitation to increase the tempo but rather as suggesting inner excitement. (*Agitato* for Chopin is an indication of character, not of tempo.) A too-fast tempo at this point would take away from the grandeur of this section. The problem for the right hand is the correct presentation of the typical eighths-and-triplet rhythm and the short melodic motives. These two elements should contrast in touch, in tone, and in expression. The eighths-and-triplet motive is like an obsession here: it dominates the section rhythmically while the melody motives in singing legato are more expressive. The left hand adds to the excitement with the slur between the second and third beats. The accuracy of the fifth finger on the bass notes is greatly aided by an appropriate fingering like:

measures 492-494

It is obvious that the use of the fifth finger is exclusively reserved for the bass line wherever it is held (measures 503–508).

At measure 517, the D-flat major subject of the scherzo section reappears triumphantly, this time in E major. Its second version is particularly difficult because of the violent fanfare rhythm in the left hand (measure 525). Synchronization of this rhythm with the run gives some players a bit of a problem. The solution is more a matter of dissociation of the hands than one of coordination between them.

The final crescendo toward the climax of the development (and of the whole scherzo) begins in measure 528, and the left hand takes the preponderant part in this climax through the expressive character of its legato chords and octaves; the left-hand part contains a difficult tenth chord, which can be broken, if need be. In the same measure 540 begins a "stretto" of the figure between the hands with offbeat accents on the first notes of each motive to reach the climax at measure 544. "Sempre con fuoco" is Chopin's indication for this section, which requires the utmost in both dynamics and expression. For the first eight measures (544–551), the left hand needs practice above all to assure the accuracy of the octaves and the clarity of the fourths and thirds on the last beats of the measures. In the right hand, the eighths-and-triplet motive has to be rendered with utmost clarity.

Complications begin at measure 552: following the typical eighths-and-triplet motive, which is played in unisono here, both hands have to jump—the right hand to a broken chord and the left hand to an octave. The performance of these chords and octaves is often spoiled—not only by inaccuracy but also by a hasty jump, which produces a dry, inarticulate noise. Spreading the typical eighths-and-triplet figure out slightly and taking a little time for the jump in order to get a well-balanced chord without hardness is probably the best solution. The section between measures 552 and 576 is the most difficult part of the work; it needs patient, slow practice with the arms relaxed from the shoulders in such a way that only the hands execute the jumps, without involving the body in lateral movements. There is only little value in practicing this section hands separately.

The important decrescendo should start early enough (at measure 566) and bring the dynamics down to *quasi niente;* the decrescendo should be coupled with a rallentando that continues to the last convulsions and complete disintegration of the typical figure.

The recapitulation brings an important novelty to the opening triplet figure: sorrowfully the last note is held for two measures. Otherwise the scherzo unfolds as before until measure 697, where a chromatically built closing phrase is inserted. The left hand has difficult problems to solve in these measures. Already tired by the long and difficult accompaniment, it has to cope with increasing gaps between the fifth and third fingers. From measure 702 on, the use of the fourth finger is necessary. The right hand has a somewhat simpler problem in finding the position of the middle fingers solidly.

The surprise coda, with its deceptive cadence, starts with a real explosion of virtuosity and vigor. In the midst of the frenetic activity of the right hand, some players forget to repeat the low A in the left hand on the last beat of measures 719 and 723, thus changing the harmony to the dominant for no reason at the end of those measures.

In the following section (measures 724–732), it is difficult to achieve accuracy, especially in the right hand. The passage should be played correctly in rhythm, without any distortion. In preparing the fingering of this passage; note the very simple fact that when the third and fourth finger is used in the upward arpeggiation, 3 or 4 is to be used on the ending third, accordingly.

measures 724-732

The left hand plays as legato as possible; the playing should be quite light in order to avoid covering the right hand. At measure 732, in spite of the più mosso, the triplets should not be distorted into inarticulate jerks, and they should still begin on the third beat of each measure. In the contrasting chords (measures 737 on), the middle voice has to be singled out like a solo trumpet.

At measure 749, a stretto is added to the più mosso. In order to be able to complete the last crescendo, a meno forte should be adopted at this point; a fortissimo can thus be arrived at again at measure 756, where the virtuosity explodes once more. The shaping of the motive at measures 764–769 is quite important. During the violent hammering of chords at measures 770–771, the repeated notes of the chords are to be played each time. The brilliant succession of closing chords ends with a risky jump. It should sound brilliant, and the jump should be fast enough to suggest risks. The elbow should be kept in a natural position, close to the body during the execution of the jump, and the hands should be turned slightly outward. It is impossible to make such a jump secure by practice; its execution always involves a certain amount of risk. Chopin certainly calculated it to make this ending sound as brilliant as possible.

The difficulties are multiple and various in this scherzo. They encompass virtuoso runs, chords, singing legato, and difficult accompaniment figures, as well as poetic feeling and refinement in tone. The length of the piece calls for a good sense of construction and for physical endurance. Once again, the popularity of this scherzo can be the greatest difficulty for the performer to overcome. Patient, attentive work can lead to a performance that restores nobility and brilliance to a work often mistreated in performance.

CHOPIN
Ballade No. 3, Op. 47

The *ballade*, a new kind of expression rather than a musical form, is certainly among the most original creations of Chopin. Because it is possible that Chopin's ballades were inspired by ballads of the Polish poet Adam Mickiewicz, many attempts have been made to relate each of the four Chopin ballades to specific poems by Mickiewicz. The attempts have been not only unsuccessful but unnecessary. The Chopin ballades have hardly any programatic element—definitely too little to tie these poetic compositions beyond any possible doubt to the ballads of Mickiewicz.

The musical forms of the four ballades have little in common except their 6/4 or 6/8 time signatures and their epic character. Their form is perhaps best described as "mixed," showing elements of Lied, rondo, sonata, and variations.

Form: Mixed		MEASURES
A		1 – 52
	A_1	1 – 8
	A_2	9 – 36
	A_1	37 – 51
B		52 – 115
	B_1	52 – 65
	B_2	66 – 103
	B_1	104 – 115
C		116 – 144
	C_1	116 – 135
	C_2	136 – 144
B		145 – 212
	B_1	145 – 156
	B_1 (varied)	157 – 183
	Development	184 – 212
Coda		213 – 241

This ballade (like the second one, in F major) does not begin with an introduction. It immediately reflects a serene, happy mood. The opening eight measures have often been referred to as a conversation between a girl and a boy since the sections of this first phrase appear in the ranges of female and male voices. The important rhythm ♪ ♩ appears immediately in the second measure and dominates the entire piece rhythmically. There is no general dynamic indication for the first eight measures: it is customary to play a singing piano, and the first and last sections (measures 1–2 and 7–8) usually have expressive crescendo-decrescendos.

The forte exclamation at measure 9 introduces a new section, which is already entirely dominated by the characteristic rhythm. A perfect rendering, without "limping" one way or the other, is fairly difficult. In order to assure a more carefree rendering of the rhythm, the octaves of measure 10 can be played with the help of the left hand, as follows:

measure 10

The same solution should be brought to measure 14:

measure 14

The nervous precision of the rhythm throughout the ballade has to be the object of constant care. The slightest deviation from it could have serious consequences. If the sixteenth note is played too short and the rhythm thus becomes too sharp, it will imprint a theatrically heroic character upon the playfulness of this first part.

Also it will prevent the rendering of the longer line appearing at measure 17. At this point, and especially from measure 21 on, the music becomes more and more narrative and gets into the complication of maintaining good tonal balance. Measure 22 contains a difficult grace-note chord that (usually) distorts the characteristic rhythm almost unrecognizably. The execution of the grace note should draw time away from the preceding sixteenth note chord in order that the last eighth-note chord may fall in its right place in the bar. In addition to the rhythm, the articulation is also very important: the grace note should sound softer than either the preceding or the following chord, thus melting into the melodic line.

At measure 25 for the first time, the rhythm gives up its playfulness and takes on the menacing expression of an oracle. The arpeggios in the following measures need practice, especially by those who have neglected the regular practice of scales and arpeggios in contrary motion. First firmly establish the placement of the two first fingers, as shown and then play the octave:

The wrist constantly remains loose, especially when the player is jumping to the octave at the beginning of measures 27, 29, and those following. From measure 28 on, the excitement coupled with the crescendo pushes the tempo slightly ahead. However the rhythmic proportions of the measure should remain consistently correct: the trill lasts one eighth note and the ensuing arpeggio is still composed of sixteenth notes.

The volume decreases quickly, and the passage dissolves in a splendid C-major arpeggio grouped in hemiolas. The tenor has a significant role in the cadence (measures 34–35). The rising and falling arpeggio line has to be played with ease and airiness, avoiding accents on the double notes. Two elegantly played legato octaves (measure 36) suffice to lead back to the original key, where the A subject is presented again, extended by a sequence, and spread larger on the keyboard. The small sforzandos marking the beginnings of the sequences are expressive rather than violent. Good part playing is very important in these measures (42–44), just as it is in measures 46 and 47, where the A-flat middle voice has to be played anew in each chord in the right hand. The closing chord in measure 50 has to ring like a bell; well-balanced and magical in sound, it not only closes one section but also opens the next.

Section B is built almost entirely on the characteristic rocking rhythm. Fluency is a problem mainly in the left hand, where the slurring of the chord to the single bass note is quite difficult. It is advisable to practice the left hand alone, like this:

measure 54

and so on, then

then

Only after the notes have been learned separately can the chord be put together. The right hand is somewhat easier, although the player has to realize that the melody descends to the lonely C every time. The grace note in measure 55 melts into the melodic line while the thumb stays down. In spite of its technically easier task, the right hand has the difficulty of rendering the melodic line without excessive interruption or overphrasing. The role of a flexible wrist in playing this undulating phrase is of great importance. It helps the tonal balance, the rocking rhythm, and the fluent articulation.

The meaningful middle voices of measures 63–64 lead into the second part of section B—a darker, more insistent subject in minor, showing longer legato lines. The left hand has the same problems as it did previously. The longer lines of the right hand include a difficulty of legato interrupted by rests that should be rigorously respected. In other words, the eighth-note chords in measures 67 and 69 have to have their precise length; they must be played without dryness, and they cannot be prolonged by either hand or pedal. Attention should also be drawn to executing the grace notes in a liquid manner wherever they appear.

In measure 71, the left hand adds an expressive commentary to the melody. Its articulation is complicated but has to be followed exactly. Just beware of a too-short, humorous type of staccato: the right touch is much closer to serious portamento. The doubling of the melody in the tenor in measures 73 through 80 can be effective in making the line expressive. The rhythm which can easily succumb to limping here, needs constant care. Also the differences in the lengths of the chords in the right hand have to be clearly rendered, even if these differences are not audible because of the use of the pedal.

The crescendo does not begin until measure 77; it reaches a dramatic fortissimo at measure 81, where the second part of section B is presented in full bloom. The tone should be well balanced—full but not brutal. Although the articulation mark in the left hand changes here, the legato character is still recommended. The grace-note octave in the right hand is to be played ahead of time in measure 82 as well as in measure 86;

yet it should be very expressive and part of the melodic line. Some editions indicate forte at measure 86. Forte is certainly a letdown for the succession of chromatically falling chords representing the total collapse of the subject and of the universe it stood for. Fortissimo is preferred for this emotionally climactic measure.

There is an inconsistency in the dynamics of the subsequent measures as well: most editions, as well as the original manuscript, indicate piano as early as measure 89. Then, through a series of diminuendos a piano is reached again at the obviously lowest point, at measure 95. Quite a sonorous piano, somewhere close to a mezzo forte, at measure 89 would allow the gradual decrease prescribed to the real piano reached at measure 95. This passage (measures 88–94) also has syncopated chords (the first even has a sforzando), which constantly give a hasty character to the music. It is very important that the chords have their correct duration; otherwise the syncopation will not be felt as such. The decrescendos marked after each one of the chords refer not only to the general decrease of the sound but also to the tonal shaping of the melody: when playing the single notes after the chords, the performer has to take into consideration the decay of sound in order to make a line of the melody.

The long and uninterrupted line at measure 95 has to be free of limping in the rhythm. The left-hand chords in measures 97–98 are very wide and have to be discreetly arpeggiated. The grace-note chord in measure 98 can easily cause technical and rhythmic problems. The recommended execution is:

measure 98

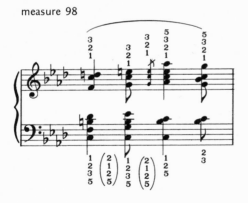

The following short bridge passage leading back to the B subject contains one of the most disputed points in this text of Chopin. The reference is to the first note of the tenor in measure 102. The E flat slurred over from the preceding measure makes a false relation with the E natural of the soprano appearing later in the measure. Some editions advocate an E natural as the first note of the tenor instead of the E flat. This would avert the false relation, but it would also break the slur clearly indicated by Chopin between the E flats.

Even more important than this question is that of the proper sound of the bass notes that should ring through those measures like bells. Special care has to be taken with the grace notes; they should be played in a relaxed, harmonious way. In the ensuing restatement of section B, there is an expressive tenor line to be brought out, without obtrusiveness, in measures 109–112.

The new subject (measure 116) introduces flowing sixteenth notes into the piece that will play an important role in the further development of the work. The rocking rhythm remains the main feature of the new subject and has to be correct throughout, in spite of the difficult large, broken chords later. In the sixteenth runs, the right hand displays a gentle, sweet melody instead of virtuosity; these runs are best rendered by a relaxed hand without excessive finger articualtion. Passages over the thumb have to be especially effortless to avoid bumps in the sound. The grace-note arpeggios have to be played ahead of the beat, more in the style of smoothly broken chords than of virtuoso arpeggios. In measures 118 and 122, a solution involving both hands can be recommended:

measure 118

The relaxed grace of the figure should not be spoiled by playing the sixteenth notes nervously, especially when they follow the dotted quarter notes. A refined, small stretch to mark the dissonances between soprano and bass at the beginning of measures 117, 119, 121, and 123 adds to their charm.

The new section of the subject (measures 124–135) contains many difficulties. The rhythmic difference in the left hand (a change from ) has to be shown, but without heaviness on the quarter-note chord. In the right hand, clarity and lightness are the required qualities, without aggressive virtuosity. The passage is difficult to finger. Lateral flexibility of the wrist is necessary to insure legato in figures like the one in the second half of measure 124. Sliding the thumb from the D flat to the C between measures 125 and 126 and from the G flat to the F between measures 129 and 130 is in accordance with Chopin's original fingering and facilitates the performance a great deal.

measures 125-126

For those who are not familiar with this sort of fingering, some practice is necessary to avoid sliding so much weight that a bump results. Actually all that is involved in sliding is very little finger weight. If it is well executed, this sliding produces the most perfect legato.

The left hand adds meaningful chords with a countermelody in the tenor in measures 126–127. In measure 130, avoid the often-observed reading mistake: the third sixteenth note of the right-hand scale is an A flat; the other A's in the scale are naturals. The meaningful chords appear here too; they have a nervous rhythm in measure 132 that should be perfectly synchronized with the right hand and avoid disturbing its fluency. Again the trills are more expressive than virtuosic, and they always begin on the main note. The left hand is only accompaniment here and should avoid heaviness.

The sostenuto of measures 136–144 applies both to the sound and to the tempo. The right hand here has to be able to produce a rich, singing legato tone without hardness. The wide arpeggio accompaniment of the left hand is particularly difficult: it needs a laterally flexible wrist and very little finger articulation. The extended arpeggio at measure 140 is like a longer wave: it elevates the melody an octave higher. The fingering in measures 141–142 is particularly uncomfortable; the recommended fingering is:

measures 141-142

The grace note in measure 143 can too easily be jammed into the chord: it has to be treated melodically, even though it is played ahead of the beat.

At measure 144, the rocking B subject is back, and with it the meaningful tenor line. It is followed by B₂ in a varied form that combines the motive with a sixteenths motion in the left hand. The main interest remains with the right hand; however the left-hand figurations with frequent chromaticism add an interesting counterpoint. The correct articulation of the right hand, including the correct length of the chords must be secured. The chords marked staccato should be mellowed to a more gentle portamento for the sake of the line.

The left hand occupies the musical foreground in the next section (measures 165–172), while the right hand is reduced to a technically difficult upper pedal point. The length of this passage combined with the following section (measures 173–183) severely taxes the endurance of the player. To cope with the difficulty, the hand and forearm should remain as loose as possible throughout the entire passage—in spite of the stretched position of the hand. The following exercise (which should be practiced first) shows that a constant stretching of the hand is not needed for the execution of this passage:

measure 165

and so on.

The moment that the thumb is substituted for the fourth finger, the narrow position of the hand should bring welcome relaxation every time it occurs.

Measures 165 through 172 also include a tremendous increase of sound, which prepares for the fortissimo entrance of the B_2 subject at measure 173. The technical aspect of the right hand's role is complicated here by the presence of the theme outlined in the figuration, in double notes and chords. The left hand returns to the rocking accompaniment in easily *overplayed large chords;* in addition to their technical problems, these chords further tax the right hand with problems of tonal balance. The falling sequence (measures 179–183) is particularly dangerous in that it adds considerably to the already existing fatigue of the player and tenses up his hands even more. Usually the tempo also gets out of control at this passage, and the breakneck speed adopted can cause total disaster. The patient study of this sequence is strongly recommended, starting with the following exercise:

measure 179

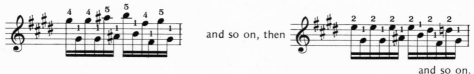

and so on, then

and so on.

The recommended fingering is as follows:

measures 179-182

(cont.)

measures 179–182 (*cont.*)

The left hand seems to be less of a problem. It should be played lightly, with its accuracy secured by the guidance of the thumb. The fifth finger only is to be used on the octaves; the sixths are to be played with 1–3.

The ensuing development is also full of technical problems. To begin with, the accompaniment in the left hand is most uncomfortable and tiring, although the dynamic remains piano throughout. (The fifth finger in the first six measures is helped by a side motion of the forearm and by a flexible wrist.) Great difficulty is encountered in measures 189–191 and 197, where the distance between the fifth and third (or second) fingers becomes a seventh. Only players with very flexible wrists can make a sufficient lateral motion to cope with the interval. The usual fault here consists in unduly prolonging the first note of each group in order to allow enough time for the hand to change position. If the accompaniment is rhythmically distorted, the melody cannot evolve in a relaxed manner. The left hand has to maintain a constant piano, which is only interrupted by the unfurling of the chromatic waves. Players with narrow hands are particularly disadvantaged here; their salvation lies only in their ability to change position quickly on the keyboard.

Even the right hand has problems of extension, which are complicated by grace notes, in measures 190 and 198. The required sotto voce makes things only more complicated because it does not allow the often-heard crashing on the chord. The musical problem of this development consists in the difference in character between the hands' roles: the melody controls only with difficulty the agitated assaults of the accompaniment. By degrees the right hand is finally carried away; eventually it starts the chromatically rising chords (in the best Wagnerian tradition), which reach the apotheosis of the A subject at measure 213, the true climax of the piece.

Both hands are involved in severe difficulties here. The right hand has to have the full, singing tone, without harshness, needed for the melody. At the same time, it has to make the part playing clear by keeping the chords and double notes that do not belong to the melody below the level of the melody. In measure 215, the middle-voice G should stay down. It should naturally be played with the second finger: this fingering will turn the hand to the best position (with the fingers slightly outward) to play the rest of the chords in strict legato. Also the grace note has to have the same melodic importance as before.

The fingering in the left hand should be well established. The recommended
fingering is:

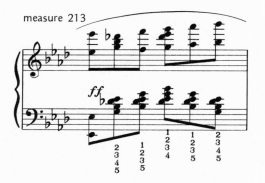

measure 213

From measure 222 on, beware of playing the sixeenths too short and thus giving the
rhythm too sharp a character. The allargando at measure 225 means that there should
be time enough to deal with both the melody and harmony. The stretto (measure 227)
means play faster, not as fast as you can.

The coda is marked più mosso; nonetheless the accurate rhythm in the rocking accompaniment chords has to be maintained. The grace-note arpeggios here are also to
be played ahead of the beat. Particular care should be taken about the correct length of
the trills in measures 235 and 236; they are often played hurriedly and short. The
arpeggio downward in measures 237 and 238 is often a victim of inaccuracy. The
fingers on black keys should play fairly flat. If the result is still unsatisfactory, dividing
the notes between the hands is acceptable for the sake of accuracy. The closing chords
have to be played with the greatest conviction.

One of Chopin's most popular pieces, this work seems to be the easiest, technically, of the ballades: it does not contain a difficult fast coda, as the others do. But
technical difficulties still abound, and only experienced, well-prepared players can
take on such a piece successfully. Besides the technical demands, there are also great
musical difficulties that have to be dealth with with equal ease. Most of them are in the
usual realm of difficulties in Chopin, and they require the following traits: a sense for
freedom, or rubato; a sense for proportions; refinement in tone and expression; and,
above all, taste.

CHOPIN
Berceuse, Op. 57

~~~~~~

Chopin's Berceuse is a most ingenious combination—a basso ostinato one measure long containing the tonic and the dominant and a four-measure theme that is subjected to a number of variations. It is also one of the rare pieces by Chopin that gives some linking of a program; in character it is close to a nocturne.

Form: Variations (chaconne)

	MEASURES
Introduction	1 – 2
Theme	3 – 6
Variations 1–10	7 – 46
Coda 1 (variations 11–12)	47 – 54
Coda 2 (variation 13)	55 – 62
Coda 3	63 – 70

The rhythm of the introduction (the accompaniment figure alone) gives a hint of the rocking of a cradle. Its monotony suggests that interest will be concentrated throughout on the right hand. The introduction also establishes the pedaling for the rest of the piece, with a few exceptions in the coda: there will usually be two pedal changes per measure in the coda, but the number of pedal changes depends on the changes in the harmony. In order to keep the introductory measures in a colorless sonority, the use of the left pedal is recommended.

The theme comes in simply and dolce; it has no coloring crescendos or decrescendos and is completely devoid of any sort of plain cantabile character. The quarter note in measure 5 is a resting stop for the melody and will recur in the first two variations.

The first variation starts with the miraculous appearance of the second voice on the upbeat of measure 7. (Chopin seems to have had a special affection for the sudden, "out-of-the-blue" emergence of second voices; they commonly vanish no less miraculously only a couple of measures after they appear. In the Berceuse, Op. 57, many variations have two voices or contain suggestions of them.) The double notes need good tonal balance and a refined sense for rubato in order to avoid a possibly too-mechanical unfolding of the phrase.

Variation 2 encroaches upon variation 1 (variation 2 begins at measure 11), and only its second measure (measure 12) shows the melodic pattern of the theme. The encroachment measures (measures 10 and 11) have a sequence pattern in which the upward step of a fourth is to be voiced very sensitively every time.

238

Variation 3 (measures 15–18) has a beautiful effect of unreality. The theme is hidden in the grace notes over an A-flat pedal point. The grace notes should be played in a very relaxed manner, *molto armonioso,* on the beat to underline the melody. A slight rallentando in measure 18 enhances the charm of the swaying.

In variation 4 (measures 19–22), an expressive crescendo-decrescendo appears for the first time. The touch should be *jeu perlé*—light but still legato and without finger virtuosity. In measure 22, the top of the crescendo can have a more detailed melodic line, which is achieved by means of a slight broadening of the tempo.

In variation 5 (measures 23–26), the double thirds have the freedom and natural rhythm of speech: the group of six thirty-seconds at the end of measure 23 should not be played in correct time but with the flexibility of a gentle question, like the group of eight in measure 24. The chromatic double thirds should be played without explosive finger virtuosity or a driving crescendo. The tone should be more legato and the sound somewhat muffled.

Variation 6 (measuers 27–30) displays the same magical effect as variation 3. Over the harmony the melody exists only as a gentle suggestion. Here also the double notes should be played in a very relaxed manner, exactly on the beat. The triplet rhythm warns the player that the figure should not be jammed in, and it should especially not be reminiscent of the rhythm of the grace notes in variation 3. Otherwise the same magical tone is to be applied.

At measures 29–30, a light crescendo begins that leads to variation 7 (measures 31–34), where the double thirds again should be lacking in noisy finger virtuosity. The refined descending chromatic run should be heard as an uninterrupted subtle cascade of notes. The fingering of this passage is difficult; the recommended fingering is:

measures 31-32

The role of the thumb in measures 33–34 should not be predominant; the recurring A flat is only a pedal point.

Variation 8 seems to have cost Chopin considerable effort: he rewrote and corrected these measures several times before reaching this final solution. The variation is composed of two different elements—two measures of chordal texture, rhythmically almost in the style of improvisation *senza rigore,* followed by two measures of refined passagework in thirty-seconds that are more steady in tempo. The problem of this passage is the smooth repetition of the same note occurring in every group of thirty-seconds. This difficulty is even more prominent in the first group of thirty-seconds in measure 38, where the distance between the A flat and the C prevents the use of the easy, natural fingering applicable to all the other groups. Both proposed solutions have their weaknesses: one turns the hand in the wrong direction; the other entrusts the repeated note to a possibly clumsy thumb.

measure 37

A vaporous tone quality coupled with the lightest possible touch is needed for the triplet thirty-seconds in variation 9 (measures 39–42). The fingering for the first two measures, a constant 2-5-2 1-4-1, invites a gentle rotation of the hand. The top notes should emerge slightly, forming a muffled melodic line.

The four-measure pattern of variations breaks down at this point and is replaced by two two-measure patterns (measurs 43–44 and 45–46), both showing more definite cadential tendencies than the preceding variations of the melody. Both pairs of measures contain severe musical and technical problems for the performer. The even, pearly quality required for the scale in measure 43 presupposes faultless passing over the thumb; the included extra note obliges us to use the fourth finger at every passing. This fingering is both a simplification and a complication—a simplification in that the regularity of the pattern makes it easy to learn, but a complication in that every other passing of the fourth finger over the thumb involves two neighboring white keys. Only well-trained, relaxed hands can assure passages without bumps. The fourth finger should play on the fingertip. Only a supple, flexible thumb fares well under the palm of the hand and can allow the fourth finger to be in the necessary position at the moment of passing.

The ensuing trill in the same measure (measure 43) is often misread: it involves the notes C flat (not B flat) and B double flat. The next trill involves B flat and A flat. These trills have to be played lightly and effortlessly, with generous length. The long fiorituras of measure 44 have to be played against the second and fifth eighth notes in the measure; furthermore they should be laid out generously and without undue rushing. The tempo of the measure can be slower and more cadencelike. There is some controversy concerning the first note of the second fioritura: some editions have a G natural; others (concurring with the manuscript) have a G flat.

The next two-measure period, variation 10 (measures 45–46), again has the vaporous thirty-second-note triplets. Since the preceding two two-measure periods have an important cadencelike function, they make the last section of the work sound, emotionally, like a coda.

From here (measure 47) on, the tempo becomes sostenuto and the tone more of a personal comment. The more frequent stops on certain notes of the melody also show that the music is running out of its previously felt gentle drive. Variation 11 (measures 47–50) slows the speed to regular sixteenth notes.

In the next variation (variation 12, measures 51–54), the correct speed for the triplet sixteenths should be observed; a too-fast rendering would give the false impression that something new was beginning here. Measure 53 has gentle accents in cross rhythm on the A flats, recurring once in measure 54 also on the same A-flat, the sixth note of the scale.

The following eight-measure period (measures 55–62) begins with a subdominant turn of sufficient magnitude to change the harmony for the only time in the entire piece (measures 59–60). The C flat responsible for the change in harmony, repeated as frequently as possible in the figure, lends a truly magical effect to the passage. The program element in the music appears strongest here when the melodic outline becomes more repetitious, as if consciousness were sinking into sleep. The performer has to be able to play these eight measures with great delicacy and refined expression. There should be a decrescendo, especially after the appearance of the dominant chord (measure 61). Also a slight broadening in measure 62 will help one slide smoothly into the last appearance of the theme at measure 63.

The unreal quality of the subject is only emphasized the more by the disappearance of the dominant harmony from the accompaniment. The calm is complete; then the melody also starts to fade out. These last eight measures call for constant diminuendo, which is possible only if the performer can have the utmost control over the tone. The last two chords have to be played in a way that suggests deep sleep.

There is no indication of pedal in the manuscript, but this certainly does not imply that no pedal should be used. Different editions give different suggestions on this subject, some indicating pedal for the first half of each measure only and others indicating two pedal changes per measure, with some exceptions. These exceptions are in measure 28 and measure 43, each of which has three pedal changes in accordance with the changes of harmony. After measure 55, the pedal can be used for complete measures; the playing of measures 57–58 on one pedal can even be considered.

Besides the usual ingredients to be coped with in the style of Chopin (freedom of rhythm and sense for legato and line), there is an added new dimension in the Berceuse—an undeniable impressionistic character. The tone, never exceeding mezzo piano, has to have the versatility to deal with all the different types of runs, some of which surround the gently present melodic line in a vaporous atmosphere. Everything in the Berceuse is a question of tone color; therefore it is necessary to approach it through the ear and the imagination.

Franz Liszt

Born 1811, Raiding; died 1886, Bayreuth

The generous Romanticism of Liszt's musical style has its roots in the gypsy music of his native Hungary (even though he never studied the language itself); in the classical style assimilated during his years of early training in Vienna; and in French influences, which were mainly literary. This latter strand, which was probably the most important, was superimposed on the others; on it, the foundations of his "program" music were laid. On this point, Liszt advocated music's ability to express something specific—the recollection of a literary experience, the contemplation of a work of art or a landscape—in an unmistakable manner.

Programmatic elements appear in Liszt's music as early as 1835, in the *Album d'un voyageur*, which was inspired by the scenery of the Swiss Alps. Keen inventiveness and eagerness for novelty forced him constantly to explore new directions. Liszt's harmonic experiments, often pointed out in his late works, show up in his earlier works as well and lead to the blurring—and finally to the total abolition—of the tonal center. In this respect, Liszt points far ahead, influencing many composers of the twentieth century, particularly Bartók.

Liszt's output as a composer was enormous: he wrote about twelve hundred works, and approximately five hundred of them are transcriptions. His original works for the piano include the *Années de pèlerinage*, the Sonata in B Minor, the two *Légendes*, the two ballades, the études, the *Harmonies poétiques et réligieuses*, the *Hungarian Rhapsodies*, and the concertos, to mention only the most important ones.

A new field was opened by his transcriptions for solo piano. Not satisfied with simple piano settings of operatic airs, organ works, symphonies, and songs, he "translated" their musical content, with astounding inventiveness, into completely new compositions.

While Liszt the composer has been appreciated in varying degrees, his supremacy as a pianist has remained unquestioned. His absolute mastery of the keyboard and his tendency toward technical overcomplication make his piano writing seeming to be unsurpassable. Paganini's persisting influence as a virtuoso compelled him to draw effects from the piano that no artist could have drawn before him.

In performing Liszt, one cannot ignore suggestions to imitate the sounds of orchestral instruments, of the human voice, or of diverse natural sources from the waves of the sea to forest murmurs and bird songs. It is obvious that Liszt's new sound effects needed a new piano technique. Liszt's revolution fundamentally changed the approach to the instrument. In addition to total independence of the fingers (also advocated by his contemporaries), he required use of the wrist, forearm, upper arm, and even the torso. His pianistic arsenal contained chords and octaves in quick succession, leaps into distant areas of the keyboard, octave scales and trills alternating between the hands, tremolos, unusual accompaniment figures, and above all, the utmost ingenuity in emphasizing a melody appearing intermingled with different layers of accompaniment. Virtuoso piano technique is rooted in Liszt's works and remains practically unchanged since he first formulated it. No composer since Liszt has added significant novelties to this technique, but many have capitalized on his discoveries.

In our day, it is fashionable to oppose "musicality" to "virtuosity." In Liszt's art, these terms are in perfect agreement because his technique grew out of the necessity to find new ways to express new ideas.

LISZT

Sonetto 123 del Petrarca

Petrarch's Sonnet 123

~~~~~~

All three of Liszt's settings of Petrarch's sonnets share the same interesting history. They were first conceived in 1838–1839 for voice and piano and were later transcribed for piano solo on two occasions—the first time probably as early as 1839 and the second in 1849, when they were incorporated into the *Années de pèlerinage, deuxième année* in their definitive versions. The setting for sonnet 123 is truly inspired in its melody and refined in its harmony. Liszt urged his publishers to print Petrarch's poems with the music to help performers and listeners understand the placid mood of the music.

Form: Two themes alternating, with
introduction and coda

	MEASURES
Introduction	1 – 14
First theme	15 – 29
Second theme	30 – 40
First theme	41 – 48
Second theme	49 – 60
First theme (combined with introduction)	61 – 75
Coda	75 – 84

The outward peace of the introduction should be established by the left hand reaching very calmly over the right. The melody is in the high register; however the initial bass note belongs to it, at least rhythmically; it marks the downbeat of the measures and thus gives the incoming melody the necessary syncopated feeling. The right-hand triplets in sixths create difficulties for hands with a limited extension. No matter which hand this figure appears in, a soft, colorless sonority is to be maintained for it throughout the piece. Musically the motive is two measures long; it should have a slight shaping crescendo-decrescendo that climaxes on the downbeat of the second measure. This crescendo-decrescendo should be purely a shaping device; it is kept almost imperceptible so as not to disturb the placidness of the mood. In addition every measure should have a pedal for its full length.

From measure 5 on, the right hand shows a convinced fervor in the soaring octaves; the left hand is in charge of both the significant bass notes and the triplet motion. In the execution of the sorrowful dotted rhythm, mathematical exactness should be the least of one's preoccupations. The ideal solution lies in the natural flow of metrical speech.

The fervent tension emphasized by the chromatic contrary motion between soprano and bass relaxes resignedly with the resolution of measure 7 (the tonality is F flat major!). The short phrase interjected into measures 8–9 is like an apprehensive question. Its three upbeat eighth notes are spoken, with the freedom of a recitative, rather than played on the keyboard. The question dies away with a ritardando at the end of measure 9.

After a rest of generous length, a stronger phrase begins in measure 10 with more intense questioning that leads to the introduction's final suspension, at measure 14. The speed of the quarter-note triplets of measure 10 should contrast well with that of the eighth-note triplets heard up to this point in the accompaniment. From measure 11 on, the top line stands out, while the low voices of the right hand and the left-hand chords are subdued. The rhythmic subdivision is very important in these measures: each quarter note of the measure is divided into a triplet. The melodic notes appear on the main beats of the measures, while the accompanying chords are played on the last triplet of each group; a strange limping in the rhythm results. The pedal is to be changed carefully with every melodic note; capturing even the feeblest resonance of the preceding accompaniment chord should be avoided. The rendering of the expressive slur between the third and fourth notes of the melody in measures 11 and 12 is of the utmost importance: the fourth note is to be played very softly. The crescendo appearing in measure 13 is passionate, and it even pushes the tempo ahead; still, the odd limping in the rhythm is rigorously continued. The rinforzando of measure 14 applies to the C's of the melody. The fermata is meant to be held, in the best vocal tradition, and the ending B flat is to be pronounced, not too short, but very softly.

The first theme, which has a visionary character, keeps the same slow tempo. The difference between the eighth notes and the triplets of the melody is to be rendered without hardness, in an expressive manner. The performance must do justice to the difference between portamento and legato. The chordal accompaniment, which is reminiscent of the bardic harp, is to be kept soft. In measure 17, the chord followed by the familiar triplet double-note figure contains an especially difficult task for unskillful, heavy thumbs. It is possible to divide this figure between the hands in the following manner:

measure 17

This solution is not unreservedly recommended, since it involves the danger of playing the accompaniment notes entrusted to the right hand with the color of the melody. In its second half, measure 17 also has the problem of assigning a smooth fingering to the longing melody triplets.

In measure 19, the imitation in the left hand has to be brought out in the manner of a harp. The upbeat to measure 20 consists of eighth notes—not triplets—in expressive portamento; the tempo may linger slightly here. The performance of measure 20 should be focused on the change of the bass note in the middle of the measure, which switches the musical events into a new direction.

In measure 21, the accompanying triplets are to be played particularly softly, in sharp contrast to the ensuing octave melody, which soars to passionate heights. The sensitive suspensions of measure 22 are often performed inexpressively, without the implied decrescendo between the slurred octaves.

The rest at the beginning of measure 23 wears a paradoxically heavy accent in performance. The pedal of the preceding harmony has to be sharply cut at this point. The length of the rest may be more generous than exact in order to underline the change in character between the decisive strength of the preceding measure and the resigned slackening that appears here. The C flat (the minor sixth of E flat major) is the source of the sadness and is to be played with poignant sensitivity. The triplet accompaniment figure in measures 23–25 does not take part in this expression; it is reduced to the softest murmur and does not disturb the repetition of the resigned phrase in the tenor, which should sound like muted horns.

Starting from this low dynamic point in measure 25, the music again pushes in a new direction. The dotting of the triplet on the last beat of measure 26 is reminiscent of the natural flow of speech previously mentioned. The broad phrase of measure 28 is very expressive and significant, for it closes the first section. The two-note appoggiatura in measure 29 should coincide with the third triplet of the accompaniment and be played in a way to suggest a human voice.

The dignified calm of the cadence in G flat major is in strong contrast to the second theme, which is stirred by passion. The melodic line has a characteristic dotted rhythm coupled with an upward leap, and it curls chromatically downward from this point. It should be well differentiated in tone from the accompaniment, which contributes to the growing excitement with animated motion.

The fermatas in measures 31 and 33 have the same role as the rest in measure 23: they separate the entranced mood of the phrase from the sad resignation of the falling chromaticism; therefore their length should be generous.

From measure 34 on, the subject evolves in a new direction. The melody, which is in octaves from measure 35 on, is even more involved in chromaticism, while the bass line shows contrary chromatic motion. The passion rises and explodes in measure 37, where the tonality finally settles in E major. The technical difficulty of the passage is vested in the double notes. Though they have the most important role in raising the tension, they should not overpower the melodic line. Choosing an adequate fingering is of great importance; there are two main possibilities:

measure 35

At measure 37, the two hands join to play a triumphant outbreak of the accompaniment figure; it should keep the rhythmic feeling of the triplet even though it is
slurred in pairs. The fingering for this difficult passage has to be firmly established
from the very first reading and consistently adhered to during the practice period. The
only possible fingering is:

measures 37-38

To make it even more difficult, the tempo—constantly stirred by passion—gets somewhat faster here; great caution is recommended on this point, for a too-wild tempo
may rob this triumphant outbreak of its conclusive force. The "vibrato" in measure
38 means that the phrase should be played with vibrant expression.

Large broken chords like the one in measure 39 sometimes occur in Liszt's music
and are considered proof that one needs exceptionally large hands to be successful in
performing Liszt. This rolled chord can be played without noteworthy difficulty with
the fingering 1-2-3-4-5 by a supple hand of any size if the wrist is loose enough to
allow the necessary twisting.

The key of E major is strongly confirmed in measures 39-40. Notice that the rising arpeggio contains triplets, while the repeated E's of measure 40 are eighth notes.
Both measures need a well-gradated diminuendo, reaching the softest possible sound
that is still hearable by an audience. The effect of the repeated E's leading to the
celestial reappearance of the first theme is poignant.

The tempo at measure 41 should be slower than it was previously, and the theme
should reflect heavenly calm and serenity. At measure 45, the melody should be

played as if it were a cello solo (with a "human" tone); piano instead of the preceding triple piano is recommended, while the accompaniment figure is played as soft as possible, the hand barely caressing the keys. To avoid the danger of crashing heavily on the thumb of the left hand in the rolled chords, the following distribution of notes between the hands is recommended:

measures 45-48

The passionate second theme is introduced by the eighth-note figure following the fermata of measure 48. It appears here somewhat altered, though its typical features—the dotted rhythm and the expressive leap upward—are unchanged. As it does in its first appearance, the accompaniment here stirs the growing passion. In the melody, the last two triplet chords of measures 49 through 51 should linger slightly in tempo and in tone, in reminiscence of the sadly falling chromatic scale of measure 31. The low voice of the right hand should not cover the melody at this point.

In spite of the prescribed accelerando and the growing passion, the speed reached at measure 52 should still allow complete control of the melody in the left hand; the left hand also has the job of playing a bass note and then immediately leaping to the chord on the third beat of every measure—a difficult leap that is very risky to execute in a too-fast tempo. Accuracy is also the main difficulty for the accompanying right hand, which has to perform quick changes in position on the keyboard.

The climax is reached at measure 58. The suspension in the melody, reinforced by the right hand, has to be heard as such in spite of the fortissimo. The ensuing succession of falling double notes should be played portamento espressivo, with a prominent melodic profile. Particularly sensitive is the intense chromaticism at the end of measure 59 and in measure 60, showing contrary motion between soprano and bass.

As in previous double-note passages, a stable fingering is one of the keys to successful performance. The recommended fingering is:

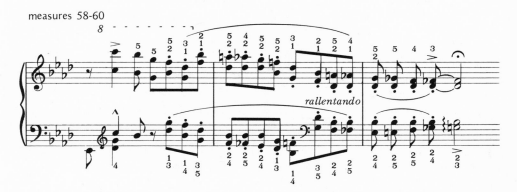

measures 58-60

The falling passage may have some diminuendo in measure 59; a small crescendo, with an important ritardando and a sorrowful accent on the fourth eighth note of the measure, follow in measure 60. The sound is suspended while the left hand corrects the harmony.

A long, dramatic rest follows. The first theme, appearing here with simple chordal accompaniment, seems to be cleansed of all human passion. The G-flat bass note in measure 63 is most significant and sets a new path harmonically. The figuration of the melody in this same measure is like an improvisation and leads to the tone of unreality that imbues the ensuing four measures. The trill introduced by an arpeggiated chord should fill out the full length of measure 64, and the remarkably inventive ten-note scales should rise up from it. These scales are frequently played too fast. Notated in groups of five with one group on each beat of the measure (hardly faster than ordinary sixteenths), they will have an improvisatory character if the tempo is kept approximately accurate. Furthermore the appropriate tempo will enable the left hand to play the entry of the melody on the last beat in an expressive manner.

In measure 66, the diminished-seventh chord of the left hand is most sensitive; the following two-note appoggiatura is to be played the same way as it was in its previous occurrences. Meanwhile the trill of the right hand requires an effortless dolcissimo, and a fast speed as well. The cascade of notes in measure 67 follows just as effortlessly. The unusually large span needed between the second and fourth fingers frequently stiffens the hand and precludes a delicate and easy performance. If the fingers are not raised high above the keys, the wrist will preserve its looseness and will allow (by moving laterally) an easier execution of this graceful run. At the indication ''quasi niente'' (''almost nothing''), the spinning turns slow down, preparing for the triplets that lead back to the motive of the introduction and to the world of reality. The absence of syncopation makes the phrase only the more serene.

A different tone color is essential at measure 70 to emphasize the addition of a higher octave to the melody. A crescendo will not appear until measure 72, and it will raise the sound to the level of an intense recitative. The fermata of measure 74 is to be played as if it were being sung in the operatic tradition.

The coda is built on the longing eighth-note motive and the sensitive suspension of the first theme. Harmonically it turns toward the subdominant key. Measure 78 needs an especially sensitive treatment. The right hand delicately caresses the keys with a fingering that insures perfect legato. In the middle of the measure, the mood grows darker when the minor key appears. Except for the bass note, the left hand is reduced to the softest murmur. The "perdendo" of measure 79 refers to the quality of utmost delicacy, with a slight lingering of the tempo.

The eighth notes of measure 80 emerge from the mist and lead toward a daring harmonic turn of Liszt's. The music hesitates between the dominant of A major and the tonic of A flat major; each chord is followed by a sensitive suspension in the melody. The performance has to do full justice to the rhythmic complexity of this passage. The rests and the rolled chords are eighth notes, while the suspension sighs are triplets—a difference that has to be rendered in a supple way. After each rolled chord, the left hand should reach toward the first note of the sigh without undue haste, in perfect calm. The sighs climb higher in measure 83, and the highest, in measure 84, involves a half note with a fermata that should last as long as it takes the sound of the B flat to die completely away. If the fermata is held this way, there is no need to change the pedal in the last measure. Thus the piece ends with the harmonious prolongation of the A flat chord slowly dying away.

Acquaintance with Petrarch's poem is an absolute precondition for the interpretation of *Sonetto 123* because mood in Liszt's works not only determines the sonority, dynamics, and tempo, but it also dominates the technique and the form. Technically the greatest difficulty lies in the accurate performance of the double-note passages, for which the consistent use of the adopted fingering has to be urged again. Still the true difficulty of the performance lies in the choice of the different tempos, in their gradual increase or decrease, in the extent of the crescendos and decrescendos, in the variety of tone in the delicate passages, in the lengths of fermatas and dramatic rests, and in general in devices that—if used in the right proportion—can unify the performance.

LISZT

Waldesrauschen

Forest Murmurs

~~~~~~

Waldesrauschen, from *Deux études de concert,* is the perfect illustration of Liszt's conception of the étude. He aimed, not to develop or improve, but to display the technique of the performer. Also he never limited any one étude to only one kind of difficulty, as his contemporaries—including Chopin—did. Furthermore, for Liszt the
poetic element distinctly took over; the pedagogical purpose was almost entirely
dropped. *Waldesrauschen* and its companion piece, *Gnomenreigen* ("Dance of the
Gnomes"), were composed in 1862–1863 in versions that became definitive.

Form: Ternary

	MEASURES
Main subject	1 – 29
Middle section (development)	29 – 60
Recapitulation (with cadenza)	61 – 86
Coda	87 – 97

The first difficulty to overcome is in the smoothly flowing accompaniment figure
of the right hand. It will become obvious from the first attempt that finger motion
alone won't do justice to the ethereal murmur. The position on the keyboard immediately suggests a slight, supple motion of the hand forward and backward on the
keyboard, a sort of "push-and-pull" motion. The hand is in the deepest "in" position
when the lowest note is played with the thumb and in the maximum "out" position
when the interval of a third is played with the fingering $\frac{5}{4}$. The motion should be very
slight and continuous. Simply pulling on the fifth finger and pushing abruptly on the
thumb would give an adverse result. The difference between "in" and "out" should
be minimal, and the positions should be linked by a continuous motion so that the
fingers can be brought into the most comfortable position on the keyboard. If well executed, this "rolling" will insure, not only metrical evenness, but tonal evenness as
well.

The first appearance of the figure, deliberately begun after an initial rest, shows a
rhythmic ambiguity that should be dissipated on the downbeat of the second measure
by slightly stretching the A flat of the accompaniment figure. Thus the syncopation of
the entering melody in the left hand will become evident. This first note of the melody

also clarifies the harmony. Measure 1 may be understood by the listener as simply being in A flat major; the transformation into the dominant seventh of D flat takes place with the entrance of the left hand.

Furthermore this first note of the melody—a syncopated quarter note—points to the formal symmetry of a phrase made up exclusively of eighth notes that ends, with a suspension, on quarter notes in measures 4 and 5. The descending part of the phrase is accompanied by dominant harmony, the ascending by tonic harmony; the ascending melody has far more importance in the further development of the piece.

In the restatement of the first phrase (from measure 6 on), the embellishing grace notes are to be melted into the melodic line and played without hardness, ahead of the principal note. A subtle enharmonic modulation leads from D flat major into E major. Especially refined are the harmonies of measures 12–14, where the tonal center of E major is almost totally effaced by the chromatic motion shown in the right hand's figure. The difficulties in the right-hand fingering are prominent in those measures because of the interval of a fourth, which appears at this point for the only time at the top of each figure. The suggested fingering is:

measures 12-14

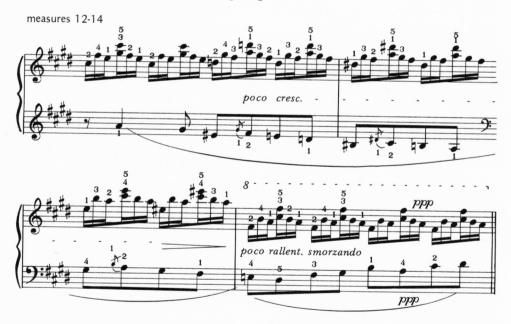

Only an agile and flexible thumb, ready to creep under the fingers in the second half of measure 12 and the first half of measure 13, can assure a smooth execution. Any excess weight of the arm—even the slightest—may be harmful. The wrist, completely loose, should be moving laterally. A word of warning may be useful at this point against a simplistic fingering of measures 12–14 consisting of continuous

1-2-3-3-2-(1)-1-2-3 and so on. While this fingering may seem promising at the slow practice tempo, it will never have the necessary smoothness at the final tempo.

At measure 15, the same enharmonic procedure plunges the music again into the soft waters of D flat major, with the melody on the top. The accompanying left-hand figure can only be executed with a laterally flexible wrist that gently marks the lowest and—even more softly—the highest notes of the figure, thus underlining the harmony. The bass notes, which first occur at quarter-note speed, begin to move in eighth notes at the end of measure 16; their faster pace requires careful control of both hand and pedal. Some of the bass notes are clearly marked suspensions that demand a sensitive rendering of the delicate harmonic frictions involved. The right hand has the difficult task of producing a fluid melodic line in octaves. The key of D flat major favors the use of the third and fourth fingers alternating with the fifth on the top of the line; meanwhile the hand and arm are to be kept as quiet as possible.

A new feature of the melody—the insertions of triplets in measures 16, 19, and 20—makes the line even more fluid. The phrase follows its previously established path as far as measure 25; here a lingering, hesitant phrase appears, gains assurance with its repetition in octaves in the next measure, and approaches F major (by an ingenious chromatic modulation). This new key is finally confirmed by a strong cadence on the downbeat of measure 29. The arpeggios of the left hand in measure 27 are, to say the least, unusual. The uncommonly large span between the first two notes (to be played with 5–3) makes it difficult to begin them smoothly because the fifth finger is frequently kept stiff in this stretched position. The arpeggios roll up and down the keyboard like waves—an effect that is better approached by a sweeping hand rather than by excessive fingerwork. The melodic line becomes triumphant at measure 28. A slight easing of the tempo in this measure helps to bring the phrase to an exultant conclusion.

In measure 29 and similar measures, the utmost lightness is assured if, instead of attacking from high above the keyboard, the hands are held close to it. In measure 30 and similar measures, the grace note represents a tonic pedal point. At measure 34, the main melody (still in the left hand) is enveloped by a countermelody appearing on the top of the right-hand figuration. The notes should be rung like little bells, though not so as to draw full attention away from the left-hand melody.

After a similar exposition of the same passage in A major (measures 37–44), an imitative development section (illustrating Liszt's taste for counterpoint) is reached. Two elements, the first and the last measure of the main idea, are opposed in every measure, and they appear alternately in the soprano and bass. The key center often changes in the subsequent measures (measures 45–60). The first measure of the main idea, with its typical syncopated opening, is the leading motive. This motive will emerge victorious in measure 51, in the midst of increasing passion. However the execution of the secondary motive is more difficult, especially in the form in which it appears in the left hand, where the span between the fifth and second fingers may stiffen smaller hands and thus make the sound uncontrolled.

Measure 50 contains the difficulty of a new figure for the right hand that has to be played with the ease and fluidity of the preceding measures. The agitato that began at measure 45 reaches a passionate boiling point at measure 51; yet the tempo should quicken only a little because an accelerando awaits at measure 53. At this point, the left-hand octaves should be quickly rolled, with the beat preserved on the top note to keep the rhythm strong; the contrary motion between the bass line and the fifth finger of the right hand should be clearly shown.

The emotional and dynamic climax is to be reached at measure 55 and maintained through the rest of the section up to the double bar, measure 60. The tempo, animated by the preceding accelerando, should be fast and overwhelmingly virtuosic. The "martellato" indication applies to the left-hand octaves. If the right hand's single notes are played too loud, the impetuous figure will sound unskillful and bumpy. The triplet octaves—somewhere on the crossroad between brilliant cadenza and meaningful recitative—are best entrusted to the left hand alone, as written. This solution will insure the clear enunciation of each octave instead of the heavy legato character that the solution with two hands may impart to it. An easing of the tempo, without diminuendo, makes the end of the recitative more eloquent.

A special difficulty for the right hand in measures 55–57 must be pointed out: it concerns the arpeggio figure, which frequently sounds inarticulate if the fingers are jammed in the octave position. It can be avoided if the octave span in the hand is released at the precise moment when the fifth finger succeeds the thumb on the same key. The hand passes flexibly from extension to contraction in a fraction of a second, and it then extends again.

The recapitulation, "un poco più mosso," is triumphant in character. Effortless ease in the execution of the accompaniment figure yields a carefree soaring of the melody, which leads to a new cadenzalike section at measure 71. The left hand in particular is tested here by a leaping accompaniment figure. Patient practicing is needed for finding the different chord positions on the keyboard without previously preparing the hand over the keys. One essential condition of success here is the fingering: the use of the fifth finger should be restricted to the lone bass notes. Thus the hand is forced to turn slightly outward while the torso leans to the right as much as possible. Raising the hand too high above the keys puts a brake on the high speed of delivery necessary here and only adds to the risk of inaccuracy. Throughout the passage, the right hand's movements remain calm, thus making possible full concentration on the left hand. The performance should display exhilarating virtuosity in a brilliant, enthusiastic fortissimo, at a speed that should seem "breakneck" to the listener.

In measures 77–78, the left hand coincides with the upper notes of the tremolo. It is recommended that this passage be practiced by playing the full text of the left-hand part accompanied only by the top A's of the right hand in order to realize the correct speed of the tremolo, which is usually played much faster than necessary. Similarly the "quasi trillo" does not mean that one is free to play any number of notes in measures 79–80. The constantly accelerating speed (stringendo from measure 71 on) reaches its climax here. The use of the left thumb in these measures or in the following two measures would be uncomfortable in this position on the keyboard or in the accompaniment to the virtuosic cascade of the right hand (measures 83–85). It is better to play this latter figure with 3–2 and 4–2 fingering. At this point, the right hand should display the utmost virtuosity, producing an evenly flowing run without grouping accents and with a well-gradated diminuendo.

Measure 86 is in the free style of a vocal recitative. The fermata, preceded by the grace note in the manner of a vocal slide, should be long held. Notice that the fermata of the left hand is on the rest: therefore the F in the right hand has to be heard alone. The ''a tempo'' in measure 87 should be slightly slower than the initial tempo, and the first note of the measure (the resolution of the preceding passionate recitative) should be slightly prolonged. The right-hand figure is readily executed if the thumb, once used, does not stay in position but promptly joins the other fingers in preparation for its next use. The entering melody, with a tonic pedal point in the grace note, shows calm and tranquility. The gently comforting motive rises higher and higher on the keyboard and finally evaporates.

One of the characteristics of Liszt's late style was the tendency to liberate the music from enslavement to a tonal center. The imaginative, colorful *Waldesrauschen* exemplifies this penchant. Perfectly solving its manifold technical difficulties is only a part of the requirement. A convincing performance should do justice to the poetic beauty, the soaring lyricism, and the shimmering tone colors of the piece as well.

LISZT

Paganini Etude No. 5
La Chasse

The Hunt

~~~~~~

The *Grandes Etudes de Paganini,* commonly called "the Paganini études," ex-
emplify the magnetic effect Paganini had on his contemporaries and particularly on
Liszt. The concert Paganini gave in 1831 in Paris was a shattering experience for the
nineteen-year-old Liszt. In response he practiced in complete seclusion up to fourteen
hours a day until the keyboard relinquished to him its most hidden secrets.

Each of the six Paganini études based on the Caprices for solo violin by Paganini
has two versions, except for the fourth étude, which has three. The first versions of all
six, of almost unplayable difficulty, date from 1838. Revised and simplified to the
forms in which we know them, they were published in 1851.

Form: Rondo

	MEASURES
Subject	1 – 32
First episode	32 – 52
Subject	52 – 68
Second episode	68 – 107
Subject	107 – 125

The indications "imitando il flauto" and "imitando il corno" have their roots in
the art of Paganini, who—as part of his staggering technique—was able to draw
sounds from the violin that had never been heard before. The main subject, which
features typical horn fifths depicting the hunt, is divided between the hands, with the
right hand playing the lighter sixteenth notes and the left hand the tenuto eighths. The
closeness of the hands on the keyboard obliges the left hand to play in a position above
the right hand. The fingering for the opening figure is: R. H. 3 2 $\begin{smallmatrix}5&4\\2&2\end{smallmatrix}$ 1 $\begin{smallmatrix}4&3\\2\end{smallmatrix}$. The
L. H. $\begin{smallmatrix}4\end{smallmatrix}$ $\begin{smallmatrix}5\end{smallmatrix}$
player should avoid the use of the left thumb, which would disturb the right hand in
such a close position.

The forte at measure 8 means that a darker color (imitating horns) rather than a
great amount of sound should be used. The sudden interventions of the flute piano
may be slightly delayed, as if for breathing on a wind instrument. The new version of
the main subject at measure 16 is supposed to imitate the harmonics (or flageolet, as

they are sometimes called) of the violin. It is very difficult to play the accompaniment softly. Heaviness in the thumb is disastrous for this figure; it has to be performed with a loose, laterally moving wrist that will help the thumb or the fifth finger to find the outlying notes. In measures 19–20 and 23, the left hand should keep close to the keys to avoid unwelcome bumping on the double notes. The right hand deals with the whole subject. The recommended fingering is:

measures 16-20

The left-hand part of measure 24 is to be executed with a lateral motion of the hand, with the following fingering:

measure 24

The first episode has the subject in the tenor, divided between the hands; for this reason, the chords of the right hand should have the weight on their lowest notes, carrying the melody. The melodic line will suffer if the prescribed accents on the main beats are excessive and swallow (so to speak) the ensuing sixteenth notes. On the other hand, if the sixteenths played by alternate hands are too loud and fail to match the sound of the preceding eighth notes, the effect is equally ruinous. Accuracy in the passage is difficult to achieve, especially for the right hand, which has to jump from the last sixteenth note to the ensuing chord. The problem arises from the necessity of using the second finger on the sixteenth note; great elasticity of the hand is needed to play the chord that immediately follows accurately. The left hand should play the white-key sixteenth notes *sotto* ("under") and the black ones *sopra* ("above"); these notes should always be played with the second finger. Both hands should use thumbs on the chords and then twist the wrist left to reach for the sixteenth notes with the second finger without lifting the hands away from the surface of the keys. Only in measure 42 may the left hand attack the three successive octaves with a slight swinging of the arm.

In measure 45, the melody gains more ardor with the sequential motive. Closeness to the keys and absence of heaviness on the beats remain essential.

The second episode needs audacious virtuosity. Because of the initial double octaves, dynamics are often pushed to extremes. A brilliant forte is more effective at this point than a heavy, thunderous fortissimo. The real problem, though, consists in the rhythmically correct execution of the sparkling glissandos. Every pianist has his own way of (or finger for) playing glissandos. Here the second or third finger in the right hand and the third finger in the left seems to give the best result. A rich, even glissando is executed with a loose hand; remember the sound you can draw from the piano while dusting the keyboard with a cloth. Pressing stiff fingers down hard on the keys painfully rips the skin off without producing an exciting, brilliant sound. Practice should begin by playing the glissando softly, and barely touching the surface of the keys until the skin hardens and can take more punishment without much pain.

Two other difficulties concerning the glissandos are distinctive here. One is that throughout the blazing glissandos, the hands should remain a sixth apart. To pull both hands along at the exact same speed is a difficult task. A good result may be secured by the simple trick of linking the two thumbs together, thus insuring a firm span between the hands executing the glissando. The third finger should be used in both hands. Arriving on an accurate interval of a sixth on the last note of each glissando is of the utmost importance.

The second difficulty is the preservation of a solid tempo throughout the glissando measures; for example, the glissando should begin immediately after the second beat of measure 70 and conclude on the second beat of measure 71, on a distinct eighth note that will be followed by two sixteenth notes. The most often-heard mistake here is a hurried execution of the glissando that lasts less than its required two beats. The speed of the glissando is difficult to control, and it is especially so for inexperienced players, whose fingers may get tangled in the keys if the glissando is not pulled up at the highest speed.

But there are more complications to follow in measure 72. First of all, the trill in the right hand has to be executed with weak fingers. Needless to say, the trill has to have the accurate length of one beat. The left-hand downbeat of this same measure is further complicated by the grace note's distance from the chord it ornaments. Its execution is very difficult, and the left hand needs great agility to play it accurately. The difficulty is somewhat lessened if the following fingering is adopted:

measures 71-72

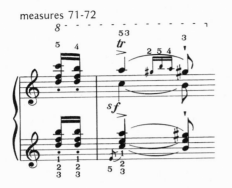

From measure 75 on, the bravura that is called for consists of finding the different positions on the keyboard with ease and elegance. The left hand crosses over the right, *sopra*. The five-note figure of the right hand is to be fingered a steady 4-3-2-1-2, thus best insuring the simultaneity of the last note of the figure with the accompanying chord of the left hand. The tempo is often rushed at this point, robbing the passage of its elegance. The fingering for measures 81–82 is:

measures 81-82

In measure 85, there is a rolled chord instead of the grace note that appeared in measure 72. The execution and fingering should be the same as in measures 71–72. From measure 89 on, elegance, ease and a solid tempo are constant requirements. The motives in the higher register from measure 95 on should produce a sort of whistling sound that imitates the harmonics on a violin; these passages should always be played somewhat lighter than those in the lower register. The same dazzling effect is to be given to the higher-register motives from measure 99 on, and undue heaviness should be avoided in spite of the initial and concluding double notes.

From measure 102 on, the figure of the right hand is to be considered the main motive; the left hand's role is only that of accompaniment, and it should be played with the utmost lightness. When the left hand yields to the right, it should not be lifted away from the keyboard lest there be attacking accents on the figures. The crescendo leads to a light forte on the downbeat of measure 106, and from here the arpeggio evaporates in diminuendo. The fingering for measure 106 is:

measures 106-107

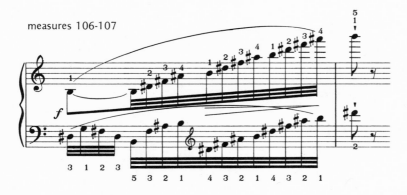

The interval of the sixth has to be clearly heard throughout this arpeggio.

The animated tempo from measure 107 on should not exhaust the reserves of the performer. If the last brilliant appearance of the main theme sounds as if a breakdown were near, the transcendental effect will be totally missed. The main reason for possible fatigue lies in the new repeated-double-note accompaniment figure. It is, indeed, very difficult to execute it elegantly without contracting the muscles in the arm. Furthermore accents on the first interval would chop the right hand's phrase into beats. These repeated intervals are to be performed from the forearm; the wrist should be loose, the upper arm relaxed and hanging from the shoulder, and the hands kept as close to the keys as possible. The "perdendosi" of measure 123 includes a slight retard with the diminuendo. The last chords are in tempo again; their rhythm should be accurate and sharp, and they are to be played forte.

La Chasse, with its concise writing, recalls the style of some virtuoso harpsichordist of the Baroque period. Liszt's transcription, which exploits the exhilarating virtuosity of Paganini's violin technique, is remarkable. The difficulty of the étude, evident mainly in the episodes, is by no means insuperable. The solution of its technical difficulties lies in the unrestrained, elegant domination of the entire four-foot length of the keyboard, on which the hands should find the required positions with extreme quickness and ease. It also lies in the use of shimmering tone colors capable of evoking the sounds of the violin, flute, and horn.

Johannes Brahms

Born 1833, Hamburg; died 1897, Vienna

During three distinct periods of his creative life, Brahms was predominantly interested in the piano. It seems only natural that the young piano virtuoso would have consecrated his first works to his own instrument: 1852 to 1856 is the period in which the three piano sonatas and the Scherzo, Op. 4, were composed. Though youthful works, they plainly show the typical Brahmsian piano style, which can be labeled "symphonic."

The second group (approximately 1857–1862) includes mainly sets of variations, most important among them those on Handel and Paganini themes. This is a period of exploring the technical possibilities of both the piano and the pianist.

Finally, the third group begins in 1878 with opus 76; this can be called Brahms's romantic or contemplative period. Comprising musical miniatures modeled after those of the Romantic composers, works of this period are distinguished by great simplicity and refinement of style.

A surprising turn lies in the trend of this development. The Romantic composer usually started off by composing small character pieces before trying his forces on large Classical forms. Brahms proceeded in the opposite direction, at least insofar as his piano music is concerned.

The main requisite of his piano style is a rich, warm sound. Massive chords and melodies in octaves abound in his writing, while finger technique and filigree work are almost nonexistent. His melodic inventiveness, one of his strongest qualities, was deeply influenced by North German folk music. The traditional accompaniment for this music came from doublings in thirds or sixths, and this custom accounts for the many double-note passages in Brahms's music, some of which involve uncomfortable stretches between the fingers. Brahms's *51 Exercises* treats this problem and also provides lessons in good legato playing. Another specific difficulty of Brahms's piano style, its extensive rhythmic complexity, is also represented at length among the exercises.

Brahms's absolute belief that Classical forms can be adapted to Romantic expression remained unshaken during his life. Did he intentionally keep the flow of his expression within the bounds of his forms or is it that Classical balance naturally fitted his refined artistry? The question cannot be answered unequivocally.

BRAHMS

Capriccio in F Sharp Minor, Op. 76, No. 1

Of the eight piano pieces forming Brahms's opus 76, there are four contemplative, introverted intermezzos and four capriccios, which are more animated in movement and passion. The set was composed between 1871 and 1878. The Capriccio in F Sharp Minor was a gift to Clara Schumann on her fifty-second birthday, in 1871. It is one of the most difficult capriccios, but it is also one of the most appealing.

Form: Ternary, with two main ideas

	MEASURES
First part	1 – 26
First idea	1 – 13
Second idea	14 – 26
Development	26 – 51
First part (Recapitulation)	52 – 71
First idea	52 – 63
Second idea	64 – 71
Coda	72 – 85

The reign of a mysterious, tormented atmosphere is established from the very outset of the piece. The contour of the melody emerges from the last three sixteenth notes of each measure and the following downbeats, while the rest of the figure sweeps restlessly through the keyboard, insisting on three descending diatonic notes. These notes will have an important role in the further development of the piece. Brahms's notation, implying an uncomfortable hand crossing, can be simplified without harm for the first eight measures in the following way:

measures 1-2

and so on.

Throughout measures 5–8, the crescendo has to be very carefully gradated, with a meaningful last crescendo and rinforzando at the end of measure 8 to reach the full fortissimo at measure 9. At this point, the three-note motive that has been confined to the lower register until now breaks through the barrier and furiously sweeps up and down the keyboard. Accuracy is difficult to acquire for the figure in these measures (measures 9–11). In the ascending form of the figure, the problem lies in the sudden expansion of the hand, which is necessary to deal with the leap of a tenth, followed by an elastic contraction, which is needed to play the three-note motive with the fingering 5–3–1. The following exercise is useful in gaining the quickness and elasticity needed for the expansion and contraction:

measure 9

and so on.

Even small hands can make good use of the following fingering for the descending arpeggio:

measure 10

Throughout the receding wave, the dynamics remains fortissimo; in fact, there is still a crescendo in the upward splashing eighth notes at the end of measure 11 leading toward the sforzando of measure 12, where the diminuendo originates.

The plaintive melody of the second idea is accompanied by the typical three-note motive. Metrical clarity is hard to maintain in measures 14 and 15. The time signature 6/8 requires that the six sixteenth notes of a half measure be felt in three groups of two notes instead of two groups of three notes. The erroneous grouping is caused by an unwanted accent on the last sixteenth note entrusted to the right hand. From measure 16 on, the melody has a more active role; its separation in tone from the accompaniment part should be accomplished in a refined manner.

The animation reaches forte at measure 20, where the downbeat has to be stretched expressively by a slight delay of the first accompaniment note. The downbeat of measure 22 needs even more stretching in order to underline the new harmony.

From measure 23 on, the melody is in duet; in spite of the diminuendo, the restless agitation still prevails. Measures 26–27 and 30–31 have a problem in part playing. Ceaseless pushing on the third finger, which is held down for two measures, spoils the independence of the other fingers in their arpeggio figures. The motive, outlined lightly at the top of the arpeggio, appears hazily after the initial sforzando. The piano dynamic indication for measures 26–33 has to be obeyed: the menacing crescendo-decrescendo appears only in the left-hand motive.

From measure 34 on, a new strain of agitation pushes the tempo ahead with a driving crescendo. The off-beat melody should be slightly delayed, adding a somberly passionate note to the excitement. The theme in augmentation (measures 38–41) has the character of a fervent statement and is played in tempo. This version of the theme is twice as slow as before and it should be clearly rendered so that the crossrhythm (or hemiola) in measures 42–48 will have the most interesting, apprehensive effect. The hemiola effect is upheld by the accompaniment sixteenths, which are heard in two groups of three notes and conflict with the inversion of the second idea grouped in the normal duple meter. The melodic note on the fifth eighth note in measures 44–46 is best entrusted to the thumb of the left hand. It is needless to point out that the second idea appears here in inversion.

The dynamic climax is at the forte of measure 48; from here the sound dies away quickly. The crescendo-decrescendo of measure 50 has limited proportions: its only purpose is to underline the main motive hidden in the inner part of the right-hand chords—E–E sharp–A–G sharp. From measure 52 on, the technical difficulties increase considerably when the hands exchange their previous roles for the recapitulation of the first idea. To begin with, the right hand has the problem of elastic/expansion and contraction already encountered in measure 9; however an ethereal piano is required at this point.

Very soon the right hand gives up the three-note motive and takes up a typical Brahmsian figuration, with one pitch extending over a broken octave. The solution for this figuration is much the same as that for the previous difficulty—quick, elastic expansion and contraction of the hand. The difficulties for the left hand include using the fifth finger after the thumb in a rising arpeggio figure, another typical Brahmsian device. It is obvious that twisting the hand so that the fifth finger can reach over or under the thumb to obtain a "perfect legato" is harmful to the fluency of the arpeggio. Here also a quick contraction of the hand is necessary. In this position, the fifth finger reaches for the next note over or under the thumb, according to the latter's location on a black or white key, only suggesting the legato. Extensive hands-separate practice is strongly suggested for this passage until the necessary ease and accuracy are secured. When the hands are put together, it is useful to realize that the fifth fingers of both hands are used simultaneously in the passagework. Thus the contractions of the hands intervene at identical times.

Here the crescendo does not lead to the furious outbreak that was heard previously. The climax is not dynamic but emotional; it culminates at measure 60 in an expressive lament. The notes played with the top part of the hand form a line from which the notes entrusted to the thumb are almost entirely excluded. It is obvious that contracting the hand is not necessary here. However the hand should stay in an extended position without stiffness. The ritardando and the metrical slowdown of measure 63 need a good sense of proportion.

The second idea appears in measure 64 in a simple, chordal version accompanied by the three-note motive in augmentation. Measure 71 is frequently the victim of an insufficiently developed rhythmic sense. The division of the left-hand part (six eighth notes in a 6/8 measure) is obscured by the tie that makes the fourth eighth note of the measure silent. It may be helpful to disobey the tie at first and play the silent beat in order to realize that it coincides with the third chord of the right hand. Another frequently heard mistake is the sudden adoption of a faster tempo for the measure because of rhythmic insecurity. If the tempo changes at all here, it slows down rather than accelerates.

The coda combines the first and second ideas. The figure in the right hand involves the expansion-contraction difficulty already discussed in detail; however the task here is even harder because of the frequency of black keys. Stiffening of the hand occurs frequently when weak fingers in expansion have to strike black keys. The reason for it is usually that the fifth finger tries to play in a position scrupulously parallel to the keys instead of in the natural position, when the fifth finger is at an angle to the key without the danger of slipping off a black key. The preparatory exercise previously recommended is very useful here as well.

Measure 77 has a new difficulty. The only possible fingering for the first three notes of the measure is 3-2-1, and this fingering involves stretching the hand drastically and turning it to a position in which the bumpless use of the immediately following fifth finger on the E sharp is troublesome. The theme in the tenor should be soft but penetrating. In measures 79-80, it is impossible to hold the augmented second in the middle of the right hand for its full value. To have recourse to the pedal is impossible, for the pedal would mix the changing harmonies of the right hand. The obvious solution is to hold the E sharp with the second finger for its full value, while the D played by the thumb is released, since the thumb is involved in playing the sixteenth-note figure. In measures 81-82, the low part of the right hand is to be brought out without obtrusiveness. Hands unable to strike the chord in measures 84-85 simultaneously may adopt the following solution:

measures 84-85

This sombre tone poem, held high in the esteem of his contemporaries, represents the turning point in Brahms's piano style. Beginning with opus 76, Brahms relinquished such Classical forms as the sonata and theme and variations, and adopted the

Romantic idea of character pieces. The mood of this capriccio is an unquiet and agitated one to which the concluding major key only brings a small amount of peace. The technical difficulties associated with the unusual expansion and contraction of the hand must first be eliminated entirely before one can expect an acceptable performance.

BRAHMS
Rhapsody in B Minor, Op. 79, No. 1

Before publishing his *Two Rhapsodies*, Op. 79, in 1880, Brahms had sent them in the early summer of 1879 to his intimate friend Dr. Theodor Billroth, who praised them in enthusiastic terms. The Rhapsody in B Minor, totally different from Liszt's rhapsodies, has a scherzo-trio-scherzo form and contains none of the improvisatory or fantasia elements so typical of rhapsodies. Nevertheless the term Brahms chose to identify this piece is fully justified by frequent rhapsodic changes of mood.

Form: Ternary

	MEASURES
First part	1 – 93
First idea	1 – 29
Second idea	30 – 39
First idea	39 – 93
Second part (Trio)	94 – 128
First part (Recapitulation)	129 – 218
Coda	219 – 233

The powerful, passionate first idea and its various developments dominate the entire first part of the composition, with the exception of the second idea. A strong presentation of the main theme presupposes a strong right hand and fingers coupled with a strong sense of rhythm; this is especially true for the first half of measure 1, where the dotted quarter note has to have its accurate duration and the ensuing triplets must be laid out with the utmost clarity. The long melodic line of the right hand is punctuated by a panting accompaniment. The octaves in the accompaniment should have some emphasis, though a too-heavy accent would be detrimental to the melodic line. The accompanying motive is played with a loose wrist, balancing laterally and tying the three notes together into one motion.

In measures 3 and 4 of the right hand, an uncomfortable figure forces the second finger to negotiate a wide stretch. In measure 5, the first motive of the first idea appears in the left hand below a syncopated chordal accompaniment. In the next measure (measure 6), the right hand regains full importance melodically; the left hand's accompaniment has only the rhythmic quality of the main subject. A good legato is required for the eighth-note figures of the right hand. The suggested fingering for measure 6 is:

measures 5-6

In measures 9–10, the first motive appears again in the left hand. A chromatic modulation and syncopation in the right hand raise the passionate feeling to the forte of measure 11, where the staccato chords of the right hand should be played without excessive shortness so that their melodic importance can be insured. Meanwhile the left hand gives the sensation of slurs (actual slurring is impossible) by moving from the octave to the chord on the surface of the keys without rising high above the keyboard. Accurate rhythm in the left hand is very important in measures 11 and 12: the eighth-note chord should not be played too soon merely to give the hand more time to reach for the octave in the lower register.

A sudden drop in the dynamics on the downbeat of measure 13, will insure a greater drive toward the crescendo octaves and, together with a slight easing of the tempo in measure 15, will render the ending strong.

The staccato indication for the left hand in measures 16–17 should not be followed literally. Portamento (appearing at measure 18) is the right touch for the left hand, playing throughout in the *sopra* position. The right hand plays the F sharps with a flat finger and hand so that the left hand's crossover will be easier. In measures 19 and 21, it is advantageous to play the second and fourth notes of the left-hand part with the right hand, in the following manner:

measure 19

The sudden appearance of the major key in measure 22 lends generous warmth to the music. The section beginning at this point needs perfect part playing in the right hand, which must hold the notes accurately and, what is more important, project different colors for the different layers of the texture. In particular, it is only too easy to overplay the syncopated F sharps with the thumb in the lowest voice of the right hand whereas the voice moving in quarter notes in the middle of the texture needs to be inflated expressively with the crescendo-decrescendo of measures 25 and 26.

The lower D of the left hand is slurred over from measure 28 to measure 29; only the higher D is to be played again on the downbeat of measure 29.

The second idea, appearing at this point, is apprehensive and anxiously questioning. Beneath the main melody, which is in the first plane, the moving middle voice is to be rendered evenly, passing without a break in continuity or in tone from one hand to the other. The dynamic shading of the idea is not to be overlooked; the section should be played as follows: in measures 30–31, there should be local, small, coloring crescendos; in measures 32–33, a driving, expressive crescendo-decrescendo; in measures 34–35, again the motion seems to be less animated; then in measures 36–38, a crescendo-decrescendo points in the most expressive manner to the downbeat of measure 38 and finally dies away with a ritardando.

The a tempo brings the first idea back with an explosion of forte, lasting for a short time only. The piano of measure 43 should be introduced by a sizable diminuendo. After the triumphant explosion, the character of the music becomes mysterious and tormented: the persistent syncopation and the alternation of hands express anxiety. Changes between higher and lower registers will be exploited for orchestral tone color possibilities. The crescendo reaches forte at measure 49, where the first motive of the first idea blazes through the keyboard in exciting imitation. The execution of this passage, though possible, is awkward because of the uncomfortable hand crossings involved. The two substitutions of the right hand for the left suggested here may facilitate a clearer and easier rendering of the passage:

measures 49-50

This solution may yield good results if the right hand does not attack the triplet motive with an accent.

After the rinforzando (which should be interpreted here as a sforzando), a sudden meno forte will make the following long crescendo (with a climax at measure 60) possible. These measures have an irresistible effect if they are well performed. The left-hand octaves, rising chromatically in ceaseless motion, punctuate the rhythm, thus emphasizing the offbeat chords and octaves of the right hand. A slight broadening of the tempo in measure 59 helps to achieve the passionate climax of measures 60–61.

The previous suggestions for measures 49–50 can be applied here as well. The last triplet figure of measure 61 has a dramatic broadening that also allows for greater clarity in the low register.

The scales in measures 62–66 have to be played in strict tempo and with the utmost clarity and brio. The half or whole note preceding the scale should get its accurate length. Whereas the first scale winds up with a short staccato note, the second concludes on a whole note, the source of a frequent blunder. Entrusted with playing the whole-note F sharp, the right thumb should be prepared immediately after its last employment in the scale by opening the hand to the octave span. Once the accuracy of the whole note is secured, pedaling should be used to sustain the sound.

The first idea returns here, unchanged as far as measure 81; here great difficulties are suddenly met with in the left hand. The large broken chord in più forte is often an unsurmountable task for smaller hands. The following suggested redistribution of the notes between the hands will facilitate the precise execution of the passage:

measure 81

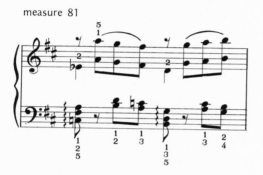

The second finger of the right hand crosses over the thumb, while the hand is kept as close as possible to the octave position.

The alternation of the hands in measures 83 and 84 does not need the clarity of short staccato. Measure 86 includes a quarter-note rest, a frequent victim of miscalculation. It must consist of silence; the prolongation of the preceding chord by the pedal is intolerable here. After the silence, the sforzando chord is the dynamic climax of the entire passage. The ensuing alternated chords and octaves have to be played with the utmost power and conviction, each harmonic turn adding more significance to the splendid cadence. At measure 89, the octave in the low register should be broken to avoid a possible harsh, crashing tone. From this point on, ritardando and diminuendo calm down the excitement and lead to the open question of the fermata, whose length should be generous enough to allow for the transformation from the minor key into the major.

Although the middle section does not wear a new tempo indication in the original edition, it is customary and utterly justified to adopt a slightly slower tempo for it. The theme has its roots in the second idea, which has been only briefly handled in the first section. Transposed into the major key, the subject has a reassuring, warm, lyrical character. Some technical difficulties await the player in the moving eighth notes of the left hand. Their solution requires a good, bumpless passage of the thumb, a relaxed hand, and the avoidance of excessive finger articulation. The notes moving concurrently with the melody may be held longer; the left-hand part would split into two voices. The end of measure 100 should keep the calm, even motion of the eighth notes, in spite of the distant C sharp on the downbeat of measure 101.

In the second part, the modulation on the last beat of measure 107 has to be displayed with clarity; from this point on, the upper pedal point becomes syncopated and needs good care. The dynamic shading reaches its greatest importance. The crescendo that began at measure 106 reaches a first climax at measure 110, where only minimal diminuendo is allowed. From there it leads to the most important crescendo and a slight easing of the tempo in measure 112 and emphasizing the climactic downbeat of measure 113. There, further lingering of the tempo brings the first idea of the section back.

The rhythmic complexity of measures 118 and 119 often ruins an otherwise acceptable performance. Measure 118 is usually easier to figure out because it contains difficulties most performers have already met. The nonconformity of measure 119 leaves even the best mathematicians puzzled. A further complication arises from the wide figure of the left hand, which is very difficult to play metrically evenly without limping. The only solution is in the ear and in a knack for dissociating the hands. The triplet extended for the full measure has to be evenly placed; this condition can be fulfilled only if a one-measure pulse has been established (the left thumb should avoid giving the feeling of a second beat in the middle of the measure by making any inadvertent accents).

The middle section calls for generous use of the pedal; it should be changed with every quarter note throughout, except for measures 117–119 (pedal by half measure); measures 120b and 121b, the second ending (pedal the first half of measure and then pedal the two quarter notes); and measures 125–126 (one pedal is held through both measures). The correct lifting of the pedal should be a constant concern, and the ear should relentlessly control every change to prevent blurring.

The coda is built on the sorrowful second idea, which is played over a tonic pedal point that causes problems of tonal balance for the left hand. The right hand weaves a delicate accompaniment over the melody with an evenly flowing triplet figure. The countermelody, appearing only at measure 223, has already been implied in measure 221. The melody shows the same shaping crescendos-decrescendos as it did on its previous appearance; however at this point their extent should be severely controlled, since the melody appears in a low register. To avoid the uncomfortable position change of the left hand in the middle of measures 230 and 231, the following execution is suggested:

measure 230

In measure 232, the low B in the middle of the measure is more effective if it is entrusted to a right hand crossover. In these measures the coda dies away in Olympian calm.

The main parts of the rhapsody stir dark, menacing passions; these are contrasted sharply with the idyllic middle section—a truce between raging storms. Ingeniously handled the same themes disclose different expressions at various points in the work. Technical difficulties are to be found in chord and octave playing, and these difficulties are intensified for small hands. The tone, which is full and round and without hardness in the fortes, should remain weighty and well focused throughout the softest pianissimos. The middle section needs a good sense of proportion and warm musicality. The Nordic character of Brahms's earlier works—passionate impetuosity opposed to tender expression—is plainly displayed in this rhapsody.

BRAHMS

Capriccio in G Minor, Op. 116, No. 3

Together with opus 117, opus 116 was composed almost entirely at Ischl, Austria, where Brahms generally passed the summer months. Published as *Fantasies* in 1892, opus 116 consists of seven piano pieces (four intermezzos and three capriccios). The extraverted capriccios differ from the intermezzos in having a vehement, impulsive character. In this respect, the Capriccio in G Minor is a typical example of its genre.

Form: Ternary

	MEASURES
First part	1 – 34
Second part	35 – 70
First part (recapitulation)	71 – 104

From the very first moment, the listener is plunged into a wild, tempestuous turmoil that will last through the entire first part. The confusion seems even more widespread as harmonic resolution on the tonic is consistently dodged until the end of the section. The first figure of the right hand has an irresistibly driving crescendo toward the sforzando chord in the middle of the first measure. The following entry of the left hand should be slightly delayed; then every step of the rising arpeggio is to be punctuated. Tonal balance is difficult to maintain; the right-hand part should constantly dominate the texture.

The motive in measures 3–4 comes as an answer to the first two measures and should be similarly conceived, except for a little easing of the tempo and sound at the end of measure 4. The repetition of the two motives (measures 5–8) shifts the sforzando from the chord to the entrance of the left hand. In measure 6 great emphasis should be given to the highest note of the melody with an expressive extension.

From measure 9 on, the turmoil is further increased by the sinuosity of the unison line. The first note of every measure needs expressive prolongation and has to be separated from the preceding measure by a clear interruption. From measure 10 on, the stepwise ascent of the motive builds the tension toward measure 12, where the repeated G's (which are more prolonged at each repetition) prepare for the reentry of the main idea in augmentation at measure 13.

The unison passage following at measure 21 first descends chromatically into darker regions. The separation of the measures and the prolongation of the first notes is just as important as before, especially from measure 25 on, where the chromatic ascent of the top line begins, coupled with a roaring crescendo. The dramatic rests in measures 28–29 should not be miscalculated. The chordal ending of the section shows hopeless despair. From measure 31 on, the bass line in octaves is to be treated as melody, and the frictions between tonic and dominant harmonies are to be sensitively brought out. In measure 33, a fresh pedal is needed on the chord even if it means the loss of the low bass note. The substitute note one octave higher in the next measure has to be played emphatically.

The middle part begins after a noticeable silence, which is called for by the fermata on the double bar closing the first section. The atmosphere changes drastically. Solemnity and an almost religious fervor emanate from this choralelike middle episode. The theme is taken from the top part of the first subject. A recurrent feature is the triplet motive, which is also taken from the first subject (the soprano of measure 2) and was already used in the closing measures of the preceding section. It is a counterpoint to the chorale that monopolizes the motion in the section; it also has an important part in the further unfolding of the chorale.

The tone drops to piano for the first time; however the quality remains full and weighty. The crescendo beginning almost immediately has to be carefully gauged, and an imperceptible progression should be made until the forte is reached, led by the triplet figure that intrudes into the melody in measures 41–42. These and similar measures are the only technically taxing passages of this section. A clear rendering of the voices in the middle of the octaves may occasion problems for narrow hands. The fingering for measures 41–42 is:

measures 41-42

Below the triplets, the rhythmic independence of the left hand is to be preserved.

In measures 43 and 44, the sforzandos on the downbeat are like bell strokes; the dissonances involved should be fully sensed and brought out. From measure 45 on, the phrase regresses to the initial piano. The fingering for the first and second endings is:

measures 46a–46b

A new, mysterious character appears in the second section with the sudden entry of G major. The motion is totally dominated by the triplet figure. The crescendo raises the tone gradually to the forte of measure 53 (the misleading ''più forte'' in measure 51 means ''louder than the initial piano'').

The surprise appearance of the minor key in measure 54 has to be brought out in a sensitive way by a slight hesitation and a somewhat more cantabile tone. The descending sequence from measure 55 on introduces a meditative sentiment; it is broken into by the sforzando of measure 59 (like a terrifying ghostly apparition), and it then dissipates with the diminuendo and resolves into the recapitulation of the chorale.

Two poignant sforzandos in measures 65 and 66 attract attention. They are followed by descending leaps of a sixth that lend sorrowful resignation to the phrase, which ends in quiet solemnity. The lightning of the opening motive strikes again even more powerfully and is sustained by a broken chord in the left hand in measure 71. It seems impossible to add more passion to the storm of the first section recapitulated here, but Brahms accomplishes the task successfully. Instead of the previous unison passage, the left hand adds furious waves to the raging passion (measures 79–82).

Measure 83, the augmentation of the first motive, also has a violent wave as accompaniment. Furthermore on the last beat the lowest C on the piano is added to the texture, opening a wide gap between the hands. From measure 95 on, the mirrored motion between the hands stirs the passion frantically. After the dramatic rest, the fortissimo appears for the first time, clearly pointing to the dynamic climax of the piece in a final exclamation of revolt.

This capriccio, reminiscent of the young Brahms in style and general tone, was most probably composed before 1892. Its performance needs power, both physical and expressive, and a full, round tone able to render the loudest forte without hardness.

BRAHMS

Intermezzo in B Flat Minor, Op. 117, No. 2

The *Three Intermezzos,* Brahms's opus 117, which were composed and published in 1892 (the same year as the preceding opus), are comparable to autumn sketches. Typically for the intermezzos, they show meditativeness, profound sensitivity, and often sorrowful resignation. The second intermezzo of the series is the most gratifying and counts among the most universally admired piano pieces of Brahms.

Form: Ternary

	MEASURES
First section	1 – 22
Second section	22 – 38
Transition	38 – 51
First section (Recapitula-tion)	51 – 72
Coda	72 – 85

The top notes of a lacelike arpeggio texture carry the melodic line, clearly marked by short slurs. Pale in color, the main theme has to float over the accompaniment, which is played lightly and without obtrusiveness; the accompaniment itself, even in tempo and in tone, appears in a dark second plane. While the melody is suspended, the rising initial semitone step of each left-hand arpeggio has to be hinted at delicately. This rising semitone will have an important role throughout the intermezzo.

The rising melodic turn between measures 2 and 3 needs sensitive rendering. From this point on, the melody gains more intensity and needs more coloration. The symmetry of the melody, established previously, is suddenly disrupted in measure 5. Here the phrase shows more impetus; then, in total contrast, its shorter version with dominant harmony in measure 6 gives the impression of a most bitter resignation. The legato required in the melodic line at measure 7 is best served if the last notes of the thirty-second groups are played with the left hand, matching the tone of the other accompaniment notes.

Measures 8–9 have to be played with metrical freedom, stretching the first note slightly and using the tone of the harp. In this measure, the left hand needs a bumpless passing of the thumb. At the lowest point of the arpeggio, another elongation and a clean change of pedal are necessary to make the new harmony comprehensible. The rising arpeggio figure should dissolve completely in diminuendo, with a considerable easing of the tempo.

The reentering main subject at the end of measure 9 is in tempo again. In the second part, a new height is reached with the B flat of measure 11. The ensuing descending chromaticism and harmonic sequences display more intensity in the required espressivo. Asymmetry recurs in measure 14 and is followed by sad resignation. At this point, the reign of the new key, F minor, seems well established, when a desolate convulsion in measure 17 sends the music toward gloomy G flat minor. The deceptive cadence of measures 21–22 (the lowest low so far as the mood is concerned) dies away in diminuendo and rallentando. The D flat in the middle voice of the right hand on the last beat of measure 21 is emphatic and turns the triad into a seventh chord.

The subject of the middle section, though seemingly new, is the same short, slurred motive the first section has dealt with. Here the warm espressivo in the major key drives the low spirits away and lends a comforting character to the section. If the two-note slurs in the melodic line are overdone, they may lack earnestness and disturb the fervent seriousness of the phrase. Whenever the melody pauses on a long note, the left hand pronounces, with great emphasis, the same semitone step that has already been pointed out in the first section. The broken chords of measures 24–25 are very difficult to play with a stiff wrist or hand. Only a loose and laterally moving wrist is able to blend the broken chords into an uninterrupted melodic line.

The phrase ends on the last sixteenth note of measure 26. A real separation between the phrases is not welcome at this point; a slight difference of tone color is sufficient. The question whether the melody is in the soprano or in the middle voice for the following four measures (measures 27–30) is difficult to answer because both lines are of fundamental importance. The sinuous line of sixteenth notes and the other voices often clash in expressive, dissonant suspensions. The most important feature of the phrase, however, is the billowing crescendo and ebbing decrescendo that transform the sixteenths' line into a large arc.

After the phrase has died away in ritardando and after a slight pause, the first idea resumes. The subdominant harmonic turn of measure 32 darkens the atmosphere considerably. The crescendo-decrescendo, reinforced almost to the size of a tidal wave, reaches forte for the first time in measure 37. The resolution of measure 38 closes the section with a considerable ritardando.

The mood suddenly and totally changes here. The warm melody gives way to the apprehensive, short slurred first motive. The transition section—in fact, a short development of the first motive—for the first time gives the complete motive to the left hand (measures 39–41). Rendering it is not easy, for the zeal to bring out the motive with the fifth and fourth fingers often stiffens the hand up so that it is unable to control speed or tone. The forearm, the wrist, and the fingers should be kept perfectly relaxed here, thus insuring the clarity of the motives imitating each other in the soprano and bass. Although it is very inviting to start it early, the crescendo should not begin before measure 42; only a small breeze, it should be followed by a sudden piano in measure 43.

For the following four measures, the main motive—the two thirty-second notes, one on separate stem and the following in each slurred arpeggio—should stand out.

The arpeggio itself should be very soft, but it should still be played with clarity and the utmost evenness in spite of changing hands. The distribution of the arpeggios between the hands, carefully marked by Brahms, should not be changed. The fingering of measure 46 is:

measure 46

From measure 46 on, the motive in augmentation with its chordal accompaniment alternates between the hands in an atmosphere of lament. The last motive in augmentation, which consists of the single sixteenth notes of the left hand in measure 48, is to be brought out fully with a slight ritardando, even though it is slurred to the ensuing thirty-second-note-wave. Measures 49 and 50 are very difficult. The main danger lies in a heavy left hand that may clumsily spoil the delicacy of the right-hand design. The crescendo-decrescendo is only minimal and climaxes in measure 50, at the pause of the right hand. Therefore it is the left hand's responsibility to achieve it. The pause in measure 51 should be a silence, generous in length.

The main motive, returning here in the minor subdominant key, is imbued with even more sadness than it had before. The same deep sorrow emerges at measure 60 in a true lament of the right hand, over the left's arpeggio. This measure is to be treated with expressive freedom by an emphatic prolongation of the highest note in the right hand and a hesitation in the tempo for the rest of the figure.

From this measure on, the subject explores a new harmonic path with a crescendo driving to the climax. Measures 67–71 are the most difficult in the intermezzo. Instead of an easy diminuendo, measures 67–68 should have a well-sustained forte, with the melody blended into a perfect legato line. The execution of the appoggiatura chord often sounds like a major earthquake. A slight easing of the tempo at the end of measure 68 will permit an easier insertion of the appoggiatura into the texture. The rinforzando of measure 69 should be extended through the whole measure, and it should especially apply to the expressiveness of the leap between appoggiatura and main note. The melodic line should be perfectly legato, with a well-gauged diminuendo, and the left hand should be in the tone of an accompaniment.

The coda, built on the middle episode, begins as a reminiscence of happier days. The short recitative laments have to be soft and played with expressive freedom in a parenthetic way between the fragments of the motive. The meaningful left-hand semitone step shares in the interest. In measure 76, it turns into a desperate forte that begins a long, expressive line that dies away little by little, persistently punctuated by the semitone step in the left hand. The chords on the third beat of each measure bear poignant dissonances, with resolutions on the downbeats of the following measures. The pedal can be held without harm throughout the concluding three measures. The last two octaves in the right hand should be played with a slight coloration on the fifth finger, yet very softly.

This momentous intermezzo shows much inner agitation and profound sadness. The difficulty of the performance lies in the subtleties needed in three separate areas—tone, dynamics, and rubato. The separation of the melody from the arpeggios needs a polished tone. The dynamics—soft throughout with two fortes only—call for a good sense of gradation and colors. However the most important difficulty lies in the proportions of the rubato applied. Without expressive freedom, most of the harmonic implication would be lost. On the other hand, excessive, tasteless rubato would impinge on the natural flow of the thirty-second-note arpeggios and ruin this exquisite miniature.

BRAHMS

Intermezzo in A Major, Op. 118, No. 2

Brahms's opus 118, a set of six piano pieces (four intermezzos, one ballade, and one romance), was completed and published in 1893. The natural flow of the songlike melody of the Intermezzo in A Major makes it a favorite among Brahms's short pieces. It is built upon two themes—the first gently wistful and the second frankly emotional.

Form: Ternary

	MEASURES
First section	1 – 48
Second section	48 – 76
First section (Recapitulation)	76 – 118

The key to this piece's mood is the "teneramente" indication. The two eighth-note upbeats are often separated from the downbeat by a gap that occurs while the hands are clumsily searching for the new position. The impulse of the upbeat drives straight to the downbeat, which may be slightly stretched by delaying the ensuing eighth note of the alto. In measures 2 and 3, the dotted rhythm needs careful handling. Overdotting the rhythm or accenting the dotted eighth notes even slightly would be harmful to the melodic line, which is inflated here with a crescendo-decrescendo. The task is further complicated by the use of the same key for the sixteenth note and the ensuing dotted eighth, and by problems of tonal balance.

A slight delay of the third beat in measure 4 enhances the phrasing. A longer delay should be interpolated before the third beat of measure 8. Notice here that the repeat of the main idea is pianissimo. Therefore the extent of the crescendo-decrescendo involved in the phrase should also be reduced. Due emphasis should be given here to the slight changes in harmonization, such as the F natural of measure 10 and the suspension eighth notes of measures 10 and 15.

From measure 16 on, the second part takes leave of the initial placidity. Over an animated accompaniment, the melodic line displays straightforward lyricism. A perfect rendering of details such as part playing and the contrary motion between soprano and tenor at measure 19 enlivens the performance. The expressive upward leap of the melody at measure 23 is to be played with a slight delay, conforming with the vocal traditions; the wave of the accompanying left hand is in the second plane.

From measure 25 on, as the sound grows fuller, the driving phrase shows more and more eloquence. The coordination of the hands in playing the eighth-note accompaniment figure needs particular care: it is very easy to produce a bump when the left hand takes over the figure. The climax at measure 30 is reached with a slight broadening of the tempo, following which a little time is needed for ending the phrase. The major and minor key for the same motive (measures 30–34) makes the interpretation obvious even without Brahms's indications—espressivo for the major key, and piano, diminuendo, and calando for the minor key.

The main idea in inversion returns here with a mournful smile. If rolling the chords at measures 34 and 35 is unavoidable, it has to be done in a harplike, mellow way. The animation from measure 39 on should not be out of proportion, just as the più lento should not be excessively slow. At measures 42, 43, and 45, the fourth and fifth eighth notes of the accompaniment have a slight but meaningful emphasis. The succession of notes forming the concluding broken chord is often played at too slow a pace without real connection between the notes.

The middle section brings contrast, not only by the introduction of the minor mode, but also by a more outgoing, almost passionate lyricism. The introduction of triplets into the accompaniment figure also lends more agitation to this section. Though marked piano, the melody in the right hand should be played with a rich, singing, legato tone, making the decrescendo required in measures 55–56 natural and possible. For the left hand, elastic looseness is a requisite for dealing with extended and contracted positions intermittently. The individual notes of the arpeggios are to be melted smoothly into harmonies. The canonic imitation of the melody appearing in the tenor is best played without crude obtrusiveness.

At measure 57, the seemingly lost serenity is found again. The una corda puts a stifling damper on the sound; still the top part should be brought out slightly and the imitation in the tenor barely hinted at. The fullness and the perfectly simultaneous attack (individually and between the hands) of each chord should be in the forefront of one's preoccupations. Impeccably rendering this "easy" passage is more taxing than it appears to be at first glance.

At the recapitulation of the lyrical subject, in measure 65, the soprano and tenor interchange their previous roles. An impatient crescendo inflates the phrase to the exultant forte at measure 69, where the soprano regains its full rights with a new, bold gesture. In measures 70 and 71, a heavy second beat may ruin the suspensions implied between the first and second beats. The tonal balance in favor of the melody should be preserved throughout measure 72, in spite of the uncomfortable position and low register.

In the ensuing short transition (measures 73–76), the ascending triplets provide the necessary calm in which to bring back the first section. The fermata of measure 76, which is approached with a ritardando, should be held for a long time—almost until the decay of the sound is total. The recapitulation of the first section contains new accounts of phrases and different harmonies, such as the rinforzando descending sixths in measure 78; these intervals are very difficult for hands with a small span. They should be fingered as follows:

measures 78-80

There is a real danger of heaviness in measure 82 in its thick texture coupled with a crescendo-decrescendo.

The mood expressed is tenderness and simplicity in the first section and fervent lyricism and serenity in the middle section. There are no complications so far as interpretation is concerned. The main technical difficulty involved is an ultimate and refined control of tone.

BRAHMS
Ballade in G Minor, Op. 118, No. 3

~~~~~~

Incorporated into opus 118 and published in 1893, this ballade was probably composed as early as 1879. Its positive tone and definitely Nordic character associate it with the piano works of Brahms's earlier periods.

Form: Ternary

	MEASURES
First section and transition	1 – 40
Middle section and transition	41 – 76
First section (Recapitulation) and coda	77 – 117

The heroic character of the main theme is best served by strong rhythm and crisp chord playing. The sustained top line should not be disturbed by the vigorous accompanying chords, which should be kept in strict tempo; the slightest deviation in them from perfect regularity is intolerable. The staccato chords halt with a sforzando on the tenuto quarter-note chord in the middle of each of the first two measures. The weight of these tenuto chords almost equals the importance of the downbeats.

In measure 3, the melody should be clearly projected, and the eighth notes should be melted into the line instead of standing out improperly. The rising motion of the accompanying chords is best rendered with an audacious crescendo in measure 5. After the repetition of the theme, at measure 10 a mysterious piano is reached. The chords, which are played in a subdued, legato manner, contrast with the previous pulsating staccatos. Notice the difference between the portamento and legato upbeats (measures 10–11 versus those beginning at measure 12). The melodic line of measures 15–16 is often disturbed by a noisy accompaniment or by undue accents on the eighth notes. The danger is even greater here, where the right hand strikes only one note on the heavy beats.

The crescendo at measure 18 has to be carefully gradated and the forte reached only at measure 23. The syncopations of measures 21 and 22 should be played in the enthusiastic spirit of the growing crescendo: especially overwhelming is the sforzando on the first syncopation of measure 22.

The recapitulation of the first idea brings a new majestic turn in measure 27, with its three upbeat chords proudly raising the melodic line a third above its previous height with a spirited crescendo. At the close of this section, the chords gain more independence, once the melody stops on the tonic at measure 32. The harmonies in the middle of the measures carry great importance. The forte preserved up to the end of measure 35 fades to piano almost without artifice, solely through the natural decay of the sound. The arpeggio motion appearing in measure 38 should be played very softly, with a diminuendo.

An additional comment must be made about the use of the pedal for the entire section. The absolute prohibition of the pedal is frequently advocated here on the basis of the staccato marking of the accompanying chords. But the powerful character of the main subject requires a strong, colorful tone that can be provided only by judicious pedaling. A short pedal of about a quarter note's length is suggested in the forte sections for every melodic note longer than a quarter note. Fastidiousness in applying the pedal has to be insisted upon. The pedal has to be pushed down in such a manner that it does not catch the resonance of the preceding harmony. In the piano passages, the legato mark allows more generous pedaling, which is usually well indicated in the music.

With its generous melody in smooth legato, the middle section contrasts sharply with the first section. The fingering of the double notes in the right hand should serve the purpose of the legato by avoiding changes in hand position between the eighth notes and the ensuing dotted quarters. The suavity of the melody should suggest the perfect legato and tonal balance of two clarinets. Strict obedience to the dynamic markings is of the utmost importance. The total absence of dynamic shading in the unmarked measures will bring the short crescendo-decrescendos to full effect when they occur. Smooth legato in the accompaniment is as much a requisite for the left hand as it is for the right hand. The fingering recommended for the left hand of measures 45–46 is:

measures 45-46

The brief appearance of the main subject in measure 53 has an expressive swell with a driving crescendo-decrescendo. At the end of measure 56, the three eighth notes, into which the grace note has to be melted, should be played with a slight ritardando.

In the second exposition of the theme, measures 67–72 are particularly difficult. The natural flow of the phrase is slowed down in measures 67–68 by the greater activity of the melody coupled with the disjunct motion of the left hand. The right hand may slow the tempo down slightly to bring out the harmonic details of these measures and to prepare for the smooth execution of the broken tenths in measures 69 and 70, where the top notes should be played together with the left hand, on the beat. The length of the fermata in measure 72 is in proportion to the preceding ritardando.

A breathing pause should be interpolated between the fermata and the short transition; this transition should begin in a slower tempo and accelerate toward the recapitulation, where the tempo should be no different from that of the first exposition up to measure 108. At this point, the turbulent accompanying chords triumphantly confirm the G minor key in the only fortissimo of the piece. The left-hand figure in measures 112–113 is reminiscent of the triumphant outbreak of the chords and is to be played with great sensitivity. Measure 116 is to be played without pedal; however the intense legato of measure 117, with its tempo slowing down, is better served with a pedal on each eighth note.

This ballade requires a strong, impetuous interpretation in the first and last parts and poetic delicacy in the middle section. The main difficulty of the stormy part is in the chord playing. The component notes of the chords should be struck with perfect simultaneity and good tonal balance. Dramatic sense and overflowing enthusiasm are also necessary for a convincing performance. The middle section requires smooth legato, a feeling for long line, and care for details.

Claude Debussy

Born 1862, St.-Germain-en-Laye; died 1918, Paris

The pianistic output of Debussy is remarkable not only for its size but also for the novelty of its musical language and for its forms, harmony, and pianism. Even today, six decades after Debussy's death, it is difficult to grasp his importance and his effect on twentieth-century music. He is generally considered to have been an Impressionist. The word is borrowed from art history; it means that the artist does not paint objects as they are but rather as they appear under the influence of surrounding nature. The Impressionism of Debussy is mingled with a strong influence of literary Symbolism and the musical Classicism of the French harpsichordists.

To escape the predictability of a harmony based on the major and minor modes, he adopted the whole-tone and pentatonic scales; these scales opened up a brand-new harmonic language where chords, liberated from their tonal harmonic function, often progress in parallel motion. Harmonic functions are further enriched by adding overtones—ninths, elevenths, and so on. Obviously the new harmonic language could not fit into the existing musical forms—particularly not into the sonata form. Instead Debussy adopted a free style of construction in which (most of the time) traces of A–B–A form can be detected. Like Chopin he created his own musical forms to meet his own needs. Classical forms, such as sonata and the étude, do not appear in Debussy's music before his late years.

Debussy's piano oeuvre—*Two Arabesques; Suite Bergamasque; Pour le piano; Images* (two series); *Estampes; Children's Corner; Préludes,* Books 1 and 2; and the twelve études, to mention only the most important works—reveals an original piano style, whose most prominent characteristics are great elegance and delicate tone quality. The pedal plays a particularly important role in creating the appropriate hazy ambiance. It is most unfortunate that Debussy omitted all pedal markings (as well as all fingerings) in his original editions. His scores contain only hints for pedaling—slurs reaching out to rests. To obtain more clarity, he liked to notate his scores on three staffs, an interesting idea related to the different layers of sound built into his compositions. This device was used mostly in his preludes. He also has an unusual power to create dazzling virtuosic effects, comparable only to the instrumental fascination of Liszt.

The often hazy, undefined disposition of Impressionistic music has provided a pretext for interpretations that approximate rather than fully convey Debussy's intentions. However clarity of the musical thought is essential for both rhythm and melody, and "Impressionism" should be confined to an imaginative and sensitive tone quality that is able to render strong and lively colors as well as delicate half-tints.

DEBUSSY
Prélude

Pour le piano

~~~~~~

Published in 1901, Debussy's suite *Pour le piano* (a prélude, a sarabande, and a toc-cata) is regarded as marking an important stage in the musical maturing of the composer. Modeling his work on that of the clavecinists of the seventeenth and eighteenth centuries as far as clarity of ideas and form is concerned, Debussy added a new harmonic language using unresolved harmonic progressions, parallel fifths and octaves, and whole-tone and modal scales. This prélude was composed for and dedicated to a Miss Romilly, to improve her piano technique.

Form: Three parts and a coda-cadenza

	MEASURES
First part	1 – 58
Introduction (Second theme)	1 – 5
First theme	6 – 42
Second theme	43 – 58
Second part (Development)	59 – 96
First part (Recapitulation)	97 – 133
Coda-cadenza	134 – 163

"Assez animé et très rhythmé" means "with considerable animation and very rhythmically"; the tempo should be M.M. ♩ = 120–144. The "non legato" indication applies to the leading left hand for the initial five measures. It exposes the motive that will become the second subject at measure 43, and here it is given a full forte tone. The passage is played from the forearm without the unwelcome stiffness in the wrist that would produce a too-dry or short sound. The right hand plays the toccatalike figure in a sonorous legato; however its sound should be more biting when the hands alternate at the end of measure 2.

In measure 5, the diminuendo brings with it a legato touch for the left hand, together with a broadening of the tempo preparing for the main subject "un peu retardé" (somewhat slower). The theme from measure 6 on calls for a mysterious, yet intense, sonority, which is obtained by the total absence of senseless hammering and excessive fingerwork. The sound of the low A bass is preserved by means of the middle pedal. (If it is not available, the fifth finger holds on to the key as long as possible; from measure 9 on, the higher A—held by the fifth finger substituting for the thumb —will supply at least part of the required resonance.) The melody in the left hand has to be played in the best possible legato, with the sound of bell strokes still clearly separated.

Tonal shading (crescendo and decrescendos) has to be used with extreme caution, since it may lend a Romantic flavor to this dignified, Classical melodic line. However general crescendo—a growing of the sound—was certainly among the intentions of the composer and can hardly be avoided in performance; for example, the double notes from measure 14 on will naturally increase the expressive intensity together with the volume of sound.

In measures 16, 21, 23, and 35, the entire sixteenth-note figure on the first beat has to be executed by the right hand, since the left hand is repeating the low A. The recommended fingering for the figures—1$\begin{smallmatrix} 2\text{-}3\text{-}5\text{-}3 \\ \end{smallmatrix}$—presumes that the right hand avoids the use of the thumb on the last beats of the preceding measures. In measures 24–25, the hands should have an easy, bumpless coordination; the rest on the first beat of measure 26 must have an accurate duration.

After a second, shortened exposition of the first subject, a new difficulty arises at measures 41–42. The four-note figure is best played with a slight swaying motion of the wrist and forearm; fingers alone cannot do justice to this passage, which includes a massive crescendo. The right hand will play *sotto* in these measures (that is, the right thumb crosses under). The chordal second theme at measure 43 should stand out as one of the main dynamic climaxes of the work. Its character is that of proud, radiant strength. The quarter-note chords show a clear-cut accent, while the ensuing eighth chords are to be played slightly softer to match the sound. Without being stiff, the fingers have to be solidly prepared to give the keys (and consequently the hammers) great initial speed, thus securing a brilliant color for this passage. The best fingering is $\begin{smallmatrix} 5 \\ 3 \\ 2 \\ 1 \end{smallmatrix}$ for the right hand and $\begin{smallmatrix} 1 \\ 2 \\ 4 \end{smallmatrix}$ for the left hand, on every chord.

From measure 51 on, the left-hand fifth finger needs a strong accent at every single use. From measure 55 on, the same fifth finger is used on the appoggiatura, which is to be played as a sixteenth note preceding the beat. This solution keeps the tempo steady and secures simultaneity of the chords; meanwhile changes of the pedal are to be linked accurately with the fifth finger to make the harmonic progression clear. Some printings of the music have an erroneous B natural as the last note of measure 58; it obviously should be a B flat.

Measures 59 through 71 are best played with the fingering 2–3 in the right hand; the tone should be that of a soft murmur, yet the metric outline should not be blurred. The left hand, in a distinctive staccato, has the leading role. As at measure 43, the quarter notes bear definite accents. From measure 67 on, the right hand is in the *sotto* position, and the hand and fingers should be kept as flat as possible so as not to interfere with the left hand's reaching over it. The fingering 5–2–2–5 is recommended for the left hand to avoid an uncomfortable use of the thumb, which is too short for use here. The touch is a short portamento, close to staccato. At measure 71, the right hand's trill figure is reduced to its softest murmur, and the accented A flats flash one after another like beams at night. The last beat of measure 71 is difficult because of the sudden upward leap of the right hand. There are several possible ways to change the distribution of notes between the hands, but none is really satisfactory; the best solution is to follow Debussy's text at this point.

For the trill figure in the left hand, a useful solution may consist in playing it throughout the passage (measures 71–90) with the fingering 2–1, provided that the right hand plays the upper A-flat bells of measures 76, 78, and so on with the thumb; the sound is sustained by the pedal, which is changed with each measure. The right hand leads the whole-tone, gamelanlike melody, enunciating every quarter note clearly with a rather short portamento touch. Rhythmic precision is quite difficult to secure in measures 79–82 and 87–90, especially if the mathematical approach is used in placing the triplets over the sixteenth-trill figure. The musical solution, which takes into account the similar duration of the sixteenth groups and the triplets, is much preferable at this point. Measures 87–90 are particularly difficult, for the minute slurs over the triplets further complicate the rhythm with a flavorful hemiola that often influences the left hand to abandon the steady sixteenths for temporary triplets. Well-developed hearing and rhythmic independence of the hands are prerequisites for a perfect realization of this passage.

The hand crossing in measures 91–96 may be uncomfortable for some players. It can easily be avoided if the hands simply exchange their assigned roles. In order to reach the slower tempo of the recapitulation, the ''perdendosi'' indicated may be coupled with a ritardando. The recapitulation contains only a few differences from the exposition. One of these is the anticipated glissando in measure 118, where the four left-hand octaves should strongly punctuate the rhythm, firmly keeping the tempo. Another difference is the toccatalike text in measures 127–133, which poses problems of good coordination between the hands. The left hand plays longer and slightly louder than the right in these alternated-chord passages.

The transition part is similar to the passage in measures 59–71. A new difficulty is the interval of a ninth on the downbeats of measures 137 and 139. Performers with small hands may take the trill figure into the left hand for the duration of the first beat. Measures 142–147 contain what is no doubt the hardest passage of the work. The difficulty lies in the double notes and in the changes between arpeggio and tremolo figures, which may possibly cause stiffness in the hand and forearm. It is advisable to finger all thirds with $\frac{5}{3}$ throughout, watching to see that the first third of the arpeggio figure is released promptly. Keeping this third down would irremediably stiffen the hand and thus make smooth execution impossible. Furthermore the extremely soft dynamic required (triple piano) has to remain unaltered to measure 145, where the crescendo, coupled with a progressive ritardando, first begins; it reaches the forte at the fermata of measure 148.

''Tempo di cadenza'' suggests a fair amount of rhythmic freedom even though the proportions of the metric elements involved have to be respected. The bar lines are the boundaries of the musical units or phrases. The first two measures of the cadenza are to be played in a declamatory recitative style. The sixteenth and thirty-second notes are expressively legato, while the eighths (slightly faster than their accurate speed) contrast with them in a radiant staccato that is without dryness and very close to a portamento. In measure 149, the appearance of quarter notes is a printing mistake; they should be eight notes as before, with a ritardando. The half notes from measure 150 on should have a generous duration; they should last about two and a half beats of the adopted tempo (the suggested M.M. is $\bullet$ = 88–92), and the top note of each ensuing scale should coincide with the fourth beat.

For the execution of the glissandolike scales, the left-hand fingers should be prepared on the appropriate keys in *sotto* position (under the right hand). Every single note of each scale has to be articulated to obtain the effect of the harp glissando, and special care must be taken to insure coordination between the hands. The first two scales have bursting crescendo-decrescendos; those of measures 152–153 are to be played unvaryingly softly. The dotted half notes have some emphasis like a pedal point under the soft scales. In measures 154–155, the scales are no longer interrupted by the longer note, and have a continuous crescendo.

The first note of measure 156 is entrusted to the left hand's second finger, in *sotto* position. Every note of this measure should be sonorous, but without harshness; and the tempo should slow down gradually ("retenu"). Measure 157 should be quite long, and some additional time should even be included for the double bar. The majestic chords of the closing measures have to be given separate pedals, keeping the bass-note appoggiaturas resonant. The tempo indicated is the opening tempo: the performer may fit the chordal motive of measure 43 in, mentally, for each measure. In the concluding measure, the right hand may play the third and fourth appoggiatura notes with the fingering 2–5; the left hand follows, with a 5–3–2–1 fingering, in a gradual broadening.

In spite of its distinctly archaic flavor, the prélude displays impressive modern virtuosity. Above all the performance should have the utmost clarity, while still allowing for mystery and magic in certain passages. Only a few measures are unusually difficult technically: measures 79–82 and 87–90 require perfect metric independence of the hands, and measures 142–147 include unusual figures.

DEBUSSY

Jardins sous la pluie

Gardens in the Rain / *Estampes*

In 1903, soon after completing *Pelléas et Mélisande,* Debussy published the suite entitled *Estampes* (''Prints''), which included *Pagodes, La Soirée dans Grenade,* and *Jardins sous la pluie.* The titles suggest evocations of past memories, though Debussy had never seen the fabulous buildings of the Orient or spent an evening in Granada. In fact, on his only visit to Spain, he stayed a couple of hours in San Sebastian (which is several hundred miles from Andalusia!). *Jardins sous la pluie* is built upon two French folk songs—*Dodo, l'enfant, do,* a lullaby, and *Nous n'irons plus au bois* (''We'll Go No More to the Woods''), and it is the only piece of *Estampes* that was inspired by Debussy's native land.

Form: Three parts

	MEASURES
First part	1 – 74
Second part	75 – 99
Third part	100 – 157

The utmost clarity, both in the melodic line of the left hand and in the toccatalike sixteenths motion of the right hand, is the first condition for an acceptable performance. The tempo of the movement is M.M. $\decrescendo$ = 84–96. For the left hand, the proximity of the right-hand figure compels the adoption of the following fingering for the first three measures: 1–1–3–2– | 1–3–4–2. | 1–1–2–2 (the vertical lines indicate the bar lines). The left hand should be in sopra position. From this point, the bass note held with the fifth finger enforces the use of similar fingering. The right-hand figure calls for a light, nonlegato, accurately detailed touch; yet the individual fingers should not be raised excessively high. Both hands will participate in the small dynamic swells of measures 4 and 5.

From measure 8 on, the broken-chord progression has the first general crescendo, which is followed by a sudden pianissimo. Compliance with this dynamic marking is an absolute must. From measure 10 on, the last sixteenth note of the group on the second beat is revealed to be part of the melody and is to be brought out as such; at measures 14 and 15, the fourth beat as well as the second beat has to be played in this manner.

From measure 16 on, the melody in the left hand gains importance that is supported by the expressive swells. The right-hand notes played with the fifth finger on the first and third beats imply a countermelody that should complement rather than cover the main melody. Technically this passage is somewhat more difficult than the previous ones, in that each figure is played twice—once descending and once ascending. The hand has a tendency to remain rigidly in position and to become stiff, this is particularly true of hands with a small span. In measures 20 and 21, the left hand plays the first sixteenth note of the last beat *sopra,* using the second finger, and it repeatedly takes this position wherever it is needed (for example, on the first beat of measure 22 and in measures 25–26. The entire passage progresses with a driving crescendo toward the climax at measure 25.

The appearance of the major mode at measure 27 brings out the light, playful character of the folk song. The left hand consistently occupies the *sopra* position and therefore should avoid the use of the thumb. The recommended fingering for the left hand from measure 27 on is: 2-5-2-2 | 3-5-2-2 | 3-5-4-3 | 2-3-4-2 |.

Dynamics and character change abruptly at measure 31 with the reappearance of the minor key, which is like a sudden, furious spattering of the rain. In measures 33 and 34, the left-hand half notes alone compose the melody; the notes on the second and fourth beats, although entrusted to the left hand, belong to the moving figure and should not be played with the same tone as the melody. In mesures 35–36, the last sixteenth note of each second and fourth group again has melodic importance.

From measure 37 to measure 43, there are three distinct melodic layers—one on the top notes of the right-hand figure, one in the tenor, and one in the bass line. The persistent expressive swells increase in each measure and always fall back to the required piano at every bar line. The forte at measure 43 should not be a display of roughness in the left-hand chords. At measures 45–49, the left hand had better use the fingering 5-2 (*sopra*) instead of the thumb, which is too short for use here. From measure 50 on, the melody should be softly sustained in the left hand by bringing only the top part of the octave out. The use of the second finger of the left hand for the single notes of measures 52–55 is recommended. The two-measures-long crescendos of measures 52–53 and 54–55 should have ample force and be followed by a sudden piano. At measure 56, the direction means "animate the tempo and increase the sound little by little."

Throughout this passage, up to measure 71, the right hand leads the melody in the top notes of the figures; they should be effortlessly played, and excessive finger articulation and swaying the wrist laterally should be avoided. The choice between the third and fourth fingers for the thirds should be determined by the various positions on the keyboard. The process of learning this passage should include playing the figures as solid chords in order to become familiar with the notes and positions. In the left hand, the use of the second finger for the single notes is once more recommended. The tenutos of measures 59 and 63 are best fingered so as to confer an almost legato, expressive character to the line, which should also have a dynamic swell. The conclusive crescendo and accelerando begins at measure 64 and darts toward the climactic G sharp in measure 71.

There are a number of misprints in this passage. In measures 64 and 66, the last note of the right hand is an F natural instead of an F sharp. In the last group of triplets in measure 67, the right hand should play an A natural instead of A flat. The last two right-hand groups in measure 68 should be identical with the same groups in the preceding measure.

After the forte in measure 72, the sound dies away quickly, and the tempo calms down; in measures 73–74 the whole-note F sharps ring through in a bell-like manner. From measure 75 on, the trill motion of the left hand is to be kept solidly in tempo, with perfect evenness, while dynamically it is reduced to the level of a soft murmur. The line below the soft trill is difficult to bring out. It has to be played louder than the soft trill motive, almost as part of the right-hand melody but without bumping out the coinciding note of the trill motive. The melody in the right hand has transparent clarity, and the individual notes of the line are played in a smooth portamento, without dryness. Of course, pedal is used throughout, concomitant with the bass line.

In measure 82, the right hand has to be ready over the F sharp key to assure a flawless takeover of the trill figure and prepare for the change in the motive occurring at the beginning of measure 83. The left hand should not be permitted to stiffen while negotiating the three intervals of a ninth because the quality of the tone may suffer. (Small hands have to play the bass note imperceptibly ahead of the top note and catch it in the pedal.) The reappearance of the trill figure in the left hand in measure 90 is to be prepared for by changing from the thumb to the third finger on the held-over E; the small ritardando at measures 88–89 will grant more time to execute this substitution.

The terrifying pianissimo of measures 98 and 99 should not be spoiled by accents on the downbeats. At measure 100, the light arpeggio figures set out on their ramblings in the mysterious depths of the lower register. Their rising and falling motion requires a liquid legato achieved by contracting the hand at the points where the thumb and fifth fingers are used in succession on the same key. The notes marked with an accent in measures 103, 105, and so on have to be played with the second finger of the left hand; the pedal should only be changed when an octave occurs in the bass.

The motive appearing in the left hand at measure 112 leads with an explosive crescendo to a cadenzalike passage. It begins with an awkward appoggiatura to a chord in the left hand that should be "clicked in" ahead of the beat, with the fingering: $4\begin{smallmatrix}2&1\\&3\\&5\end{smallmatrix}$. The right hand, in brilliant precipitateness and crackling articulation, imitates the furious downpour of the rainstorm. At measure 122, the trill in piano, like thunder rumbling in the distance, should have the appropriate duration in a gradually slowing tempo. At measure 126, the glitter of the lightning has to be rendered with the utmost brilliance. The right hand takes the G sharp (the first note of the tremolo) and extends it slightly; then the left hand takes over, dropping the sound almost immediately to piano. The triplets of the right hand in measures 128–129 are best played with the fingering 1–2–3; then the thumb passes over the third finger while reaching for F sharp, the lower note of the octave.

Measure 133 should be practiced hands separately first, keeping the count in cut time. Before attempting the full text with both hands, it is recommended that the right-hand figure be reduced to only four C's per measure while the left hand plays the leading motive in its entirety. The finished execution should be overwhelmingly exuberant, reaching a sparkling ("éclatant") fortissimo. The following "scherzando" measures contrast sharply; they are in light but still precise tone.

The final crescendo begins from the piano of measure 147. The leading motive is in the top part of the right-hand figure; the staccato points imply firm but small accents. In measures 147 and 149, the thumb is to be used on two keys at once to play the interval of a second. The appoggiatura notes appearing on the last two beats of measures 148 and 150 are to be played in the manner of rapidly broken chords. From measure 151 on, the growing excitement brings an accelerando along with the crescendo. The last note (D sharp) of the very fast arpeggio divided between the hands is often a blunder if the fifth finger on this black key is kept fastidiously parallel to the key instead of in a slightly oblique position that prevents sliding off the key. In the concluding measure, the fingers have to be carefully prepared on every single key before the attack, while the eyes are already aiming at the top E, which will be played with the third finger of the left hand.

In fact a radiant toccata, *Jardins sous la pluie* unites poetic inspiration with technical brilliance. The main difficulty, which is by no means insuperable, consists in playing quick arpeggios with extreme clarity and perfect coordination between the hands. The programmatic element—the evocation of a rainstorm—is intermingled with personal feelings and impressions that keep the musical interest unwavering. Study of the "Gardens" is eminently rewarding to those who have already had previous experience with Debussy's style.

DEBUSSY

La Cathédrale engloutie

The Sunken Cathedral / *Préludes*, Book 1, No. 10

This prélude's title refers to the legendary cathedral of Ys, engulfed by the waters of the Atlantic Ocean some fifteen centuries ago but said to rise to the surface from time to time. Debussy's narrative depicts such an occasion.

	MEASURES
Presentation of two themes as motives	1 – 27
First theme	28 – 40
Transition	40 – 46
Second theme	47 – 67
Transition	67 – 71
Recapitulation of first theme	72 – 83
Coda	84 – 89

The expressive indication at the start of the piece, which is translated as "Profoundly calm, in a softly sonorous haze," sets the scene deep under the surface of the water. The time signature 6/4 = 3/2 indicates the interchangeability of these meters, with the length of the quarter note remaining constant (however see the comment on Debussy's own performance at the end of this chapter). The tempo is M.M. ♩ = 60–66.

In the opening measures, an implication of the Phrygian mode and the intervals of open fourths and fifths lend an archaic flavor to the music. The dotted whole-note chords should be carefully differentiated in timbre from the series of rising chords suggesting the muffled sound of the various bells still submerged. A slight predominance to the notes played by the fifth finger throughout the initial six measures is recommended.

At measure 7, where the atmosphere becomes "soft and fluid," the second theme appears in 3/2. The upper pedal-point E represents the horizon for the emerging melody, which has to be played in an intense legato. The dynamic swell of measures 11–12, though plainly discernible in performance, has only limited proportions. From measure 16 on, the bell chimes are "little by little emerging from the haze." The dotted whole-note chords on the downbeats are the heavier strokes. The left-hand triplet

figure, combining the sounds of the different bells, has to be carefully fingered to obtain a smooth legato. The suggested fingering for measure 16 is: 1-2-5 2-5-2 5-3-1
5
1
2-3-5 1-2-5 2-5-2. The suggested fingering for measure 19 is 5-1-2 2-2-1 1-5-2
1-2-3
4   ⅞ etc.
5

In the short, running figure appearing for the first time in the middle of measure 19, the sixteenth notes and sixteenth triplets need to be perfectly timed and played with ease. At measure 20, the indication means "increase [crescendo] gradually without accelerating [the tempo]." The passage in measures 22–27 contains chords that are so thick that the player has his thumb playing two keys at once; this occurs twice, at measures 26 and 27. The second finger as well as the thumb has to deal with two keys simultaneously. Musically the majesty of this passage when it is well played is overwhelming. At this point the cathedral literally emerges from the waves like an entrancing vision.

At measure 28, the first theme makes its climactic entrance "without harshness." The bell chimes appear in the bass and punctuate a melody that has the rich, full sound of the organ. The parallel triads are to be played with the utmost simultaneity, with the fingers close to the keys and the weight of the full arm. The dynamic level remains fortissimo throughout the theme; the only dynamic swelling points to measure 38, but it does so without endangering the beauty of the sound.

At measure 41, the sound decreases rapidly, and the following modulatory passage bears the careful dynamic markings of a step-by-step diminuendo, which have to be rigorously obeyed.

At measure 47, the indication means "a little less slow, with increasing intensity of expression." After its sketchy exposition in measures 7–13, the second theme appears here in full. First exposed in the dark color of the low register over a persistent pedal point, the theme repeatedly expands in crescendos and then falls back to piano or pianissimo. The largest, most important swelling of the sound is aided by canonic imitations of the theme in the left hand in measures 55–58. The bass notes played as grace notes to the downbeats of measures 59 and 61 have to be caught by the pedal and ring through these measures. They should be executed as if they were the last eighth notes of measures 58 and 60—quickly enough not to hinder metrical continuity.

After the climax at measure 61, the sound decreases promptly toward the doleful phrase of successive dominant seventh chords, which are to be played in an expressive portamento. During measures 64–71, the cathedral sinks back into the depths of the ocean. The first theme appears again at measure 72 ("floating and muffled, in the tempo of the first section, like an echo of the phrase heard previously"). It is wrapped in the soft waves of the left hand. This accompaniment, made up of intervals of the fifth and fourth, should suggest the soft and indistinct noise of the deepening waters in which the cathedral is engulfed. Notice the recurring crescendo-decrescendo of measures 80–81. Reappearing in measure 84 with C as the bass note, the opening chords clarify the tonality little by little until only C major triads are heard.

This prélude has the imposing power of a large-scale tone painting. The unmistakably programmatic narration makes "The Sunken Cathedral" one of Debussy's most celebrated compositions. Its popularity is further enhanced by the quasi-total absence of apparent technical problems. Significant difficulties, however, are located along the line of absolute tonal control and balance and refined gradation. Furthermore there is a need for a strongly musical mind—one that is capable of drafting a solid architectural plan that welds the elements of the interpretation—tempo, dynamics, and touch—into a cohesive picture.

Here are a few suggestions about using the pedals. In measures 1–7, the pedal should be renewed with the playing of every long bass chord. From measure 7 through measure 13, change the pedal with every recurring E. Measures 14 and 15 may be pedaled without a break; likewise measures 16–18, 19–21, and 22–24. Measures 25 through 27 need three pedals per measure. From measure 28 on, the sustaining pedal (the middle pedal) can be used to preserve the deep sound of the persistent low bass while the triads receive separate pedals. In measures 42–46, play one pedal per measure so that the carefully marked dynamic changes will be noticeable. From measure 47 to measure 62, the pedal is renewed only when the bass note is struck again. The ensuing dominant-seventh chords need separate pedals. Measures 72–84 will have a separate pedal on each triad; from measure 84 to the end, the pedal remains down.

The use of the soft, or una corda, pedal is justified in the first fifteen measures, in the passage encompassing measures 42 through 52, and from measure 70 to the end.

Debussy's own recorded performance (in *The Keyboard Immortals,* Series No. 2, Stereo A–005) raises the question of how the time signature 6/4 = 3/2 is to be interpreted. Contrary to the current view, which favors keeping the length of the quarter note constant, Debussy doubles the speed in those passages, measures 7–13, 22–84, and 86 to the end. One wonders whether he meant the 6/4 and 3/2 to be related in this manner or made a mistake in the notation. At any rate, the authority of the recorded performance cannot be questioned.

DEBUSSY

Minstrels

Préludes, Book 1, No. 12

~~~~~~

Minstrel shows originated on the plantations of the American Deep South early in the last century. Music-hall groups called "minstrels" were popular in France after 1900 and inspired painters, poets, and musicians. This prélude describes a stage act as performed by minstrels in a popular Montmartre music hall.

Form: Three sections of uneven length

	MEASURES
First section	1 – 33
Second second	34 –77
Partial recapitulation of first section	78 – 89

The casual dance begins in a moderate tempo ($\quad$ = 72–88) and is played "crisply and with humor." The "gruppetti" are to be executed on the beat, in the manner of chords rolled very quickly downward, without taking up measurable time. The tempo for the opening eight measures has a supple grace. "Cédéz" means "slow down." but the staccatos in the left hand still keep their vigorous plunked sound. At measure 9, the tempo begins to be "a little more fluent." The initial staccato octave of the left hand represents the first striking of the tap dancer's heel. The sixteenth chords should be "very detached" staccatos played with an effortlessly brilliant sound that is lightly accelerated, while the off-beat chords may be slightly delayed and prolonged, with an irresistibly hilarious accent.

The rhythmic predominance of the pianissimo chords (like drumbeats) sets the scene for the triviality of the entering cornet. A sharp staccato touch has to be applied throughout to this solo as well as to the spirited chords of the full band at measure 18. The next entrance of the cornet—in the wrong key at measure 26—has a frankly vulgar color. From measure 28 on, the first of each pair of slurred octaves is to be brought out with a firm accent, while the slurred eighth-note octaves in measures 29 and 31 explode in great hilarity with crescendos. The sixteenth notes concluding the section (measures 32–33) propel the phrase with rattling staccatos toward the final sforzando chord, which is a veritable bump.

The middle section begins in a broadened tempo, with drumbeats. The expression of the phrase marked "moqueur" ("mockingly") requires a short, almost staccato first chord and a sentimentally accented long chord that resolves into bouncy light chords, which land fairly heavily again on the half-note chord in measure 39. The prescribed portamento is closer to staccato in this phrase. The execution of the gruppetti in the following measures should remind one of the slide trombone. The gesture with the thirty-second notes in measure 44, concluding in a sharp staccato, points out the completion of an acrobatic stunt. A supple freedom has to be applied to this section (measures 35–44), which still remains jittery and animated. The fermata placed on the bar line between measures 44 and 45 has to be at least one full measure in length.

The returning tap-dance motive has some part-playing problems for the left hand. The crescendo to the exploding forte in measures 46 and 48 should not be anticipated. The muffled sound of the muted fanfare requires the use of the left pedal. Solid fingers are needed for simultaneous attacks on the chords, and the notes played by the fifth finger of the right hand should be predominant. The triplets of the drum motive from measure 58 on, obviously necessitate finger changing: 3–2–1 is suggested. Where the sixteenth notes are divided between the hands, the left hand plays longer, with an accent.

The sentimentality of the melody at measure 63 is more striking if the preceding drum motive has been kept in tempo throughout the diminuendo. The sixteenth-note motive between the lines of the melody is to be brought out (''en dehors'') in strict tempo, while the mawkish melody needs supple freedom. The recapitulation is only partial—almost a mere frame for the tone picture. The witty closing joke at measure 85 jumps suddenly to a faster tempo. The violent sforzando of measure 86 originates the accelerando (''serrez''); the concluding chords (''dry and held back in tempo'') are pompously important.

Robust humor is the quality that suits the performance of this farcical prélude above all. Energetic, nervous rhythm alternates with supple freedom as section follows section. Besides accuracy and precision, the real challenge of the piece lies in the ability to follow and render truthfully the many quick changes of mood.

DEBUSSY
Bruyères

The Heath / *Préludes*, Book 2, No. 5

~~~~~~

This mildly nostalgic prélude describes a hillside covered with heather, the evergreen leaves and purplish-pink flowers agitated by a gentle breeze.

Form: Three parts

	MEASURES
First part	1 – 17
Second part	17 – 37
Recapitulation of first part, with coda	38 – 51

"Calm and softly expressive" is the direction for the unaccompanied opening line, which is reminiscent of a shepherd's flute; the comma in measure 3 suggests his breathing pause. The tempo for the opening part is M.M.: ♩ = 66. The imitative tenor motive in measures 4 and 5 adds to the charm of the phrase ending. A new, more serious tone arises in the second section at measure 6, and chordal harmony gives more body to the sound.

The main motive, warm and smiling, appears at measure 8; it should be interpreted on a singing tone and with a fluent line in ardent legato, and the triplet should be timed accurately. The pedal has to catch the bass note, which must be played ahead as an appoggiatura. The pedal must then be changed with each harmony in spite of the sustained bass note, which can be saved only with the help of the middle (sostenuto) pedal. In measure 9, the rolled subdominant chord together with the upward-curling protamento figure needs generous timing.

Fresh warmth is to be conveyed to the recurring main motive at measure 11; the appoggiatura bass note is also sustained here in the pedal, which is to be used in the same manner as it was used at measure 8. The left hand plays the octave C on the third beat of measure 12 in the *sopra* position and then holds on to the lower note slurred over to the next measure with the fifth finger; the concluding line originates here.

The following short section (measures 14–17) is both modulatory and cadenzalike. A feather-light execution of the right-hand figure is difficult because of the extended position involved. The recommended fingering for the figure in measures 14–15 is

2-4-1-2-4   5-2-1 | 2-3-5-4-2 |
1   1   If the left hand is unable to play the chord on the
third beat in measure 16 without rolling, the A flat in the middle staff may be played
by the right hand and released before the figure in the soprano is played. The B flat of
the middle staff should be held as long as is required by using the thumb. The pedal is
changed on each of the last three quarter notes of the measure. Throughout this section, rhythmic accuracy is of fundamental importance; the thirty-seconds should be set
forth at the correct speed and not be turned into indistinct blobs. Generous timing of
the resolution E flat chord effectively concludes the first part.

The exact timing of the transition figure at measures 17 and 18 is also very important in displaying the decreased speed from thirty-seconds to quarter notes. The section beginning at measure 19 is often the victim of a heavy thumb, bumping on every
eighth note. This passage, which should be "soft and light," is one of the most delicate
moments in the performance; the dynamic swell of measures 21–22 is only a mild
breeze, supported mainly by the chordal progression in the left hand. The fingering
for the last beat of measure 22 in the right hand is 4-3-2-1 3-2-1-4.

The section beginning at measure 23, which should be "somewhat animated and
joyful," is the heart of the central part. In spite of the piano, the main motive voices
tender enthusiasm and reaches full bloom in measures 27–28 with the expressive
crescendo of the left-hand chords (in *sotto* position). The fingering of the right hand for
measures 27–28 is 4-5-4-1 3-4-3-2 1-2-3-1 | 4-5-4-1 3-4-3-2 1-4-3-1.

Suddenly a charmingly teasing dotted rhythm appears; it is followed by fragments
of the main motive that seem to have shaken free. Though the triplets here are thirty-
seconds, fast jerking is still unacceptable. The sixteenth-note upbeats to measure 31 in
the right hand and to measure 33 have to be played calmly, at an accurate speed, and
with a special melodic significance. In an inspired performance, the amiable charm of
these measures wholly captivates the listener.

The combination of a broadening tempo and a diminuendo at measure 37 is hard
to interpret, for it is followed by the recapitulation of the main motive in an exulting
mezzo forte in the next measure. The left-hand harmonies have a determining role at
measure 37 in preparing for the reentry of the main key, musically, if not dynamically.

The subdominant harmony at measure 44 presents a harmless surprise; it is held
over for two measures during the reappearance of the shepherd's flute. The tempo
broadens gradually ("en retenant") from measure 46 on, with the harmonies "softly
sustained." The last chord of mesure 47 is best played by the right hand; this way the
bass note can be kept while the pedal is changed. Measure 49 is difficult to render in a
transparent manner, without heaviness in the low register. Also the metric accuracy of
the measure is often marred by a confusing execution of the thirty-second triplets and
sixteenth notes.

Bruyères, with its nostalgia and folksonglike simplicity, belongs to the technically
easier group of Debussy préludes. Aside from preserving mellowness of tone and flexibility in the melody, there are no technical difficulties. Therefore for performers with
insufficient experience in Debussy's world, where tone and flexibility prevail, *Bruyères*
may be highly recommended.

DEBUSSY
Ondine

Préludes, Book 2, No. 8

~~~~~~

Ondine is one of the Debussy préludes that draw on mythology and embody imaginary characters. Undines were water nymphs who treacherously attracted and bewitched sailors and fishermen.

Form: Two parts, with introduction and coda

	MEASURES
Introduction	1 – 10
First part	11 – 31
First theme	11 – 13
Second theme	16 – 19
Third theme	30 – 31
Second part (development)	32 – 64
Coda	64 – 74

The introductory measures set the scene deep within the opacity of the underwater world. Despite the indefinite contours, the metrical division of these measures should be precise. The suggested tempo is ♪ = 116–132. In measure 4, the broken-chord arpeggios are difficult to execute. The triplet sixteenths must be played evenly and the left-hand chords as short staccatos; the last grace-note arpeggio is to be jammed together like a quickly rolled chord and has to have the splashing sound of whirling water. Notice how the crescendo-decrescendo in measures 6 and 7 stirs up tension while the long waves of measures 8 and 9 have only a gentle dynamic swell, along with a liquid legato sound, concluding in peaceful staccato eighths. The feeling of suspense in measure 10 is effectively increased by the ritardando, which terminates in a fermatalike suspension and a pause.

The "scintillating" grace-note arpeggio of measure 11 have the sound of water slapping. Good coordination between the hands is the first requisite; it is attained by having the fingers of both hands ready, close to the keys. The "soft" notes (in large type) with their precise legato and staccato articulation have melodic importance. The group of twelve notes should be played in the time of the fifth eighth note of the measure. It should be played with a bursting crescendo-decrescendo, and its unitary impression is to be emphasized more than distinct finger articulation.

The motive quickly runs out of drive, and at measure 14, a dreamy improvisatory passage begins; it concludes in another suspension at the next measure. The second theme, at measure 16, reveals a delicate, dancing character. The feeling of a longer line, further secured by the crescendo-decrescendo, should not be disturbed by the short slurs—or by heavy thumbs. The darting arpeggio figure of measures 18 and 19 is probably best played with the right hand alone, with the F sharp Debussy entrusts to the left hand being played by the fifth finger of the right. If the original version is adopted, one should beware of a too-heavy left-hand note that fails to match the liquid sound of the arpeggio. The crescendos of both measures remain small.

At measure 20, which is to be played "with ease," the tenor holds the attention with a longingly expressive phrase while the accompanying double notes remain light. The piano in measure 22 is suffused with expressive warmth; however the rhythm should remain accurate, especially where the precise timing of the offbeat bass notes is concerned. An extensive ritardando and diminuendo make the motive evaporate before the restatement of both the first and second themes.

A new, important motive appears at measures 30–31; it is to be "brought out in retard." It is an ominous, recitativelike motive loaded with sinister prophecy. The upward leap of the augmented fourth utters a particularly menacing threat. At measure 32, the atmosphere changes completely. The preceding sinister statement now sounds like scoffing laughter transposed into the obscure underwater world. At first glance, Debussy's intentions for the left hand seem confused by contradictory slurs and staccatos. No question, these are not ordinary slurs. Their only purpose is to prevent a dry staccato interpretation and at the same time, to secure a slight emphasis on the B natural throughout.

A clumsy left hand can easily overpower the dancing motive of measures 38–39. Measures 40 and 41 may be executed similarly to measures 18–19; supple hands won't have much difficulty in putting the thumb on a black key. The "twice as slow" indication appearing at measure 42 only makes the sinister motive more menacing. The half tempo remains in force up to measure 54; the "Rubato, slightly under the tempo" implies a further slowing of the speed. The feeling of a regular beat totally disappears in the soft murmurs of the right hand, which must not be punctuated by accents on the fifth finger. The appearance of the sixteenths related to the dancing motive further weakens the metric sensation.

In order to avoid an uncomfortable change of position at measure 49, the right hand should play in the *sopra* position from measure 44 on (that is, the right thumb should cross over the left thumb). The ominous motive at measure 46 has the character of a dream "softly marked"; it should have no rhythmic contours, and the ripple should curl up at measure 47 like an apprehensive question. The crescendo in measure 50 is to be kept within the smallest possible proportions; it is followed by a sudden, terrified pianissimo. The motive descends into the lower register, where it is even harder to maintain the pianissimo.

As if by magic, the original tempo suddenly brings the rhythmic pulse and life back at measure 54. However the tone remains at the level of a mysterious, light pianissimo. Unfortunately in most performances, it is blown up at this point to the proportions of a raging tornado. The difficulty here lies in the left hand's extended position, which makes the hand stiff and unable to execute the figure hidden in the lower part lightly. It is necessary first to familiarize oneself with the position of the thumb when it is used on two keys; practice the passage slowly with a relaxed, elastic hand. The ominous motive in the right hand, this time darting devilishly, should remain light and facile in the required pianissimo.

The offbeat octaves of measure 58 increase the excitement and the sound, which then drops back abruptly to pianissimo in measure 60. The crescendo of measure 61 is usually exaggerated. Instead of the grace-note snap, measures 62 and 63 show a single note and an octave in the left hand; if possible they should be brought out in an expressive legato, using the fifth finger for the single note and the thumb and fourth finger for the octave.

The first theme disintegrates totally. In order to play the shimmering arpeggios of the coda successfully, the hands must be prepared in their respective new positions in time to make the continuity perfect. The pedal should be changed with the bass notes: one pedal for two measures. Measure 71 and the first half of measure 72 can be in one pedal, the concluding broken chord on the second half of measure 72 needs a change of pedal. Use of the right hand may be easier at this point, playing the bass note with the third finger in *sotto* position; the figure that follows should be begun with the right hand, as printed. The left hand, crossing over the right, makes a small, bell-like accent on the concluding chord, which dies away rapidly.

From all points of view, *Ondine* is a difficult prélude. Technically the capriciously darting figure work has to be mastered first, to secure an effortless, easy performance that yields to the fluctuations of mood and color with sensitivity and insight.

Sergei Prokofiev

Born 1891, Sontzovka; died 1953, Moscow

The oeuvre of Prokofiev (131 finished compositions) includes an abundance of piano works—works of which he was a celebrated interpreter. Trained in Russia as both composer and pianist, he emigrated from his native country at the end of World War I and concertized extensively in Japan, the United States, and Europe. During this period, his style absorbed elements of the contemporary American and French music. After his final repatriation (in 1933), his works show more influence of Russian and other folk music.

His piano works—nine sonatas, five concertos, Toccata, *Sarcasms, Visions fugitives,* and *Tales of an Old Grandmother*—to mention only the most important ones—are highly energetic pieces in which rhythm and a powerful tone play important roles. They also show a distinctive lyricism and a real talent for storytelling. Prokofiev often uses mechanistic-motoric patterns that propel his music irresistibly.

Prokofiev's own virtuoso style is fully reflected in his piano writing—in the many octave and chordal passages for which large, strong hands are a definite advantage and in the many difficult figurations for which an even articulation is absolutely required.

PROKOFIEV
Tales of an Old Grandmother, Op. 31

~~~~~~

Descended from the nineteenth century's miniature tone paintings, these four narratives (composed in 1918) bear the unmistakable imprint of Russian folk music. Some of them are frightening; others are fanciful. They call forth memories of stories heard in early childhood.

No. 1: Moderato

M.M. ♩ = about 104

Form: Ternary

	MEASURES
A	1 – 28
B	29 – 44
A	45 – 52

A comfortable pace and graceful staccatos with a touch of the pedal on the first and third beats set the scene in the two opening measures. The melody entering on the long A, preceded by a soft grace note, should be gently sustained over the established pattern of the accompaniment. From measure 5 on, the mildly arpeggiated chords carry the melody in their top notes; the staccatos keep their delicacy free from dryness.

The uncomfortably wide broken chord on the downbeat of measure 8 should be executed entirely by the left hand. Measures 7 and 8 include part-playing and balance problems in the right hand. From measure 9 on, if the phrasing is executed as written, more charm will be added to the music. The grace-note chord in the right hand, like the downbeat of measure 10, is the resolution of the preceding harmony; however it has to be played ahead of the beat. Measure 12 brings the first period to a full close; consequently the duration of the closing half note should be accurate, if not generous. The doubling of the melodic line in the tenor in measures 11–12 may be gently brought out.

From measure 13 on, the music becomes livelier. On the downbeats, the chords are to be arpeggiated with the utmost grace; the following slurs should be played expressively while the staccato chords keep the gentle touch free from dryness. In this section, the pedal should be used only on the downbeat of each measure, adding color rather than weight to the accents prescribed for the arpeggiated chords. The short comment of the tenor on the last beats of measures 14 and 16 should not be over-looked; use the fingering

$$\begin{array}{ccc} 1\text{-}2\text{-}1 & \\ 2 & 3 \\ 3 & 4 \\ 5 & 5 \end{array}$$

Measures 17 and 18 require pedaling on their first and third beats. The pianissimo from measure 21 on contrasts with the mezzo forte at the first appearance of this subject. However uncomfortable the chords for the left hand on the downbeats of measures 22 and 24 may feel, they should not disturb the delicacy of the pianissimo. The right hand may help out at those points. Good part playing and tonal balance are necessary in the closing measures of the A section, where clarity and softness in the low register are hard to achieve.

Without warning, the B section of the story plunges into a frightening atmosphere. The evenly spaced, faraway rumbling of the accompaniment chords, the shy melody, and the big gap between them, give the listener gooseflesh. The melody unfolds ice cold, without crescendo-decrescendo in its first exposition; it should be pianissimo but clear. The rhythmic patterns on the last beats of measures 33 and 34 should have both liveliness and accuracy, contrasting sharply with the smooth rhythmic contours of the melody in the previous measures. The trill-like sixteenth-note figure in measure 36 concludes the phrase in a shiver.

Good part playing and tonal balance are needed in the second part. This time a prominent crescendo-decrescendo, appearing only in the alto, enlivens the phrase. It is obviously not possible to hold on to the keys in measure 37 or in measures 41–42; the continuity of the voices is secured by applying distinct colors to them. The atmosphere of fright dies away with a ritardando in measures 43–44, after which the graceful mood of the A section returns. The closing meno mosso may be prepared for by a slight ritardando on the last two beats of measure 50. The meno mosso itself again needs clarity and softness in the low register.

The simple narration of the first "tale" is best conveyed to the listener through unsophistication and spontaneous artistry. Quality and purity of tone, balance among voices, and clarity in the low register are the most important contributions of the performer. There is also need for a great deal of suggestive power in order to render the eerie atmosphere of the B section.

No. 2: Andantino

M.M. ♩ = about 96–100

Form: Ternary

	MEASURES
A	1 – 8
B	9 – 16
A	17 – 24

The delicacy of the accompaniment, moving evenly in eighth notes, must be responsible to a large extent for a faultless exposition of the melody. In measure 5, the pianissimo warns that a brusque arpeggio is to be avoided. The brief comment of the tenor in measure 6 has to be brought out clearly. The only technical difficulty of the piece appears in measure 7 in the double-note pattern; it requires very careful finger-ing to achieve a legato effect. The recommended fingering is: $\begin{smallmatrix}2 & 3 & 3 & 4 & & 5 & 4 & 3 & 2\\1 & 1 & 1 & 2 & & 3 & 2 & 1 & 1\end{smallmatrix}$. This measure may be played with a slight rubato, underlining the contrary motion between the tenor and the upper voices.

The B section brings in moderate difficulties in part playing (or voice leading); measure 9 in the left hand and the octave step in the melody at the downbeat of the next measure contain problems of this kind. The yearning dynamic swell, together with the sixteenth-note triplets of the left hand, intensifies the expressiveness of the phrase and contrasts with the next four-measure period (measures 13–16), which is to be played with a calm and transparent delicacy. The recapitulation of the A section, despite its appearance in the lower register, should remain delicate and clear.

The second "tale" is one of the most lyrical pieces in the oeuvre of Prokofiev. Its delicate lyricism is best served by a simple, unaffected, but still warm interpretation.

No. 3: Andante assai

M.M. ♩ = about 66

Form: Ternary

	MEASURES
A	1 – 17
B	18 – 44
A	45 – 52

The resemblance between the A section and *Bydlo* from Mussorgsky's *Pictures at an Exhibition* is quite obvious. In spite of the required piano, the ostinato-staccato accompaniment needs weightiness and an avoidance of excessive shortness. The melody contains the difficulty of playing a perfectly even group of five sixteenth notes. In the ponderous tempo of the passage, any deviation from evenness in the group of five can be detected; consequently the last accompaniment eighth note has to be kept from coinciding with any note of the melody. The thirty-second notes in measure 4 (and similar measures) have the bite of grace notes played on the beat; like the dotted rhythm in measure 6, they are to have sharpness and clarity. The second part of the A section has minor part-playing problems in the right hand: the alto, as well as the soprano, has to be played legato.

The bass line continues to move in eighth notes in the B section; however the staccato gives way—first to minute slurs and then to long legato lines. The chromaticism of the melody plunges this section into mystery, which should not be dispelled by loud or heavy grace notes in the bass. In measures 20–21 (and similar measures), the right-hand part has to be played imaginatively, with different coloration for the chords and the middle voice. In measures 24–25, the dotted rhythm has to have perfect accuracy together with good legato. At measure 26, the music plunges deeper into fearsome mystery. Precise part playing in this section (measures 26–28) may be troublesome for small hands; in some instances, as on the last beat of measure 28, sliding the thumb is the only solution.

The soprano in measures 30–31 is best fingered in the following way: 4-5-4-3 2-3-2-3 2-3-3-4 | 5-4-3/4-3 2 (the quick substitution of the fourth finger for the third in measure 31 is quite natural and easy). From measure 35 on, the left hand has to be kept light and transparent, in spite of the leaps and the heavier texture. The crescendo and the forte at measure 41 are mainly the responsibility of the right hand. The short recapitulation of the A section brings with it no new difficulties.

The descriptive character of the A section, with its ponderous staccato accompaniment, is quite easy to understand and interpret, while the mystery and phantoms of the B section tend to escape most players. Imagination for tone colors is a prime requisite for an interpretation that—like the story itself—should be both captivating and enchanting.

No. 4: Sostenuto

M.M. $\downarrow$ = about 120

Form: Ternary

	MEASURES
A	1 – 21
B	21 – 58
A	59 – 65

The opening three staccato chords (which should be played without excessive shortness) set the scene for the theme, a song in genuine Russian style. The tone used should be broad and singing, and special care should be taken to insure the smoothness of the eighth notes. The chromaticism in the tenor remains on the second plane. The second part of the melody soon plunges into eerie mystery.

Although the B section begins pianissimo, it contrasts strongly with the A section; the upper part contains a lightly bouncing accompaniment figure. The rhythm should be kept smooth throughout, without distortion into the sharper dotted rhythm. The melody is exposed broadly in the left hand; it climaxes in measures 33–34 and measures 45–46, where the bright sound of trumpets should be in the mind of the performer. The climactic accents at these points are to be rendered with brilliance, but without heaviness.

At measure 47, the forte of the downbeat is only moderate, to allow the following pianissimo to be heard clearly. The minute slurs appearing from this measure on indicate a short phrasing interruption after each quarter note—even after measure 49, where the right hand has minor part-playing and tonal balance problems. The melody has to be led skillfully from the thumb to the fifth finger of the right hand at measure 52. The brief recapitulation of the A section requires good tonal balance and clarity in pianissimo despite the low register.

The interpretation of this ''tale'' is made easier by the strong contrast in mood between the A and B sections. The only difficulty lies in the precise rendering of the smoothly bouncing rhythm, which should be kept accurate throughout the B section, even when the minute slurs appear.

Béla Bartók

Born 1881, Nagyszentmiklós; died 1945, New York

Only a few composers of the twentieth century are accepted and appreciated by audiences today as Bartók is. Pianist, composer, and musicologist, he excelled in all three spheres of his musical activity. The unwavering influence of his musicological research reveals itself in his compositions.

Bartók's earliest works follow the examples of the nationalist school in Hungary at the turn of the century. Soon he discovered the priceless treasures of authentic Hungarian folk music, which brought about a radical change in his compositional style. His research was limited at first to areas where Hungarian was spoken, but his interest promptly expanded to include Slovaks, Rumanians, Ukrainians, and various ethnic groups in Asia Minor and North Africa.

Traveling to remote villages in these parts of the world before World War I was truly equivalent to staging expeditions, but Bartók had an unwavering faith in folk idioms and accepted his hardships without complaint. In the earliest phase of his researches, he arranged the collected folk materials only to the extent of providing accompaniments to the songs. Then he realized that the conventional approach (as utilized by Glinka, Grieg, Dvořák, and Smetana, to mention just a few), consisting in the adaptation of the folk materials to Western musical language, could not be applied to Hungarian and non-European folk songs in general. He had but one choice—to adapt his own musical style to the folklore.

The task was enormous. Every single compositional element—form, rhythm, and harmony—had to follow the new path. The result was Bartók's mature style; in it his own melodic inventiveness yielded to the folkloristic influence to such an extent that it is difficult to determine without careful research when the material used is folk song and when it is of his own invention.

His piano works (fourteen bagatelles, two élégies, *For Children*, two Rumanian dances, four dirges, three burlesques, *Allegro barbaro*, the *Sonatine*, the Suite, Op. 14, *15 Hungarian Peasant Songs*, three études, the Improvisations, the Sonata, "Out of Doors," three rondos, the *Mikrokosmos* (in six volumes), and three piano concertos, to mention only the most important ones) were written throughout his lifetime and illustrate his stylistic development. Bartók's piano writing has often been described as primitive: the simple but exciting rhythms are hammered out with barbaric strength and the melodies have a range of only a few notes. This early view of his piano music surfaces sometimes even today despite the fact that quite a few of his pieces show great refinement in tonal coloration and soft dynamics (these qualities are probably a result of Debussy's influence). In the later works, complicated, intricate counterpoint demonstrates his veneration of Bach, whose *Well-Tempered Clavier* was taught from the Bartók edition at the Franz Liszt Academy in Budapest. Bach's influence was also determinative in the creation of Bartók's large-scope pedagogical works, such as "For Children" and *Mikrokosmos*, a series of 153 pieces ranging from the beginner level to full mastery of the instrument.

The technical difficulties involved in Bartók's piano music (not including the pedagogical works) lie mainly in octave and chord playing; the chords usually contain many notes (they are often referred to as "tone clusters") and extend beyond the octave range. Besides strong hands, a good rhythmic sense is essential for the comprehension of the many possible complications that are a result of the folkloristic origin of the motives.

The impression of barbaric hammering in Bartók's piano music has been further emphasized by note-perfect but often insensitive performances. To be sure, Bartók's style makes few concessions and is unsuitable for romantic treatment. But without spiritual involvement and an understanding of the beauty, artistry, and logic of his works, no performance of them can be entirely satisfactory.

BARTÓK
Suite, Op. 14

~~~~~~

A recently discovered manuscript proves that this suite was originally intended to have five movements. A slow piece was originally placed between the first and second movements. Folkloristic influences of very different origins can be seen in two of the four surviving movements. The first movement has its roots in Central European—probably Rumanian—folklore, which are disclosed by the regular, four-line stanzas and by its rhythmic character. As for the third movement, it clearly shows the influence of Bartók's excursion in 1913 to North Africa. The suite was composed in 1916 and first published in 1918.

1. Allegretto

M.M. $\quad\downarrow$ = 120

Form: Ternary

	MEASURES
First section	1 – 36
Second section	37 – 79
First section (partial recapitulation) and coda	79 – 117

Rhythmic angularity and evenness of tone are of great importance in the first four measures; the opening bass note is a possible exception and may have a slight accent. These four measures determine the character of the entire performance. From measure 5 on, the downbeat of every other measure carries a sizable accent, like foot tapping. Substituting for the foot tapping, there are rests on the downbeats of measures 7 and 11. The "accent" on these rests should be clearly felt by the performer so as to establish their rhythmic importance and accurate duration. The right hand needs independence in articulating the top voice, which should be played staccato and legato alternately, and the lower part, which should always be staccato. On this point, measures 8, 12, 16, and 20 are particularly difficult because the difference between the tenuto of the top voice and the staccato of the lower part is hard to render. The staccato applied to the lower voices in the right hand should constantly be remembered in this section—in fact, for better comprehension of the distribution and profile of the accompaniment, it may be useful to play the text once or twice without the melodic line.

The "pochissimo" confines the ritardando at measures 19 and 20 to the smallest proportions in order to avoid a possible sentimental mollifying of the phrase ending.

At measure 21, the change in dynamic range is evident. The accompaniment includes the strong, foot-tapping downbeat almost everywhere, infusing renewed energy and cheerfulness into the music. The left hand copes with the bold jumps better if the elbow is relaxed.

Measures 35 and 36 include a good-sized ritardando; it introduces a new, flexible tempo that fits the improvisatory character of the next passage, measures 37–52. The left hand has an essential role in this part. The staccato basses should be light, while the sixths are tenuto with a slight emphasis on the top notes; these accents, which occur in an inconsistent and quasi-syncopated way in this flexible, improvised tempo, make the passage sound like the unsteady steps of a tipsy company. The right hand interjects the upward-curling motive from time to time in an espressivo manner. At measure 47, the right hand recaptures its leading role. Measures 49 and 50 are to be played molto espressivo, with considerable ritardando and a small decrescendo to shape the line, in spite of the general crescendo. Measure 51 is exempt from decrescendo and drives forcefully toward the sforzando downbeat of the following measure. For the following three measures, the right hand has the responsibility of regaining the initial tempo without crescendo.

The leading motive of the left hand has to be carefully phrased from measure 55 on, with a distinct interruption before each accent. In measure 58, the right hand answers with an accent on the second beat, that ultimately appears off the beat in measures 60–61. Meanwhile the left hand's continuous sixteenth notes drive to the sforzando downbeat of measure 62 with a crescendo. (The last two sixteenth notes of measure 61 are easier to play in the right hand, with the fingering 2–4, facilitating a strong sforzando in the left hand on the downbeat of measure 62.)

At this point, the motive reappears a fourth higher and, at measure 70, reaches a new development that accounts for the main technical difficulty of the movement. The passage between measures 70 and 76 includes a crossing of the thumbs. In measures 70–71, the position on the keyboard calls for the right hand to be *sopra*. In measures 72–73, the left hand should be *sopra,* and in measures 74–75, the right hand should again be *sopra.* The vertiginous virtuosity required does not allow interruptions of the continuous sixteenth-note motion at points where the hand position needs to be changed. The practical solution seems to be to adopt the *sopra* position for the right hand throughout the passage and to redistribute the notes of measures 72–73 in the following manner:

measures 72-73

This solution avoids the troublesome entangling of the hands and assures the continuity of the driving sixteenths figure.

In measure 77, the following distribution allows for more strength and brilliance:

measures 77-78

The transition from the meno mosso at measure 80 to Tempo 1 at measure 87 is difficult because the increase of speed is coupled with decreasing dynamics. Notice the different articulation required for the main motive at measure 86, where the eighth note in the middle of the measure is played staccato instead of tenuto.

Measures 88–90 often cause stiffness when the thumb's rigidly extended position is unnecessarily maintained or when there is excessive finger articulation of the weak fingers. In measures 94–95, the following distribution is recommended:

measures 94-95

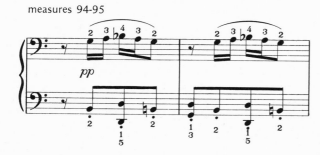

The meno mosso at measure 100 may be conceived to be considerably slower than Tempo 1. The whole-tone scales are to be phrased the way they are printed on the staff. The recommended fingering for the right hand from the middle of measure 106 is 1-2-3-4 1-2-1-2-3-4, and so on. The last seven measures show wit and verve if they are played at the required dynamic level. This caveat is especially important for the last note, which is often played roughly and too loud.

The successful performer of this comfortable Allegretto tempo-giusto dance needs the ability both to keep a solid, steady rhythm and to change the pace of the performance smoothly wherever this is required. Some affinity with folkloric popular music facilitates and enlightens the interpretation.

2. Scherzo

M.M. ♩. = 122

Form: Rondo

	MEASURES
Main subject	1 - 32
First episode	33 - 56
Main subject	57 - 72
Second episode	73 - 121
Main subject	122 - 142
Transition	143 - 162
First episode	163 - 179
Main subject	180 - 193
Coda	194 - 226

The staccato main subject is allotted alternately to the hands according to whether the stems are drawn upward or downward. Technically it is not difficult to follow this indication and still achieve perfect tonal and metrical evenness. It is also possible, however, to divide the motive in the following way:

measures 1-4

Scherzo (♩. = 132)

This solution seems stronger in performance, although it involves the danger of unwelcome accents on the downbeats in addition to the only accent required, which is on the downbeat of measure 4. (From measure 17 through measure 30, where the figure is rising, the distribution of the printed text is to be adopted without change.) A very short pedal enhances the sforzando of measure 4 (and similar measures) more by adding the color of the open strings than by real elongation of the note.

The piano at measure 17 appears suddenly, and the following crescendo should be progressively built up to the forte at measure 33. The sforzando on the last beat of measure 30 should not be overlooked. Measures 31–32 are still in tempo; the new, slower tempo begins, after a slight *luftpause,* (unmeasured rest; short breathing), at measure 33 *ex abrupto* (suddenly; without preparation). The first episode sounds irresistible, imitating the cackle of the hen in the right-hand part and accompanying this with the comically plaintive slurring of the main motive in the left hand. Accurate execution of the various accents in this section is essential. There are accents (∧) in the left hand on the downbeats of measures 33–35. There is no accent in measure 36; there is an accent in measure 37; and there are no accents in measures 38–40. The amount of sound on downbeats without accent should be distinctly less than on downbeats with accent. However the slur relation (which implies that the first note of a two-note slur should be louder than the second note) has to be plainly respected. The sforzandos apply to the right-hand part and make the cackle evident.

At the "più tranquillo," measure 49, the left-hand part shows longer lines. The dynamic level drops to fairly soft in order to allow for a driving crescendo. The right-hand part in measures 49–56 causes difficulties, especially for small hands with insufficient stretch between the thumb and fourth finger. It is useful to practice this passage first with $\frac{4}{1}$ only (omitting the fifth finger temporarily). To cope with the other difficulty of the passage—the smooth changes between the various positions on the keyboard in accordance with use of black or white keys—practice with $\frac{5}{4}$ only is also needed; omit the thumb but still keep the hand open in octave position. Further danger lies in using excessive arm weight on the longer chords, which will result in a stiff hand, wrist, and forearm that will be unable to handle the ensuing bouncing staccato adequately.

At the a tempo, the following distribution of notes between the hands may be used:

measures 57–60

This solution insures more strength and obviates the danger of playing the falling octave step legato. (From measure 65 on, follow the printed text for the distribution of notes.) In measures 69–71, the slurs cannot be prominent enough; for more emphasis, the use of the pedal is recommended.

The second episode includes a great number of technical difficulties: the sforzando grace note and a fortissimo passage in the right-hand part occurring from measure 74 on. An often-heard mistake consists of playing the grace note much ahead of the beat, which makes the passage rhythmically uneven. The solution is to play the grace note almost together with the main note, like a quickly arpeggiated interval. Meanwhile the grace-note figure in the left hand begins after the third beat, without much clarity, in the style of a trombone slide. The best approach is to use the fingering 4–3–2 for the grace notes coupled with a forward motion of the forearm that allows the ensuing octave to be negotiated without interruption on the bar line.

The grace-note figure of the left hand in measure 80 is to be fingered 1-2-3-4, and the sforzando C in the following measure should be played with the fifth finger. While the right hand plays the upper voice for the entire measure 81, the left hand takes it over from measure 82 on with the fingering 3-2-1 | 1-2-3 | 3-2-1 | and so on. This accompaniment figure is insuperably difficult for performers with small hands, who usually resort to the occasional help of the right hand or to the use of the sustaining (middle) pedal.

The nonchalant, fragmentary motive of the right hand shows strength and spirit; adherence to its articulation marks is of the utmost importance. The most taxing technical difficulty occurs in measure 96: the grace-note figure of the right hand has to be followed without hesitation by a sforzandissimo octave. Small hands are a positive handicap at this point. The execution is somewhat facilitated if the hand is turned slightly outward and the fingers involved are ready on the appropriate keys; this suggestion is important not only for the second, third, and fifth fingers on the grace notes, but especially so for the thumb, which should be poised right over (or in the closest possible proximity to) the F sharp (the octave is to be played with $\overset{4}{1}$, if possible). The "poco rit." indicated for measure 96 merely favors the positioning of the right hand. The difficulty of the execution is exacerbated by the sudden leap in the left hand. To insure accuracy, aiming for the upper C with the thumb and letting the fifth finger find the lower C automatically gives good results.

The short sixteenth-note motive that first appears in measure 108 has to be played accurately, with its first note on the beat and with a slight accent on the first of the slurred notes. Furthermore attention has to be given to the periodic repetition of the pedal-point C, which is often overlooked among the numerous difficulties of the section.

The distribution of notes between the hands suggested for the main motive may be used again at its reappearance at measure 123 and may be extended throughout its rising recurrence (measures 131–137) as well. The accurate duration of measure 138 is very important, with the grace notes clinging to the ensuing downbeat. In executing the grace notes, careful positioning of the fingers (as in measure 74) is strongly recommended along with a forward motion of the forearm to give the necessary strength to the fortissimo octave. The sharpness of the staccatos in measures 135–142 is often clouded by inadvertent slurring; this is the result of mistakenly taking measures 69–71 as an example.

From measure 147 on, the portamento touch together with the use of the pedal, will lend a quasi-legato character to the left-hand line. The recommended fingering throughout measures 147–158 is $5\text{-}3\text{-} \mid \overset{1}{1}\text{-}3 \mid$, with the third finger passing over the thumb in a legato manner. The passage has an expressive, longing character that is enhanced by the careful building of the crescendo.

The recapitulation of the first episode uses different accent markings from those in its first occurrence; however the effect should be similar. From measure 175 on, the crescendo and accelerando drive irresistibly toward the downbeat of measure 179, whose sound should be round in spite of the sharp staccato. To play the sforzandissimo chord of measure 180 without arpeggiating in the left hand is impossible for most players. One may leave out, if necessary, the chord's upper F. If an arpeggio is still needed, it should be performed with the fastest possible succession of tones, and the effect of a simultaneous attack should be aimed at.

Measures 181–183 may be played by adopting the previously suggested distribution of the notes again; the printed distribution of notes should be followed again at measure 184. The two consecutive octaves in measures 187 and 189 should sound like strong slaps. In measure 188, avoid using the thumb of the right hand on the last note: it will impair the strength of the following octave.

At the "Tranquillo" (measure 194), the sforzando entrance of the soprano will be answered in the bass in the following measure (it happens again in measure 200). Expressive portamento is required for the soprano; the staccato tenor of the left hand is kept unobtrusive. At measure 203, the accompaniment figure becomes uncomfortable—if not impossible—for small hands. Two possible solutions are incorporating the B flat into the right-hand text (which becomes very uncomfortable from the rhythmic point of view in measures 205–206) and skillfully using the sostenuto (middle) pedal to keep the bass note alive. For hands large enough to play the text as printed from measure 203 on, the fingering 3-1-2 | 1-3-1 | is recommended for the staccato part.

The a tempo should have the effect of a sudden fist stroke. Maintaining the accurate duration of the one-measure rests inserted from this point on is an absolute necessity. The previously suggested distribution of notes (measures 1–4) may serve again from measures 211 through 216 because the triple forte marcatissimo at measure 218 requires it anyway. Bartók's fingering "1 & 2" indicates that the thumb and second finger should be used simultaneously, with the thumb supporting the second finger on the level of the lower phalanx. Another, possibly stronger, solution consists in holding thumb, second finger, and third finger together, with the thumb applied against the lower phalanx of the third finger. The Scherzo concludes with three measures of rest, during which the performer should remain motionless.

Powerful staccato playing is a requisite for the performance of this witty scherzo. Although the staccato motives must be "hammered" with the utmost energy, roundness of tone without harshness should still be among the preoccupations of the performer. This is especially true for passages where the dynamics exceed forte. Transitions from one tempo to another need musical insight in conception and smoothness in execution.

3. Allegro molto

M.M. $\downdownarrows$ = 124

Form: Ternary

	MEASURES
First section	1 – 59
Second section	60 – 83
First section and coda	83 – 134

As in the first movement, the bare accompaniment figure of the four opening measures determines the flow and pulse of the entire movement. The execution may adhere to the distribution of notes between the hands indicated by the downward or upward direction of note stems in the printed score; however the following solution is probably easier:

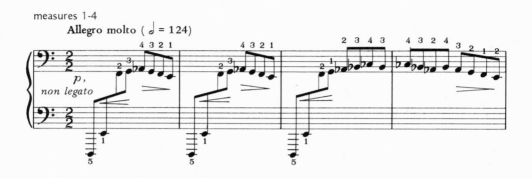

measures 1-4

The "non legato" means that a sticky legato is not needed; however "non legato" should not be confounded with staccato. There are small dynamic sways in the first four measures, which are followed by a longer and more prominent crescendo-decrescendo in measures 3-4.

The first fragment of the melody needs utmost clarity in the repeated notes. Changing fingers on repeated notes is then recommended: 2-1-3 2-1-3 should be used throughout for this motive. Meanwhile the left hand alone can handle the entire accompaniment figure if the passage over the thumb is smooth. The recommended fingering for measure 5 and similar measures is 5-1-4-3-2-3-4-1; for measure 11 and similar measures, the fingering should be 5-1-3-2-1-2-3-1. (It is understood that in measures 7-8 the right hand helps out, using either the printed solution or the one recommended for measures 3-4.) The ability to pass the fingers over the thumb presupposes a loose, laterally flexible wrist in a slightly raised position. The hand, which is open in the octave position for the first two notes, closes with the elasticity of a rubber band at the moment of passage and opens again just as easily for the use of the fifth finger. When the initial octave step widens to a ninth or tenth, the handling should remain easy and accurate. Preliminary practice of the left-hand figure is strongly recommended.

The melody is supposed to be "non legato," although a staccato would be just as improper, as was pointed out concerning the accompaniment. Notice the accent on the top note in measures 11-12 and similar measures coinciding with the height of the crescendo in the accompaniment. Particular attention has to be given to those second halves of measures where both hands play eighth notes. Their perfect simultaneity, though difficult to achieve, is an absolute requirement.

The virtuoso unison passage in measures 21-33 needs a well-established and well-learned fingering, whose choice may vary according to the hands and ability of the performer. A couple of the many possibilities is suggested here:

measures 21-33

It is evident that printing the last notes of measures 29 through 32 with separate stems means phrasing, which must not be exaggerated because this would impair the continuous even flow of the eighth notes.

At measure 34, a more difficult variant of the main subject in double notes appears. The printed fingering seems logical and appropriate for measures 34–35 but uncomfortable in measure 36. The following fingering may be more effective:

The difficulty of this fingering lies in the quick switching of the thumb from a white to a black key, which may be helped by a forward motion of the forearm.

In spite of the arm motion, the hand—especially the thumb—should remain light in the interests of faultless repetition. For the seventh in measure 36 and similar measures, the hand is turned slightly outward and then pulled back toward the body with the fingers naturally falling on the appropriate keys (the fingering for this interval is $\frac{5}{1}$). Keeping the hands rigorously together becomes increasingly difficult here, and the blame may fall on either hand—inarticulate, uneven execution in the right hand or inadvertent speeding in aiming the fifth finger toward a distant key in the left hand. For the latter problem, measures 42–47 are most difficult.

The difficulties of the large leaps from measure 50 on may be lessened if the body is kept from leaning to the left in the measures preceding leaps and if the shoulders are free and relaxed. To play measures 52–53 without leaning to the left is uncomfortable; nevertheless the central position favors the accurate execution of the following chord without noticeable delay. At measures 56–57, leaning toward the left is unavoidable; however only the arms—not the body—should be moved to play the ensuing chord.

The middle part of the movement includes the difficulty of playing fast martellato with alternate hands. Tenseness of the arms causes unevenness (the most-often observed deficiency at this point), especially when the octaves in the right hand are played with a stiff arm. The positioning of the hands is decisive for the entire passage. With the recommended fingering for the left hand ($4 \begin{smallmatrix} 3-2-1-2 \\ \\ 5 \end{smallmatrix}$ for measure 60 and similar measures), the right thumb should be inserted between the thumb and second finger of the left hand. This position is beneficial for passages in measures 60–63, 68–71, 73, and 75, including measure 69, where the left thumb plays the B flat under the right thumb. In measures 64–66, the right hand plays *sotto*. It is useful to practice the passage by playing the right thumb alone (temporarily omitting the fifth finger), together with the left-hand part, in the above-described position in order to establish the line, which should be impeccably even and clear and controlled not only by the hands but also by the ear.

In addition to the leaps, measures 72 through 76 include the obligation to alternate legato with martellato. The recommended fingering for the legato measures in the right hand is $\begin{smallmatrix} 2 & 3 & 5 & 3 \\ 1 & 1 & 2 & 1 \end{smallmatrix}$, and in the left hand is $\begin{smallmatrix} 2 & 1 & 1 \\ 4 & 3 & 2 & 3 \\ 5 \end{smallmatrix}$. Small hands that cannot cope with the chord in the left hand at measure 77 may play the top G with the right thumb. At this point, the two-note slurs have to be strongly emphasized by the sforzandos.

The recapitulation of the first section brings with it the principal technical difficulties of the piece. Measures 99–104 contain the already-mentioned problem of simultaneity of the hands. Notice the new fingering in measures 103 and 104; it requires the second finger to slide from a black key to a white key while the thumb is still relentlessly performing repetitions. The unison passage from measure 105 on necessitates long and patient slow practice for mastery of the positions of this highly unusual figure. The difficulty is further aggravated by the two-octave gap between the hands. The forte ''strepitoso'' crescendo invites excessive use of force or weight, which will not only mar the sound but also impair successful execution by straining the hands to their utmost limit. Much exertion may also originate from unnecessarily keeping the hands in wide positions. Furthermore the immoderate use of weight on the octaves from measure 112 on makes it virtually impossible to perform them. They should be played as legato as possible, without separate arm motions; the hand should be pulled with a sliding thumb, and it should be turned slightly outward so as to bring the fingers into a favorable position to negotiate the ensuing figure. When performing these measures (measures 105–116), overwhelming brilliance and consistently elegant tone are to be kept in mind.

At measure 118, the difficult leaps reappear. Again their accurate performance depends to a large extent on a relaxed shoulder. The right-hand fingering for measures 123 and 125 is

$$\begin{matrix} 4 & 5 & 5 & 5 \\ 2 & 3 & 4 & 3 \\ 1 & 1 & 1 & 1 \end{matrix}$$

, and the left-hand fingering is

$$\begin{matrix} 2 & 1 & 1 & 1 \\ 4 & 3 & 2 & 3 \\ & 5 & & \end{matrix}$$

. Difficulties are further increased at measures 130 and 132, where one hand joins the other to play the main motive after a wide leap; the closing measure is made somewhat easier by the ritardando.

No doubt the Allegro molto contains the most taxing difficulties of the suite. They derive from an unusual, almost unpianistic, passagework inspired by motives of Arab popular music from North Africa. However difficult the movement is, the performance will gain impressiveness through an easy, unforced virtuosity and a big, but still elegant, tone.

4. Sostenuto

M.M. ♪ = 120–110

Form: Ternary

	MEASURES
First section	1 – 21
Second section	22 – 25
First section (coda)	26 – 35

The opening soft pizzicato bass note, which may remind one of the vigorous foot tapping of the first piece, should follow the conclusion of the third movement *attacca*—that is, it should follow without a break. The theme is concealed in the alto and tenor and should receive softly insistent treatment. The right balance among the various voices is a subtle matter: too much or not enough insistence on the veiled melodic line are equally faults. The yearning character of the music is manifest in the offbeat entrance and in the dolorous rising-and-falling line of the main motive.

From measure 4 onward, the rising-and-falling line becomes more and more prominent, and it is emphasized by an expressive dynamic sway. On the last eighth note of measure 6, the accented soprano embarks on a comment in the manner of a flute joining the strings. The main motive, hidden up to this point amid various layers of sound, suddenly gives the impression of breaking loose to levitate into higher regions. The comment begins again even more insistently in measure 8, only to fall back sadly on the downbeat of measure 10, where the tenor (alone this time) resumes the main motive. A careful balance between the voices of the left hand is very difficult to maintain in the following eight measures; this is especially true in measure 15, where the accompaniment thirds may imprint unwelcome accents upon the melodic line. The right hand only accompanies throughout this part, except for the soft, melancholy comments in measures 16 and 18, which are voiced in a different color much inspired by the woodwinds of the orchestra.

"Orchestrating" measures 19–21 is equally important: the three layers should have three distinct colors like cellos, bassoons, and clarinets. A considerable ritardando in measure 21 prepares for the ensuing change of tempo.

The tone of the "più sostenuto" part (measures 22–25) should be one of unreal beauty; it can be achieved by playing the bass part as the most prominent layer, in the manner of an Oriental gong, while the other parts are kept colorless and incorporeal, like rising smoke. The crescendos in measures 22–23 are to be kept minimal in size, whereas in measures 24–25, the sound will grow considerably along with the stringendo; yet the previously established balance among the voices should still be preserved. Slightly more melodic importance may be given to the poignant slurs in measure 25; their wavering tone and extensive diminuendo-ritardando emphasizes the impression of heartbroken sorrow.

Control over tone becomes increasingly difficult in the last section. Most of the chords contain six notes and are preceded by grace notes, which have to be played ahead of the beat as notated; these chords have to sound mellow, while the somber motives should come out intense and well focused, yet soft. The dolcissimo octaves (measure 28) use the best notes of the instrument and sound astonishingly beautiful, even in inexperienced hands. If the tenths in the left hand from measure 30 on cannot be played simultaneously, they are best arpeggiated by playing the bass note together with the right hand and adding the top note very softly immediately afterward.

In measure 34, the right hand may play the following notes (from the top down): A, G flat, D (which is written for the left hand), and C sharp; the left hand plays the two remaining B flats. This solution yields the softest possible tone. In the right hand, the avoidance of the use of the thumb on the last three fourths improves the quality of the pianissimo; the fingering $\frac{5}{2}$ gives the best result.

The impressionistic tendencies of the intimate closing piece—mainly apparent in the "più sostenuto" section—contrast sharply with the tendencies of the preceding movements. Bartók made it evident here that control over tone can be a real difficulty, severely taxing the artistry and imagination of the performer.

Bibliography

Aguettant, L. *La Musique de piano*. Paris: Albin Michel, 1954.

Apel, W. *Brief Survey of Piano Music*. Cambridge, Mass.: Harvard University Press, 1947.

Bach, C. P. E. *Essay on the True Art of Playing Keyboard Instruments*. Translated by W.J. Mitchell. New York: Norton, 1949.

Beckett, W. *Liszt*. London: Dent, 1956.

Bie, O. *Schubert, the Man*. Westport, Conn.: Greenwood, 1971.

Bodky, E. *The Interpretation of Bach's Keyboard Works*. Cambridge, Mass.: Harvard University Press, 1960.

Bosquet, E. *La Musique de clavier*. Brussels: Les Amis de la Musique, 1953.

Chantavoine, J. *Beethoven*. Paris: Félix Alcan, 1907.

Chissell, J. *Schumann*. London: Dent. New York: Farrar, Straus & Giroux, 1967.

———. *Schumann Piano Music*. Seattle: University of Washington Press, 1972 (BBC Guide Series No. 25).

Cone, E. T. *Musical Form and Musical Performance*. New York: Norton, 1968.

Cortot, A. *Aspects de Chopin*. Paris: Albin Michel, 1949.

———. *Cours d'interprétation*. Compiled by J. Thieffry. Paris: Librairie Musicale. R. Legouix, 1934.

Czerny, C. *On the Proper Performance of Beethoven's Work for the Piano*. Vienna: Universal Edition, 1970.

Davenson, H. *Traité de la musique selon l'esprit de Saint Augustin*. Neuchâtel: La Baconnière, 1942.

Dawes, F. E. *Debussy Piano Music*. Seattle: University of Washington, 1971 (BBC Guide Series No. 14).

Downey, J. W. *La Musique populaire dans l'oeuvre de Béla Bartók*. Paris: Centre de Documentation Universitaire, 1964.

Dumesnil, M. *How to Play and Teach Debussy*. New York: Schroeder & Gunther, c. 1932.

Eigeldinger, J. J. *Chopin, vu par ses élèves*. Neuchâtel: La Baconnière, 1970.

Einstein, A. *Mozart: His character, His work*. Translated by A. Mendel and N. Broder. New York: Oxford University Press, 1945.

Evans, E. *Handbook to the Pianoforte Works of Johannes Brahms*. New York: Scribner, 1936.

Ferguson, H. *Keyboard Interpretation*. New York and London: Oxford University Press, 1975.

Fuchs, W. *Béla Bartók en Suisse*. Lausanne: Payot, 1975.

Furtwangler, W. *Gespräche über Musik*. Zurich: Atlantis, 1948.

Geiringer, K. *Haydn: A Creative Life in Music*. New York: Norton, 1946.

Georgii, W. *Klaviermusik*. Zurich: Atlantis, 1950.

Gheon, H. *Promenades avec Mozart*. Paris: Desclée de Brouwer, 1932.

Girdlestone, C. M. *Mozart's Piano Concertos*. London: Cassell, 1948.

Gray, C. *The Forty-eight Preludes and Fugues by J. S. Bach.* London: Oxford University Press, 1938.

Hanson, L. *Prokofiev: A Biography in Three Movements.* New York: Random House, 1964.

Haraszti, E. *Franz Liszt.* Paris: Picard, 1967.

Hedley, A. *Chopin.* London: Dent, 1947.

Hinson, M. *Guide to the Pianist's Repertoire.* Edited by I. Freudlich. Bloomington, Ind.: Indiana University Press, 1973.

Hughes, R. *Haydn.* London: Dent, 1950.

Hundt, T. *Bartóks Satztechnik in den Klavierwerken.* Regensburg: Gustav Bosse, 1971.

Hutchings, A. *Schubert.* New York: Octagon Books, 1973.

Iliffe, F. *The Forty-eight Preludes and Fugues of J. S. Bach.* London: Novello, 1923.

Kalbeck, M. *Johannes Brahms.* Berlin: Deutsche Brahms-Gesellschaft, 1908.

——. *Analyse der Chopin' schen Klavierwerke.* Berlin: Hasse, 1921–1922.

Leichtentritt, H. *Musical Form.* Cambridge, Mass.: Harvard University Press, 1951.

Lesznai, L. *Béla Bartók.* Translated by P. M. Young. Leipzig: Veb. Deutscher Verlag für Musik, 1967.

Lichtenberg, E. *Mozart élete és müvei.* Budapest: Rozsavölgyi, 1923.

Lockspeiser, E. *Debussy.* New York: McGraw-Hill, 1972.

Loesser, A. *Men, Women and Pianos.* New York: Simon & Schuster, 1954.

Marx, A. B. *Introduction to the Interpretation of the Beethoven Piano Works.* Chicago: Clayton F. Sunny, 1895.

——. *Ludwig van Beethoven: Leben und Schaffen.* Berlin: Otto Janka, 1901.

Matthews, D. *Keyboard Music.* New York: Praeger, 1972.

Nestev, I. V. *Sergei Prokofieff: His Musical Life.* New York: Knopf, 1946.

Neuhaus, G. G. *A zongorajáték müvészete.* Translated by D. Legány. Budapest: Zenemükiadó Vállalat, 1961.

Paumgartner, B. *Mozart.* Translated by P. Pascali. Paris: Gallimard, 1951.

Perenyi, E. *Liszt: The Artist as Romantic Hero.* Boston: Little, Brown, 1974.

Pirro, A. *J. S. Bach.* Paris: Félix Alcan, 1907.

Radcliffe, P. *Schubert Piano Sonatas.* Seattle: University of Washington Press, 1971 (BBC Guide Series No. 17).

Riemann, H. *Analyse von Beethovens Klaviersonaten.* Berlin: M. Hesse, 1919.

Rosen, C. *The Classical Style.* New York: Norton, 1972.

Rostand, C. *Brahms.* Paris: Librairie Plon, 1954.

Schmitz, E. R. *The Piano Works of Claude Debussy.* New York: Duell, Sloan & Pearce, 1950.

Tovey, D. F. *A Companion to Beethoven's Pianoforte Sonatas.* London: Associated Board, 1931.

Ujfalusy, J. *Béla Bartók.* Translated by R. Pataki. Boston: Crescendo, 1972.

Walker, A., ed. *Frédéric Chopin: Profiles of the Man and the Musician.* London: Barrie & Rockliff, 1966.

——. *Franz Liszt: The Man and His Music.* London: Barrie & Jenkins, 1970.

——. *Robert Schumann: The Man and His Music.* London: Barrie & Jenkins, 1972.

Weissman, A. *Der Virtuose.* Berlin: Paul Cassirer, 1920.

Acknowledgments

I am deeply indebted to David Pellell for his devoted help and encouragement.

Musical examples have been drawn from or based upon the following editions, which are published by Edwin F. Kalmus, New York; C. F. Peters, New York, London, and Frankfurt; G. Schirmer, New York and London; and Universal Edition (in U.S.A., Boosey & Hawkes):

Bach, *Well-Tempered Clavier*, ed. Hans Bischoff, Book 1, Schirmer's Library, Vol. 1759.
Bartók, *Suite*, Op. 14, Universal Edition 5891.
Beethoven, *Sonatas for the Piano*, Urtext edition, Schirmer's Library, Vol. 1769.
Brahms, *Piano Works in Two Volumes*, ed. E. V. Sauer, Vol. 2, Schirmer's Library, Vol. 1758.
Chopin, *Album: A Collection of Thirty-three Favorite Compositions for the Piano*, Schirmer's Library, Vol. 39.
Chopin, *Complete Works for the Pinao*, ed. Carl Mikuli, Book 1, *Waltzes;* Book 4, *Nocturnes;* Book 5, *Ballades;* and Book 7, *Études;* Schirmer's Library, Vols. 1549, 1550, 1552, and 1551, respectively.
Chopin, *Compositions for the Piano*, ed. Rafael Joseffy, *Mazurkas* and *Scherzi and Fantasy,* Schirmer's Library, Vols. 28 and 32, respectively.
Haydn, *Klavierstücke,* ed. Kurt Soldan, Edition Peters, No. 4392.
Haydn, *Sonaten für Klavier zu zwei Händen,* ed. Carl Adolf Martienssen, Vol. 3, Edition Peters, No. 713c.
Liszt, *Années de pèlerinage, deuxième année, "Italie,"* ed. Rafael Joseffy, Schirmer's Library, Vol. 911.
Liszt, *Two Concert Études,* ed. Rafael Joseffy, and *Two Legends,* ed. Louis Oesterle, Schirmer's Library, Vol. 1753.
[Liszt] Paganini, *Six Grand Études Arranged for the Piano by Franz Liszt,* ed. Paolo Gallico, Schirmer's Library, Vol. 835.
Mozart, *Nineteen Sonatas for the Piano,* ed. Richard Epstein, Schirmer's Library, Vol. 1304.
Schubert, *Ten Sonatas for the Piano,* ed. G. Buonamici, Schirmer's Library, Vol. 837.
Schumann, *Fantasy Pieces,* Op. 12, ed. Clara Schumann, Kalmus Piano Series, No. 3906.
Schumann, *Papillons,* Op. 2, ed. Clara Schumann, Kalmus Piano Series, No. 3910.